A class against itself

A class against itself

Power and the nationalisation of
the British steel industry

Doug McEachern

Department of Politics
University of Adelaide

Cambridge University Press

Cambridge
London New York New Rochelle
Melbourne Sydney

Published by the Press Syndicate of the University of Cambridge
The Pitt Building, Trumpington Street, Cambridge CB2 1RP
32 East 57th Street, New York, NY 10022, USA
296 Beaconsfield Parade, Middle Park, Melbourne 3206, Australia

© Cambridge University Press 1980

First published 1980

Phototypeset in V.I.P. Melior by
Western Printing Services Ltd, Bristol
Printed in Great Britain
at the University Press, Cambridge

British Library Cataloguing in Publication Data
McEachern, Doug
A class against itself.
1. Iron industry and trade – Government
ownership – Great Britain
2. Steel industry and trade – Government
ownership – Great Britain
I. Title
338.4'7'66910941   HD9521.6   79–41766
ISBN 0 521 22985 5 hard covers

Contents

Contents

Acknowledgements

My special thanks to

    Charmaine Collett and Alan Warde.

My thanks also to

    Melanie Beresford, Zygmunt Bauman, Geoff Mercer, Ralph Miliband, Bruce MacFarlane, Cathy Dobson, Jeanne Bellovics and to my friends in the Sociology and Politics Departments and in the Politics Office of Leeds University.

Abbreviations

BSC   British Steel Corporation
BISF   British Iron and Steel Federation
IDAC   Import Duties Advisory Committee
ISB   Iron and Steel Board
ISHRA Iron and Steel Holding and Realisation Agency
NFISM National Federation of Iron and Steel Manufacturers
NSC   National Steel Corporation

Introduction

There have been numerous studies of power undertaken in recent years, but the quality and usefulness of these has, unfortunately, been limited. Most have concentrated on the definition and characteristics of power, which they attempt to discern in abstract reflections on its general properties. Few consider the power evident in the social processes of an actual capitalist society. It is easy to despair of the conclusions suggested in such general studies whose over-ambition involves them in a search for some feature which either indicates power or reveals its universal essence. Their comments are frequently too general to be used in the analysis of the serious consequences of the conflicts and interactions of social and political life. A contrast exists between the general observations on power and its analysis, and the conclusions reached in those studies which investigate actual communities, countries or incidents. Such is the contrast between Dahl's initial articles on the study of power and the conclusions he draws about the politics of New Haven in *Who Governs?*[1] Even though the conclusions inadequately deal with the evidence presented, they are at least addressed to some actual social process and have some pertinence to a genuine social question. The comparison between Bachrach and Baratz's general comments on power, which embody both the best and the worst of this genre, and their actual study of a serious issue is unflattering in that it is not a good analysis and it fails, significantly, to use the procedures outlined in their other articles.[2] By far the best example of a pluralist account of power is not to be found in the general arguments of people like Polsby[3] but in the study by Rose which argues its points in the context of a discussion of the actions of the U.S. Government.[4] It should not be thought that the study of an actual incident or series of incidents provides a guarantee against a bad analysis. Hewitt's cavalier 'testing' of elite and pluralist hypotheses is a clear indication that a good analysis depends on the skill with which the conceptualisation of power is related to the examination of social developments.[5]

Apart from a discussion of the general character of power and the

most appropriate methods by which it may be studied, recent works
on the subject have also been concerned to judge the extent to which
the political processes of capitalist countries accord with some basic
notion of democracy. The controversy over power had been part of a
dispute about the character of western democracy. Here the two main
issues are: 'To what extent do the people control the government?',
and 'To what extent does government control social development?'
This second question has prompted arguments about the character of
the interaction between government and private capital. Marxists and
others who are suspicious of the democratic claims of the western
system have tried to show that the class power of capital is such that
governments of capitalist countries act to advance the interests of
private business to a greater extent than they meet the needs of the
vast majority of the people.[6] On the other side, there are those who
wish to defend the existing political order and who counter such
comments by what they describe as a pluralist interpretation of power
in western democracies.[7] This includes both arguments about the
meaning of democracy, often involving a substantial revision of the
term's classical usage, and an analysis of the distribution of power. In
this account they stress the fact that power is diffused throughout
society and no group possesses sufficient power to dominate society
as a whole. On the question of government action, their interpretation
maintains that governments dominate the process of economic
development and that this shows that the class or elite critiques of
liberal democracy must be wrong. Business could not enforce its
wishes on democratically elected governments, but governments
could and do impose their wishes on business.

There have been a large number of critiques of the pluralist argument and these have criticised its methodological precepts, its concept of power and its factual adequacy.[8] Though I agree with the main
points made in these critiques, I do not think that the case has been
established on as sound a conceptual base as is possible. Part of the
intention behind the study undertaken here is to suggest an alternative interpretation of the class power of capital through the analysis of
a specific interaction between a succession of governments and a
section of private capital. The main focus of the study is not, however,
on the adequacy or otherwise of pluralist interpretations. It is rather
an attempt to discover the character of power which can be seen in the
various struggles over the nationalisation and denationalisation of
the steel industry in the period between 1945 and 1967, the year in
which the industry was renationalised. There will be some discussion
of various established conceptions of power and the accompanying

methodologies, mainly to reveal the problems they have in dealing with the actions of governments. But this will serve as necessary background to an argument about the power evident in a very specific social process which was of considerable economic, political and social significance in the development of British capitalism.

Even when Britain was the dominant capitalist power in the world, the economy was not free from periodic trade crises and severe contractions in industrial production. The problems evident in the economy in its ascendancy did not diminish in its period of relative decline.[9] Certainly by the middle of the twentieth century the economy had developed a series of serious bottlenecks and inadequacies which taxed the ingenuity of those who sought to find solutions and have them implemented. The depression of the late 1920s, and the slow recovery through the thirties, revealed the deficiencies of the economy in a stark manner. Though the political defeat of the labour movement in the General Strike of 1926 effectively reduced the social significance of the high levels of unemployment in the depression, it was apparent to politicians and businessmen that problems in the economy could provide the basis for exacerbated social tensions. Attempts to overcome the main structural weaknesses of the economy were postponed by the war with Germany. After the declaration of war, there was an upsurge of production, concentrated in areas most relevant to the war effort. But Britain was financially ill-equipped for its wartime tasks and, under pressure from the United States of America, was forced to sell off various foreign assets and weaken its hold on the empire.[10] This meant that in the postwar world, Britain would no longer be able to manipulate the terms of imperial trade to stave off the consequences of the difficulties faced by the domestic economy. The increase in production during the war may have provided the basis for a period of rapid industrial growth in the initial years of peace, similar to the short boom which followed the end of the First World War, but all the main problems of the economy remained unsolved. These included a poor structure of industrial organisation characterised by many small units operating with outmoded machinery and outdated technical processes, and also a very low level of investment in industrial production. It was fairly obvious that if Britain was to prosper in the postwar world, the government would have to do something about the state of the economy.

A programme of nationalisation and welfare legislation were the two main elements in the 1945 Labour Government's attempt to counter the re-emergence of large scale unemployment.[11] Among the intended measures, the nationalisation of steel did not have the highest priority. Nevertheless, it did become the most contentious issue of the postwar period.[12] This was largely a result of the vigour with which the industry opposed its nationalisation and the effort which the Conservative Party added to the campaign. Unlike the previous acts of nationalisation, this one involved considerable drama, delay, constitutional questions and public interest. The industry's opposition and its struggle with the Government did not prevent nationalisation, which became law in 1951. It did, however, provide a very solid basis for the denationalisation of steel which was enacted by the Conservative Party when it came to office late in 1951. Denationalisation, in the sense of the actual resale of the industry to private owners, took some years. As a consequence of this, and the pledge made by the Labour Party to nationalise the industry again at the earliest possible opportunity, the status of steel remained a political issue throughout the long period of Conservative rule. Despite a changed view of nationalisation and its relevance to the Labour Party's social objectives, the nationalisation of steel was part of the Labour Party's electoral programme when it returned to office in 1964. Consideration of the Party's numbers in the House of Commons, and the threat of defection by two backbenchers, meant that the move to renationalise was delayed until the Party's majority was boosted by another electoral victory. So it was not until 1967 that the industry finally returned to public ownership. This time there was little prospect that it would ever be resold to private owners.

The nationalisation of steel and the conflicts which surrounded the ownership of the industry between 1945 and 1967 do not make it a representative example of interaction between governments and private capital. No other industry underwent such a sequence of changes or was at the centre of such important disputes about the power and legitimacy of government action. It is just those factors that make it unrepresentative which make it a good subject to be studied for the character of power in the relationship between private capital and government. Not only does the process include a number of struggles with governments of different party-political composition, but very few of the conclusions are clear-cut or contain self-evident lessons about the character of power. For instance, the initial nationalisation cannot be treated as a clear triumph for either the Government, which had to delay and compromise its plans, or the steel industry, as it was eventually nationalised. Knowledge that the industry was subsequently denationalised must add further caution to any interpretation of governmental power based on the successful nationalisation of steel. Similarly, the denationalisation of the industry was a complicated process. The delay in reselling the companies to private owners must be explained and the fact that one major firm was never sold must be taken into account. After denationalisation the industry was subject to more formal control than had previously been the case, and so it is not possible to treat denationalisation as unqualified evidence that private capital had triumphed over the wishes of government. There was a great deal of agreement between the Conservative Government and the steel industry over denationalisation. Though the outcome of the last struggle over nationalisation was definite enough, the dispute was far less dramatic than that which had surrounded the first nationalisation. Also it is necessary to consider the actual form of the nationalised steel industry before it is possible to make any assertions about the power revealed by the success of the Labour Government. In this sense, the example of relations between governments and the steel industry forms a most useful basis for the construction of arguments about the character of power as it is full of contrasting incidents and outcomes and it is a complicated process to be interpreted.

In outlining developments in the steel industry, I do not want to write the postwar history of its relations with the government as, for most of the period, there are very competent accounts already in existence. For example, Ross has published a detailed study of the conflict over the first nationalisation that provides more than enough information for an argument about the character of power evident in that process.[13] Duncan Burn has published a number of books and articles that are an extensive history of both the industry and its relationship with governments and various government-appointed bodies.[14] Unfortunately, his account stops in 1959. The British Iron and Steel Federation (BISF), one of the main participants in the dispute under consideration, commissioned an account by two of their officials which brings the story up to 1962.[15] John Vaizey, in *The History of British Steel*, provides a very brief overview of the whole period and includes information on the fortunes of the industry in the 1960s and an account of the renationalisation of steel in 1967.[16] These are the main sources of information about relations between the industry and the various governments, but they have been supplemented here by an examination of the publications of the Federation, newspaper accounts, Hansard, White Papers and Labour Party pamphlets. Overall, I have provided only as much detail about the steel industry as was necessary for the elaboration of the argument about the character of government action and the nature of power in this particular social process. My purpose in undertaking the research was not to discover new or dramatic facts about the relationship between government and the steel industry, but to reinterpret the facts which were already available in as rigorous and systematic a manner as possible in terms of an argument about government action and the processes of power in a dispute which had important implications for a mature capitalist system.

The argument has been presented in the following way. Chapter 1 is concerned with the various arguments about the character of power and the best procedures for its analysis. In the discussion here, attention has been paid to the problems that such approaches have with the evaluation of government action and the assessment of its consequences for the study of power. Various problems raised will be taken up in Chapter 2 which examines contemporary state theory and its approach to the question of class interests. Included as part of this discussion is the framework which I consider most appropriate for discussing the class interests affected by the various changes in the status of the ownership of the steel industry and different government policies for the industry. Chapter 3 begins the argument about the relations between government and the industry by looking at the events that prefigured the initial struggle over nationalisation. The setting up of the British Iron and Steel Federation and the various factors that shaped the situation of this first struggle are outlined. In the next two chapters, the details of the nationalisation of steel are examined. The first of these, Chapter 4, considers what was at stake in the dispute and what was implied by the two proposals for the future organisation of government/industry relations. Chapter 5 contains a reflection on these developments and an initial set of propositions about the character of power evident in that struggle. Chapters 6 and 7 examine the form of denationalisation and the changes that occurred in the steel industry in the period of public regulation. Chapter 8 concludes the presentation with a discussion of the renationalisation of steel and an account of the form of the newly established National Steel Corporation. Throughout the course of these chapters, there are parts of an argument about both the significance of government action and the character of power evident in the interaction between government and the steel industry. All these elements have been brought together in a concluding chapter which focuses on the general implications for the analysis of government action and the power of private capital.

To summarise then, the subject of the argument is power. It is a study of the class power of capital on the basis of a detailed examination of the nationalisation of steel. As such it is not based on a general or abstract consideration, but on the analysis of an actual social process which is, by its nature, of some importance to the development of the system. In looking at this process, I have been concerned to theorise about the character of power present in these events and to develop a conception of power which is capable of making the developments and changes intelligible. The account offered is not primarily designed to test hypotheses about the character of power. The focal point of the argument is similar to that of those previous accounts of the relationship between government and business, which, whatever their intended purpose, all probed the realities and forms of the class power of capital.

1

Problems in the analysis of power

Arguments about the definition, character and analysis of power have always played an important part in the discussion of social life. For all practical purposes, contemporary sociological arguments about power are related to the propositions put forward by Max Weber. His definition of power as

the chance of a man or a number of men to realize their own will in a communal action even against the resistance of others who are participating in the action[1]

introduced the main elements of later arguments about power: action, the realisation of goals (will), conflict and the social context. Differences over the interpretation of the terms *Macht* and *Herrschaft* are of some consequence in the framing of the discussion, for it changes the emphasis in an important way. For instance, Parsons's translation of *Macht* as power and *Herrschaft* as domination produces the following contrasted definitions:

A. 'Power' (*Macht*) is the probability that one actor within a social relationship will be in a position to carry out his own will despite resistance, regardless of the basis on which this probability rests.
B. 'Domination' (*Herrschaft*) is the probability that a command with a specific given content will be obeyed by a given group of persons. 'Discipline' is the probability that by virtue of habituation a command will receive prompt and automatic obedience in stereotyped forms, on the part of a given group of persons.[2]

If instead *Macht* refers to force or might and not power, the interpretation of what Weber meant by *Herrschaft* takes on increased significance. Poulantzas, for one, uses the definition of *Herrschaft* as the basis for his discussion of Weber's position on power.[3] Such disputes have opened the way for a detailed reinterpretation of what was implied by Weber in his analysis of legitimate domination.[4] The point of these comments is not to frame my argument in the terms outlined by Weber but to indicate the way in which such a view of the question has formed a backdrop to subsequent definitions and alternative procedures for the analysis of power.

8

That Weber's arguments formed such a background can be seen in the way American liberal scholars sought to refute the social critics who maintained that power was not distributed throughout the polity but was, in fact, concentrated in the hands of an economic elite. These scholars attempted to clarify what was meant by the concept of power and to determine the most appropriate methods for its analysis. On the basis of these conceptual and methodological arguments and with an emphasis on the way in which power was socially effective, these writers generated a pluralist description of the distribution and processes of power in American society. Though Dahl and his associates illustrated their positions by reference to the study of small towns and communities, their conclusions were treated as relevant to the interpretation of power at a national level. Such an apology for the democracy of the U.S. political system did not go unchallenged. Their findings were criticised for their factual inadequacy, the definitions of power employed and the methodologies used. Bachrach and Baratz, in their criticisms of Dahl and Polsby, opened up several new areas for discussion. Their alternative procedures did not result in a substantially new interpretation of the role of power in the U.S.A. It was not until Lukes produced his brief and incisive survey of the debate that their propositions were systematised and given a coherent exposition.[5] Lukes was not working on the analysis of any particular power situation, but brought to the dispute a concern with the question of free will and determinism which gave his arguments a distinctive flavour. He emphasised the need to increase the scope of democratic participation. Though his arguments provide a challenge to the restricted form of democracy characteristic of liberal political systems, his procedures do not represent a radical break with the tradition of power analysis that he is criticising.

Before turning to the dispute between Dahl and his critics, I want to introduce briefly the position taken by Poulantzas as it stands apart from the arguments of that exchange. The substance of Poulantzas's position will be examined further in the next chapter. There is no marxist tradition in the analysis of power comparable to that of the Weberian heritage. Neither Marx nor Engels gives an explicit definition of power, and those who argue from a marxist perspective have to develop arguments about power from the basic interpretation by Marx and Engels of the class relations of capitalist society. This Poulantzas does on the basis of his own distinctive style of theorising and produces the following definition:

By power, we shall designate *the capacity of a social class to realise its specific objective interests.*[6]

Lukes, on the basis of his concern with the attribution of (moral) responsibility to the exercisers of power, rejects Poulantzas's position.[7] He sees it as based within an interpretive system of structural determinism that undermines conceptions implicit in the language of power. Though the role of the structure in Poulantzas's analysis is important, it should be noted that the definition contains no reference to the structure, nor is it predicated on a prior conceptualisation of structure, for the basis of the class's capacity to achieve its interests is unspecified. The important thing about this definition is that it links power with classes and with interests, a focus that is not only relevant to the interpretation of steel nationalisation that I want to develop, but also intrudes into Lukes's interpretation of how power is properly to be analysed.

In this chapter I have not attempted a full and detailed survey of all the arguments about power which have been developed in recent years. Instead, I have concentrated on those that are most appropriate to the analysis of power in the relationship between private capital and government. It is my contention that most of the relevant arguments about power and the procedures for its analysis share a basic position which makes it very difficult for the proponents of these arguments to deal with the actions of governments. It is not that they are unaware of the significance of government action for their wider concerns, but that they make no attempt to relate the character of governments, as social institutions, to the basic conceptions of power being used. This has the dual effect of undermining not just their conceptions of power but also their arguments about the character of the social system. Here I want to examine first the basic positions on the conceptualisation and analysis of power put forward by Dahl, Bachrach and Baratz and Lukes, and secondly the ways in which their approaches have problems in dealing with the analysis of government action. On the basis of this discussion, I want to outline the main features that need to be clarified before the conflict over the nationalisation of steel can be analysed for what it can be made to reveal about the character of power involved in the interaction between government and private capital.

Approaches to power

Dahl

Robert A. Dahl is the major American behaviourist to have argued about the most appropriate procedures for the study of power. His arguments are, on the whole, more refined, and hence less easily refuted, than those of his popularisers such as Polsby.[8] In his articles, Dahl does not explicitly answer the question 'What is Power?' but rather seeks to establish certain strict procedures to determine who has power in closely defined circumstances. On the basis of these procedures it is possible to identify several important aspects of the way in which he actually views power. His work is clearly within the tradition that sees power as something used to gain particularly chosen or valued ends. From his rejection of the elite approach of Hunter and Wright-Mills, it would seem that Dahl regards power as a resource whose distribution differed from that of other social resources and which could be measured separately. But Dahl does not treat power as a disembodied or general attribute and is careful to define it in the context of relations between people. Though Dahl largely illustrates his positions by references to the actions of individuals, he believes that his approach is applicable to the conflicts between significant social classes and institutions. Dahl expresses his assumptions about power in a simple formula which is refined and rephrased throughout his work. Thus he states that:

My intuitive idea of power, then, is something like this: A has power over B to the extent that he can get B to do something that B would not otherwise do.[9]

The subsequent refinements of this basic formula were all based on considering power relations as a subset of general causal relations.[10] This is most evident in Dahl's treatment of the scope and measurement of power.[11] Central to his procedure is Dahl's concern to establish the behavioural changes necessary to indicate a successful exercise of power. Unlike some of his co-workers, Dahl's conception of behaviour is extremely broad and includes 'predispositions, feelings, attitudes and beliefs as well as overt acts.'[12] Dahl also works with the proposition that unaltered behaviour could be the result of an exercise of power, if, but for that exercise of power, the behaviour would have changed. His most important limiting condition is his assumption that power could only be identified in situations of overt conflict between several contending parties.[13] The difference between their initially stated positions and the eventual outcome could be used to reveal not only the existence and operation of power, but also the extent of the successful exercise of power by the contending parties. One of the consequences of Dahl's assumptions is to shift emphasis away from the unequal distribution of social resources to the skill with which these could be used.[14] Dahl's position can be simply summarised: power is evident only through its use and this is discernible primarily in the decision-making process where research concentrates on the question, 'Who prevails?'.

Bachrach and Baratz

As Dahl has developed his position through a critique of the elite approach, so Bachrach and Baratz have developed theirs through a critique of Dahl and Polsby.[15] In their comments Bachrach and Baratz explicitly side with Dahl and Polsby in their rejection of the 'sociological' approach.[16] Their first article is significant for the way in which it introduces the notion of non-decision-making as a complement to the decision-making process, thus widening the focus of the analysis of power.[17] It is interesting in that it does not challenge the basic conception of power that had been used by the behaviourists. This matter is taken up in a second article, which, though it does not focus on Dahl's work, clarifies their own definition of power and non-decision.[18] They reject the view that power is an attribute and hold that power is only evident in relationships and the attitudes of the interacting parties are crucial for the analysis of whether or not power is involved.[19] For Bachrach and Baratz, the emphasis is shifted from the question of who has power, to that of how the exercise of power is facilitated by the recipient in that power relation. On the basis of their rejection of power as an attribute they propose this as the definition of power:

A power relationship exists when (a) there is a conflict over values or courses of actions between A and B, (b) B complies with A's wishes; and (c) he does so because he is fearful that A will deprive him of a value or values which he, B, regards more highly than those that would have been achieved by non-compliance.[20]

A large part of that article is concerned with setting up 'operationally' useful distinctions between power, force, influence and authority on the basis of their relational characteristics and whether they are rational or not, in the sense that they rely upon choice for achieving their ends. In the first article Bachrach and Baratz introduce the idea of non-decision-making as a process in which power is exercised to prevent issues arising in the political arena. By the second article, however, this has been changed from a process to a situation that is defined in this way:

When the dominant values, the accepted rules of the game, the existing power relations among groups, and instruments of force, singly or in combination, effectively prevent certain grievances from developing into fully fledged issues which call for decisions, it can be said that a non-decision making situation exists.[21]

The second article makes no further attempt to show how the analysis of non-decision-making would clarify or assist the analysis of power. The general thrust behind these two articles is the attempt, first, to extend the area within which power could be analysed and, secondly, to come to grips with the way in which the context of the relationship is relevant to the examination of power.[22] This second point is roughly expressed by their concern with the established values of the social system, the mobilisation of bias, and the way in which a given situation may preclude certain grievances being expressed in the political system. Their solution to this problem was to move from the question of the context, or the nature of the ongoing social process, to an emphasis on the values involved and the attitudes of the participants. In that, they opened the way for a phenomenological reconstruction of the power relationship.

Bachrach and Baratz were alert to the problems of using their procedures for an actual piece of research and they sought to illustrate them in a study of community politics.[23] Unfortunately their account of Baltimore politics does not go very far in demonstrating the analysis of non-decisions. Crenson's study of air-pollution legislation, which would seem to be based on an affinity with Bachrach and Baratz's approach, is a much better piece of work.[24] It is at its most revealing when discussing the selectivity of different political systems rather than the question of non-decisions.

Lukes

The systematisation of Bachrach and Baratz's insights was not achieved until Lukes published his survey of the debate. He presents his argument in terms of one-, two- and three-dimensional approaches to power, a procedure that conceals his real contribution to the debate. Lukes manages to remove many of the difficulties involved in Bachrach and Baratz's formulations while advancing the debate by focusing on interests. None of the criticisms I make of Lukes are intended to detract from the real advance achieved by changing the focus of the dispute. What I want to suggest is that Lukes's approach to the study of interests restates the refinements made by Dahl at the outset of the debate.

In returning to the question of how power is identified in a particular relationship, Lukes follows Bachrach and Baratz in the need to widen the scope of analysis. His comments make it clear that the whole of social life, and not just those areas which involve politics, overt conflict, grievances or decision-making, is the relevant subject area. Like Dahl, he has a core notion for the identification of power which he states thus:

I have defined the concept of power by saying that A exercises power over B when A affects B in a manner contrary to B's interests.[25]

There is an obvious phraseological similarity between this formulation and that of Dahl. At that level it is of no consequence, but there are other, more important similarities in Lukes's procedures for identifying whether B's interests have been adversely affected or not.

Before considering the similarities, it is useful to consider Lukes's treatment of interests, although he is both brief and elliptical on the topic.[26] The articles he cites with approval do not clarify the situation.[27] From his criticism of the behaviourists for ignoring the distinction between interests and policy preferences, it can be inferred that persons or groups can be unaware or mistaken about their interests.[28] On the basis of a footnote, it is possible to see that he does not believe that interests are derived from the social location of the individuals or groups.[29] He also suggests that needs and interests may not coincide in a situation where cultural values have been inculcated by the powerful to serve their own ends.[30] Despite these occasional remarks, Lukes makes no argument that establishes the connection between people, groups of people, and their interests, in such a way that it would be possible to go from their interests to the way in which they were affected by the exercise of power. Lukes's procedures depend rather on the identification of a relevant 'counterfactual' which can be used to show whose interests are being acted against. Thus Lukes wants to discover, by use of reasoning, something to show that the observed situation, altered or unaltered behaviour, is the result of an exercise of power, by contrasting it with the same situation without the exercise of power. In doing so he echoes Dahl's concern with identifying relevant changes in behaviour, but Lukes's procedures differ both in their flexibility and in the range of situations to which they are applicable. In part, Lukes recognises the connection with Dahl by arguing that the circumstances which the behaviourists chose to study were ones that provided a ready-made counterfactual. Lukes sets up procedures for less obvious situations and argues that:

Where there is no observable conflict between A and B, then we must provide other grounds for asserting the relevant counterfactual. That is, we must provide other, indirect grounds for asserting that if A had not acted (or failed to act) in a certain way . . . then B would have acted differently from the way he does actually think and act. In brief we need to justify our expectation that B would have thought or acted differently; and we also need to specify the mechanisms by which A has prevented, or else acted (or abstained from acting) in a manner sufficient to prevent B from doing so.[31]

Though Lukes is correct in wanting to extend the range and scope of the analysis, and suggests a method that is consistent with the study of situations of overt conflict, he does not indicate what reasoning would be adequate to the task of identifying the relevant (as opposed to a spurious) counterfactual. In his illustrations he relies on the work of Crenson and the common-sense claim that people have an interest in not being poisoned by air pollution. Though superficially obvious this does not help the identification of interests in less common-sense situations.

At this stage, it is not necessary to examine the strength of Lukes's improvements on Dahl or Bachrach and Baratz. Suffice it to say that he has focused the debate on the crucial question of interests even though he has not set out sufficient indications of how the analysis of those interests is to be done. But it is necessary to show how the consensus about power extends across the debate from Dahl to Lukes. It is clear that it is not such an obvious or all-embracing consensus, as the participants disagree on many substantial issues. These include the area within which power is to be analysed, the nature and character of power itself, and indeed the terms in which an exercise of power is to be recognised and analysed. If there is a consensus it must cover different aspects of the contending approaches, and concern matters with more important consequences. At this level there are several indications of the consensus. Firstly, there is the common usage of the heuristic device of 'A having power over B'. Secondly, there is the shared lack of attention to the significance or meaning of the outcome of the power relationship, apart, that is, from finding out who prevailed and that the outcome was against the interests of one of the contending parties. Thirdly, there is the shared reference to behaviour, altered or not, as the basis for the assessment of the power involved in the relationship. This varies from the obvious in Dahl's writings to Lukes's suppositions about probable behaviour in imaginatively reconstructed conditions of greater autonomy. It is my contention that these areas of agreement have more significant consequences for the analysis of power relations than the manifest differences in approach. The different procedures that have been developed in the course of the debate appear to be the result of turning the explanatory logic behind Dahl's position, and the limitations that he built into the analysis of power, against those very limitations. By understanding what gave Dahl's procedures their potency, his critics were able to extend the analysis beyond the limits he set and to attempt to grapple with the problem of the way in which the setting of the power relation affected the actual interaction within it. If the core proposition of the consensus were to be stated briefly, it is the assumption that power relations are to be understood largely in terms of themselves and that the context and character of the interacting parties is less important than the analysis of the interaction itself. The progress of the debate and the successively suggested new procedures have brought the argument up against the consensus itself.

The problems of the dominant view of power

At the beginning of the chapter, I suggested not only that there was a surprising consensus between Dahl and his critics, but that this consensus was significantly flawed. At the level of language, it is obvious that the '*A* has power over *B*' formula is an important device used to conceptualise about power. As an heuristic device, the formula is unexceptionable as it does help to clarify certain propositions about power relationships. But it contains difficulties that are immediately evident in any attempt to view socially significant interactions in its terms. The formula invites the substitution of particular groups or institutions for the symbols *A* and *B* and it is here that such a formula obstructs the analysis of power. In some circumstances, the terms and substitution are adequate as, for instance, when dealing with individuals bound together by no bonds other than those of friendship or acquaintance. If one were attempting to measure the degree of influence that one of them had on the others, then these procedures would be more or less adequate. Unfortunately these conditions do not apply to the socially significant interactions between major social groups or institutions. The symbols *A* and *B* are interchangeable, but the major social classes and institutions are not. In a class-structured society, the major social groupings and institutions at the start of any particular interaction have a given character that derives from a combination of their structural location and the historical developments that lead them into interaction. In the analysis of an interaction, neither the structured context nor the specific characteristics of the interacting parties can be taken for granted, but must be accorded a significant part in the analysis. The analysis cannot just be concerned with the interaction itself, but must include an account of the character of the interacting parties, and the historical trajectory followed by them to produce the interaction. It is in this sense that the analysis of power is not enough; to understand power it is necessary to understand the context in which power operates.

There are also a number of problems in the evaluation of the outcomes of the particular interactions. Dahl, at the level of overt conflict, treats policy preferences as what is at stake. Lukes, still concerned with conflict, argues that it is interests that are involved. Dahl's reasoning is clearly deficient on this point. Not only does he confuse policy preferences with interests – the charge that Lukes makes – but he treats triumph in the decision-making process as an indication both of power and of who gained by the outcome. The conflation is weak just because it is not self-evident that securing the outcome will secure an advantage to the person or group which prevails. If it is admitted that a disjunction could exist between who prevails in the decision-making process and who gains as a result of the decisions taken, then the whole question of what is shown by a triumph in the decision-making process would have to be taken up again. Though Lukes does not explicitly tackle this problem, he does consider some aspects of it in the discussion of how policies might affect the interests of one of the parties. Lukes's arguments are useful since he maintains that it is possible to argue about interests and policy outcomes by intellectually reconstructing the link between actors and their interests. But Lukes is unwilling to accept that interests are an aspect of a group's or an institution's place in the social structure.

Against the position of Lukes and Dahl, I would like to suggest that interests are structurally located, that is, socially significant groups have their primary interests as a consequence of the place they occupy in the social structure. These interests are expressed in a number of different ways and there is no one-to-one correspondence between an interest and the policy preference or behaviour that may either express it or be based upon it. Such a connection could be explicitly established and demonstrated. Indeed, for the analysis of power it would be imperative to do so, especially if the notions of 'prevailing in decision-making' or of interests being 'significantly affected' by policies or outcomes, were to be used.

Though the current debate would seem to assume that power relations at all levels of social life can be analysed in the same terms, this is not a self-evident proposition. In the following passage, the remarks are intended to be relevant only to those interactions that occur between socially significant groups, classes or institutions. It would require more elaboration to show how, if at all, these arguments could be applied to the personal conflicts of everday life. The purpose of these remarks is not to establish detailed procedures for the analysis of any specific interaction, but to outline the general focus of such an approach. Firstly, a particular power interaction cannot be understood in its own terms. The analysis of power requires reference to other levels of the social whole and to other relations that are not necessarily power relations. Thus at the outset it is necessary to establish who the interacting parties are and how they are historically and structurally located and characterised. Furthermore, it is necessary to establish the extent to which this prior structure of the context 'prejudges' the interaction and sets the framework within which the relationship will be resolved and power, as such, will be exercised. It is then possible to consider the details of the specific interaction. The analysis would focus not only on who prevails in decision-making, and the shape of the political agenda, but also on the significance of the outcome as it affects the situation within which the parties interact. The question of whether one of the parties' interests are adversely affected is complemented by the question of whose interests are served by a particular outcome. It is not assumed that those who prevail in the decision-making process are those whose interests are served by the outcome.

The assessment of governmental power

For the purpose of illustrating the consequences of the tradition of power conceptualisation considered above, I will examine the way in which the pluralists and their critics treat the question of government power. I will also suggest that the procedures advocated by Lukes would not be sufficient to avoid the errors of the pluralist account. The purpose of the discussion is not to show that all accounts of the distribution and use of power are deficient but that certain inadequacies in the conceptualisation of power create certain important difficulties.

For the pluralists, the power of government is assessed as part of a refutation of the thesis that western capitalist countries are dominated by an economic elite or class which has inordinate power and this crucially affects the terms of their arguments. For instance, it is assumed that an elite may legitimately dominate in the sphere of its own competence without this having any consequence for the assessment of power in society as a whole.[32] It is assumed that power is primarily or most significantly located in the political system, and even when this assumption is not made, it is argued that power must make a marked impact upon the political process and hence it is a suitable area for analysis.[33] The government is treated as effectively controlling the economy as it is able to make general policy for the conduct of economic affairs.[34] If business does affect government policy, it is argued that the influence is not inordinate and that it is not exercised in such a way as to violate the norms which prevail in that political system.[35] Implicit in the pluralist account is the assumption that the terms of the '*A* has power over *B*' formula are relevant to the assessment of the relationship between government and business.

The assessment of governmental power proceeds in the following manner. A certain number of decisions or conflicts between government and private capital are chosen for analysis. No particular attention is paid to the character of the interacting parties or the historical or structured context within which they interact. Similarly no attention is paid to the interests that may be involved; policy differences are all-important. It is noted that in all but the rarest occasions the government's will prevails and the consequences of economic pressure are not significant. It is then concluded that the government is more powerful than private capital and that the political process regulates the economy. But the assessment is based on flawed assumptions that make a mockery of the certainty with which the conclusions are pronounced.

At an obvious level the apparent triumph of the government is misinterpreted in a number of ways. Firstly, government does not usually come into conflict with private capital as a whole or as a unified body but with a particular firm, a section of an industry or an industry. A government's victory over these subunits cannot be treated as symptomatic of government power over the class or the economic process. Further, any opposition that exists is converted into a categorical opposition. In doing so, the interests of a particular firm may be mistaken for the interests of capital as a whole (an interest which may be expressed in government policy) or short-term interests for long-term ones. Secondly, the opposition of small producers may be treated as indicating the opposition of the class while underestimating or ignoring the support of larger or more progressive sectors. In all these minor ways it is possible to overlook the fact that opposition does not necessarily mean that significant, dominant or class interests are being threatened.

These difficulties can be relatively easily overcome but there are other, more durable, difficulties. Many critics have noted the peculiar notion of government which infects the pluralist analysis. They have noted the belief that the government in some ways combines the properties of being neutral as regards competing social groups, with being a pressure-influenced body (such that the success of social groups in their interaction with government can be taken as a measure of their relative power) and a body that acts for the interests of society considered as a whole. For the pluralists, the government proposes policies, balances the pressures placed upon it by interested parties and enforces an eventual reasonable direction. It is this view which makes sense of the pluralist attempt to measure the respective power of labour and capital by the extent of their influence upon the policies and actions of the government. For the procedure to work, government must be a pressure-influenced body. This gives rise to an inconsistency in the argument. In proving that the economic elite does not have an inordinate influence it is assumed that the success of the government is significant, but it can only be significant if the government has interests of its own which are distinct from not only those of the firms that may challenge them, but those of capital as a whole. If this were the case then government ceases to be essentially a pressure-influenced body and the whole focus of the account must be altered. It then becomes necessary to discover just what the interests of government are and how they relate to the interests of capital as a whole or any of its subunits. This is a much more difficult task.

The basis for the pluralist mis-assessment of government power stems from the way in which the 'A has power over B' formula has informed the analysis of a situation for which it is manifestly inappropriate. In the assessment of the power which a government may have or exercise, it is necessary to establish what is the status of the two parties, how they came to be in a situation of conflict and what is the consequence of the interaction for the ongoing development of the social system (that is, the context within which the interaction occurs). Such a procedure would alert the researcher to the character of the part of capital opposed to government plans and provide a basis for establishing the relationship between such a part and the interests of the class of capital as a whole. It would also bring attention to the fact that the government is not a body like any other, but has a special character and place within the social whole which sets it apart. This is not the place to consider all these features, just the general properties relevant to this matter. Firstly, the government is a decision-making body; its purpose, character and structural location are all expressed in the fact that it is a body authorised and empowered to take decisions for the development of the whole of society. Such a statement says nothing about how it is authorised but it does suggest that it is not simply a body with power and interests that are peculiarly its own, and indeed suggests that the interests advanced by the state may not be its own. The character of the government affects the assessment of its power in this way. The success of the government in making or implementing a decision cannot be taken as an indication of its power over capital. Instead it indicates that the government is performing its normal role which would then have to be analysed and assessed. The treatment of this normal role of government would need to start from its context and consider the relationship of the interests expressed by the government to the interests of capital as a whole. This is not to deny that pressure is exerted upon government as a matter of course, but that its success is not sufficient to prove that the government is a class institution, nor its failure proof that government is above class.

There have been a large number of critiques of the pluralist account of power in contemporary capitalist society and the work of Domhoff[36] and Miliband[37] can be treated as representative. Both dispute the factual adequacy of the pluralist studies and the terms in which the relationship between the economic elite or governing class and capital is conceived. Miliband's work has been concerned to demonstrate that, in the interaction with labour, capital has a disproportionate share of resources that can be used to ensure that governments do not severely infringe business interests. To some extent his analysis reproduces, in refutation, the idea of government as a pressure influenced body, though the main thrust of this argument shows that the state would act in a manner compatible with the interests of capital even in the absence of such pressure. The point to be made about these criticisms is that they do not go far or deep enough in their refutation of the methods and procedures that underlie the pluralist conclusions. Thus they are concerned to establish how the situation in which the two classes interact is a predisposing factor by reference to the empirical properties that they possess. They do not note that the empirical properties are also an expression of the developed historical situation, the structural location and the character of the interacting parties. In this way the consequences of class structure and historically sedimented contexts are treated at one level removed from that of their most basic import. This does not diminish the power of their arguments and criticisms as the pluralists are wrong at the level of their conclusions, their assumptions about government and the methodologies that they employ. However, the systematic refutation of pluralist conclusions must start from and be able to utilise a critique of the assumptions about the nature of power that informs their procedures as well as their conclusions.

It is now necessary to turn to the question of whether Lukes's suggested procedures, could, as they now stand, give a better assessment of governmental power. Certainly they would alert the researcher to things that are missed entirely by the pluralist account. For instance, Lukes's approach is more sensitive to the question of the interests of those who do not immediately seem to be involved; in this case, the relevant sections of the working class who would be affected as a consequence of the policy being determined or implemented. But on the relationship between government and private capital Lukes's procedures seem unable to comment. How would the appropriate counterfactual be established in a case where private capital appeared to be successful in imposing a condition or a policy on the government? An imaginary reconstruction in the absence of the exercise of power would seem less useful than in the case of air pollution. How does a researcher establish what a government would have done? If it is a matter of falling back on the government's stated policy preference then the procedures have not been developed very far. But Lukes has not set out the criteria for working out the interests of bodies such as the government or the class of capital. In his work there are no hints given of any way to judge whether the policy preference expressed by an institution is the expression of an interest which is intrinsically its own. As a consequence, it would be impossible to show which interests were served by a government policy, or how one body could come to advocate a policy that served the interests of another. Thus, on the question of governmental power Lukes's procedures are inadequate or he must fall back on the procedures of his predecessors. Though his work would alert a researcher to a wider range of questions, it is unlikely that his suggested procedures would greatly improve the pluralist account of the power of government in its interaction with private capital.

Conclusion

In this chapter I have been concerned to show that there is a way of treating power that is common in social science research and which transcends the normal divisions between behaviourists and anti-behaviourists. This surprising consensus spans the work of Dahl and his critics, Bachrach, Baratz and Lukes. The critics definitely improve Dahl's formulations by extending the circumstances that can be legitimately studied and by improving the terms in which these could be treated. They did not reject that aspect of Dahl's perspective which treated power relations as entities that could be examined in their own terms. The consensus was flawed in such a way that it could not adequately account for the interactions between socially significant groups and institutions and, consequently, could not deal with the major developments in a class-fragmented society. The consensus position was ahistorical since it did not build into its analysis the need to locate the interacting parties in the process of their historical development. In that way, it did not make it necessary to understand how the situation in which the parties came to be interacting had developed and was structured. The consensus was further indiscriminate in that it did not stress the need to determine the character of the interacting parties and to treat them as important factors in the interaction. Thus the whole thrust of the dominant approach was to treat power relations in their own terms. The '*A* has power over *B*' formula has its virtues but so far it has carried too great a burden and has cut the researcher off from a critical appraisal of the circumstances in which the power interaction occurs.

On the basis of the work of Dahl's critics and particularly the position argued by Lukes, it is possible to determine what needs to be included in an assessment of the part played by power in a particular social process. An analysis of power is concerned with the way in which the interests of various groups and classes are affected by both the situation in which they exist and the actions of other classes, groups or social institutions. There is a relationship between the different ways in which the interests of various groups are affected and the character and form of power in particular social processes and conflicts. It is the points that Lukes has not properly established that need to be clarified before the conflicts surrounding the nationalisation of steel can be analysed. The significance of government action and the character of governments as social institutions need to be discussed further, as does the conceptualisation of interests and the framework within which these can best be identified.

2

State theory and the question of class interests

Though a large part of the discussion on the struggle over the nationalisation of steel will be related to the question of the status and significance of government action, it is useful to outline, in general terms, the way in which the character of government is to be treated. This matter can be approached through the perspective of the contemporary debates over the analysis of the capitalist state. It is true that the terms government and state are not interchangeable.[1] Government is only a part of the state system which also includes the civil service, the army, police and military, the judiciary and parliamentary assemblies. There has been some dispute over whether other institutions that enhance social cohesion should be treated as state institutions.[2] This question is not relevant here, but I prefer a narrower rather than a broader definition of the state and side with Miliband on this point.[3] There is an important sense, however, in which the government is the active centre of the state. This is not to assert that the government is *a priori* the most important part of the state system[4] but that the pattern of action and inaction of governments gives the state its distinctive policy or approach to the problems and developments in capitalist society. Again, the position here does not imply that to gain governmental office is the same thing as capturing state power, as was assumed by some social democrats who viewed the state as a neutral instrument which could be used to implement a complete transformation of the existing social order.

At a general level, all state theory shares a similar perspective. The role of the capitalist state (or the function of the state in a capitalist society) is to preserve and defend the class domination of capital. On such a basis, government action can then be examined for the part that it plays in such a process. It is important to note that state theory is almost the exclusive preserve of marxist and marxist-related scholarship. Conservatives and liberals do not have a concern that would lead them to consider the relationship between the state and the class of capital in such terms except to refute marxist interpretations. Though there is agreement on the general role or function of the capitalist state, that is all that is agreed. There are a large number of different accounts of why and how it is that the state comes to perform that role, and over the precise ways in which that task is performed. It is unnecessary, and would be exceedingly lengthy, to consider all the different strands in the contemporary arguments over the capitalist state. Though some of these positions are very important, especially those of Mattick[5] and O'Connor,[6] they are peripheral to a discussion of class and class interests and have only been referred to where necessary in the text. In this chapter I want to leave aside the general description of the state's actions and to concentrate attention instead on the arguments advanced to show how it is that the state comes to fulfil the task of protecting the class domination of capital. To that end, the works of Miliband, Poulantzas and those involved in the state-derivation debate have been examined, both for their arguments about the mechanisms which they identify to explain the congruence between the actions of the state and the requirements of capital, and for the different ways in which they conceptualise and argue about class interests. On the basis of that discussion, I have elaborated a framework for the interpretation of class interests that is relevant to the analysis of power.

Interpretations of the capitalist state

Miliband

There is a problem in identifying and classifying the different strands of contemporary debate on the state. It is clear that Miliband's *The State in Capitalist Society* marked a decisive point in the revival of a serious discussion of the character and significance of the capitalist state. Between the publication of Laski's interpretation in the thirties[7] and the appearance of Miliband's book, analysis of the state in English had been poorly argued and either saw the state as a simple instrument of the capitalist class, or one of its fractions, or as in some way fused with monopoly capitalism.[8] In both cases the state would almost automatically serve the interests of the dominant class as it was either part of the class or a creature of it. The great virtue of Miliband's work was that he managed both to refute pluralist defences of capitalist power and to break with the notion of the state as a simple instrument of the capitalist class. In doing so Miliband opened up for analysis the whole complexity of the relationship between class and state. Unfortunately, the study has not been followed up by others, though Westergaard and Resler, in their *Class in a*

Capitalist Society, use similar formulations about the state as part of a substantial critique of the class divisions in Britain.[9] These two books complement each other and can be used to illustrate one way in which the question of the state and class interests has been treated.

Miliband does have a conception of class and an explanation for why the state acts to advance and protect the interests of capital. This is not expressed in explicit theoretical formulations and it is necessary to reconstruct the definitions implicit in the analysis. On the question of interests, the reconstruction is complicated, as the term is used to mean the same thing as a class or a class fraction. He writes of the 'capitalist interest' or the 'other interest' in the manner of the nineteenth-century conception of society divided into substantive interests.[10] The matter is further complicated since, in the refutation of the pluralist interpretation, Miliband has used the term 'interest groups' to designate groups that sought to influence the behaviour of governments.[11] In that discussion, Miliband fully exposed the consequences of treating labour and capital as pressure groups like any others and of assuming that there is an equality in the influence that labour and capital can exert on governments and the state.[12]

Underneath the variety of words used to describe the phenomenon, Miliband follows Marx and defines classes in terms of their relationship to the means of production, identifying three main class groupings: capital, labour and the petty bourgeoisie.[13] Miliband is imprecise about the boundaries that can be drawn between the classes, but that does not affect the general terms of the argument. Capital is treated as divided into a number of elites, either on the basis of their specific part in the process of production, industry, commerce or banking, or on the basis of their place in the organisation of production, as owners or managers. The class of capital is seen as being unified in its opposition to the proletariat and in its defence of the existing economic, political and social order. The state acts to secure the interests of capital and most of the book is concerned to document the ways in which this is done. It is these sections that contain the implicit arguments about interests as class interests and the explanation of why the state acts to secure the class interests of capital.

Before examining the conception of class interests, it is useful to consider that explanation. It was this which was most strongly criticised by others writing on the state and which was given most emphasis in the wake of the so-called Miliband–Poulantzas debate.[14] The essence of the criticism was that in refuting the factual accuracy of the pluralist interpretation, Miliband had himself portrayed the state as a basically pressure-influenced body and that it was the disparities between the strength of labour and capital that caused the state to act in a manner favourable to capital. In such a criticism the book's title, 'The State *in* Capitalist Society' takes on a heightened significance and is juxtaposed against an analysis of the *capitalist* state.[15] Though there is a sense in which Miliband reproduces the notion of the state as a pressure-influenced body, this is neither the sum total of his argument nor the aspect which has the most explanatory power.

In considering why it is that the state advances the capitalist interest, Miliband emphasises several different factors and arguments. At one level he details the shared backgrounds of those who staff state institutions and those who are significant members of the class of capital.[16] With this as the basis, he also demonstrates that those who run the state share the same world-view as that of capital and will view problems and their possible solutions in the same terms. Westergaard and Resler make the same point when they argue that it is because state incumbents accept the legitimacy of both private property and profit that their actions will not be harmful to capitalist interests and that reforms will not endanger the prerogatives of private capital.[17] In other words, the shared ideology of capital will shape the space and the manner in which the state will act. Such an interpretation would explain how state action was directed to the needs of capital, even if not explicitly intended by the government or the rest of the state institutions. It cannot explain the success or failure of state action. State action would only be effective if the ideology of capital were true or adequate, that is, if capital were capable of recognising its own interests and formulating policies that could adequately express them. It is not clear that capital, as a class, is competent in that way or that its ideology is so adequately constructed.

Miliband uses a second, and quite different, argument which would also explain the harmony between state action and the interests of the capitalist class. This explanation relies on the notion of structural constraints which affect the scope and character of state action and ensure that its programmes do not work against the capitalist interest.[18] The fact that the state exists within a capitalist social framework means that there are certain imperatives built into the situations that face politicians, and those in state institutions, so that policies will be shaped in such a way that they do not harm capital. An illustration of the explanation can be found in Miliband's discussion of the role of governments, where the assumption is made that politicians are pragmatists who accept the logic of the prevailing

social order and who, to the extent that they have a theoretical perspective, do not think outside the limits of capitalist reality.[19] Here it
is argued that the goals of politicians, as they recognise them, must
necessarily harmonise with the interests of capital. If politicians want
to improve the standard of living of the population and increase
material well-being, these goals can only be gained by subsidising or
encouraging private capital or by improving the efficiency of the
capitalist economic system without damaging private profitability. In
other words, the overwhelming significance of economics and business within a capitalist system is such that the scope for political
action is constructed so that those who want to succeed and to deliver
the goods by which political skill is measured, must run the state in
such a way that it serves the interests of capital, whether they conceive of their actions in those terms or not. It should be noted that this
argument is directly related to the analysis of government action and
is not based on the existence of any personal connections between
members of governments or the state system and those in the capitalist class. The position is also similar to that taken by Westergaard and
Resler,[20] and Offe and Ronge[21] in their conclusion to a study of social
democracy.

Though this does not give a comprehensive account of how the
state actually serves the diverse interests of the capitalist class or how
it arranges compromises between conflicting sectional claims, it does
provide a useful framework for the analysis of state action. The extent
to which the consequences are actually the result of the existence or
operation of structural constraints is under-conceptualised but it does
provide a strong basis for arguing that a state in a capitalist society
must be a capitalist state and that its normal actions will be harmonised with the interests of capital.

Miliband does not provide any explicit consideration of the character of class interests. Many of the phrases he uses imply that interests
are closely related to the need to maintain the domination of the class
of capital, both by reasserting its cultural and ideological values and
by providing the social and material basis for its successful operations. Without a direct discussion of the question, it is very difficult to
be precise about the way in which interests are conceived. Westergaard and Resler, by contrast, do include a direct comment on the
definition and character of interests. Given the premiss that the
exercise of power is confined by core assumptions about profit and
private property, they ask 'whose and what interest do these core
assumptions favour?'[22] In a footnote they provide a more extensive
definition:

we see interests as the possibilities and potential objectives of action which are inherent in economic positions regardless of whether the incumbents of those positions in fact so define their objectives at any given time.

They weaken the argument when they note that their objective definition of interests is as open to a charge of being arbitrary as any other. All definitions and identifications of interest are open to argument; it is important to stress that they are objective, in the sense of being located in the structures of social life, rather than subjective, that is, existing only in the perception of that life. There is a link between the objective character of interests and the ways in which they are perceived by individual and collective actors, but this does not affect their objective character. Westergaard and Resler's approach to the question of interests is an instructive one and it requires a more extensive examination. The scope of the 'objective possibilities of action' needs to be established in a more detailed form so that such a conception of interests can be used consistently as an objective criterion for the evaluation of policies and outcomes.

Poulantzas

Ever since *Political Power and Social Classes* was published in France in the late sixties, it has been an important reference point in the arguments about the character and form of the capitalist state.[23] Not that the book is immediately about the state; it is not. It is about the attempt to delimit the significance and character of the political instance in a capitalist social formation. The state enters the argument when it is treated as an embodiment of the political instance and the general arguments made about that instance are transferred to the discussion of the state.[24] This produces a significant distortion in the argument and two different ways of treating most important matters such as relative autonomy (of the political and of the state) or class interest.

In the initial section of the book, Poulantzas is concerned to elaborate a highly-structured conception of the capitalist mode of production and then to discuss the significance of the political within it.[25] The form of this argument affects the way in which he treats both the state and class. In Poulantzas's argument, the relations of production are separated from the social relations of production. The relations of production constitute the structure of the mode of production which has the dual effect of distributing agents into classes and of determining the interconnection and significance of the various instances of the mode of production: the economic, the political and the ideological. It is the structure of the mode of production which determines the separation, relative autonomy and limits of each of the regional instances. The state is relatively autonomous as it is the embodiment of the political instance.

In this section of the book, he introduces the necessarily closely related definitions of power and class interests. He indicates that 'By power, we shall designate *the capacity of a social class to realise its specific objective interests*'.[26] He is not so direct about the designation of class interests. He excludes class interests from the structure, arguing that they are part of class practices, since they only belong to classes and appear in action.[27] This is a consequence of his initial separation of relations of production from social relations of production: both class and class interests are removed from the structure of the mode of production and become, instead, effects of that structure. Poulantzas provides neither a precise statement of what actually constitutes an interest as a property of a class or the content of any actual class interest. Rather he identifies interests with the limits of class action within the limits defined by the structure.

While the concept of class indicates the effects of the structure on supports and while the concept of practice covers not behaviour but an operation carried on within the limits imposed by the structure, interests certainly indicate these limits, but at a particular level as the *extension of the field* of the practice of one class in relation to those of the other classes, i.e. the extension of the 'action' of classes in relations of power. This is not any kind of metaphorical play on the terms of limits and field, but a result of the complexity of the relations covered by these terms.[28]

In actual fact, it is a metaphorical play on the words 'limit' and 'field' and this is revealed in his discussion of political action as the ability to occupy 'space' in that 'field'.[29]

In this and the surrounding discussion of class, interest is treated as being consistent with the proletariat's concern for socialism and its ability to pursue that goal under the organised leadership of a competent political party. There is no corresponding sense in which the class interests of capital can be defined using the sense of 'limits of action' unless they are defined in a negative sense by reference to the ability to contain the political action of the proletariat. The more useful aspects of his discussion of interests at this stage in the book is the indication that they are objective, rather than subjective, psychological sources of action and that they are crucially related to the problems of class organisation, power and political action.[30] The location of class interests outside the structure is not so helpful as it leaves the question of the status of the 'objectivity' of these interests unidentified and unargued.

In the later section of the book, where Poulantzas is concerned more immediately with the characteristics and actions of the capitalist state, he develops a series of arguments which do not depend on the previously elaborated concept of a highly structured mode of production. Here Poulantzas accounts for the relative autonomy of the state without reference to determination by the structure but by reference to the class situation in which the state has to operate.[31] He argues that the state must be relatively autonomous if it is to perform its role within the social formation, that is to be adequate to its theoretically defined task of maintaining social cohesion. The scope for its relative autonomy is derived from the class struggle between the two major classes and within the dominant class.[32] The bourgeoisie cannot raise itself to effective action at the political level because the political organisation of the class is handicapped by the division of the class into fractions whose interests are not automatically harmonised. The tensions in the relationship between the various fractions of capital are such that concessions and compromises need to be effected to preserve the general unity of capital even against the interest of some of the fractions. Similarly, the struggle between the dominant and the dominated class may be such that the hegemony of capital is threatened and once again this requires an institution which is capable of organising a solution that will protect the general domination of capital and maintain the social relations of production necessary for the continuation of the capitalist exploitation of labour power as a commodity. It is within the space so generated by class and class-related struggles that the state is able to act and to be relatively autonomous in its relations with the dominant class.

There is also a change in the argument about the character of class interests in this later section of the book. The emphasis on interests as expressing the limits of the structure disappears, but he retains his insistence that interests are objective, that they are not part of the structure and that they are crucially related to the problem of class organisation, power and political action. For the first time, however, he introduces the possibility that the class interests that exist in class practice may not be accurately or adequately embodied in the programmes of political parties or in the policies of the state.[33] Here he has introduced a significant distinction into the analysis of politics and one which was previously absent. There is a theoretical distance established between class and class practice, and the forms, processes and institutions of political life. Though it is important, Poulantzas does not fully consider the implications of this position. Nor does he provide evidence for what the content of a class interest might be or procedures which could be used to identify class interests.

In the later exchanges with Miliband, and in *Classes in Contemporary Capitalism*, Poulantzas indicates that there were sections in *Political Power and Social Class* whose formulations suffered from a 'structuralist deformation' which concealed the main emphasis of his arguments about the state.[34] Clearly included amongst these were the passages which implied a structuralist view of the state in his initial review of *The State in Capitalist Society*.[35] His 'corrected' view of the state, which shows both the way in which he uses the notion of class interests and his identification of the key function of the state, is summarised by the following passage:

On a terrain of political domination occupied by several classes and class fractions and divided by internal contradictions, the capitalist state, while predominantly representing the interests of the hegemonic class or fraction (itself variable), enjoys a relative autonomy with respect to that class and fraction as well as to the other classes and fractions of the power bloc. One reason for this is that its task is to ensure the general political interest of the power bloc as well as organising the 'unstable equilibrium of compromise' (Gramsci) among its components under the leadership of the hegemonic class or fraction; the other reason is that it organises this hegemony with respect to the dominated classes, according to the specific forms that their struggles assume under capitalism. This relative autonomy is inscribed in the very structure of the capitalist state by the relative 'separation' of the political and the economic that is specific to capitalism; it is in no way a function of the intrinsic nature of the state or the 'political instance' as such, but rather derives from the separation and dispossession of the direct producers from their means of production that characterises capitalism. In this respect, this relative autonomy is simply the necessary condition for the role of the capitalist state in class representation and in the political organisation of hegemony.[36]

Here we have the main elements of Poulantzas's position, class and class fractions, interests fragmented by these relations, the state as both organiser of the power bloc and the institution concerned with the social hegemony of capital, and the emphasis on power and organisation. Though I think that the main elements required for the analysis of the state are here, class, fraction, organisation and power, I do not think that the way in which these terms are defined or combined in Poulantzas's account is the most effective way to approach the question of the state and class interests. There is a need for greater clarity in setting out the criteria for recognising class interests and their role in the analysis of the actions of the capitalist state. I do not want to take up the task of criticising the theoretical basis or shape of Poulantzas's arguments on the state but rather to indicate that, even with class, fraction and interest appearing in his account, there is need for further elaboration of these terms.

The state-derivation debate

The state-derivation debate initially involved a number of people working in the Federal Republic of Germany who argued over the most appropriate method for establishing, or 'deriving', the capitalist character of the state which exists in a society dominated by a capitalist mode of production. Despite a variety of differences, all those involved sought to identify the essentially capitalist character of the state, its specific historical form, with the central contradictions of that mode of production. As a necessary part of that exercise, the various functions performed by the state were related to the categories in Marx's critique of political economy. As a result of the work of Holloway and Picciotto, these debates have been presented to an English reading audience[37] and their relevance to the analysis of the British state has been made explicit.[38] For this discussion of what the state-derivation debate reveals about the nature and behaviour of the capitalist state and the question of class and class interest, I have concentrated on three positions which represent the main strands of the argument. The positions are those taken by Altvater, Hirsch, and Holloway and Picciotto. Though Claus Offe's work is more associated with the development of critical sociology,[39] he shares many of the key assumptions of those involved in the derivation debate. He also provides a number of arguments about the analysis of interests and the behaviour of the state. For these reasons, it is useful to consider his arguments in this context.

Capital-logic is the often derisory name given to one of the main strands in the debate. In this approach the character of the capitalist state is deduced (or derived) from the categories of the capitalist economy, the process of production and accumulation. The ways in which this derivation is established are not relevant but some of the arguments used are. The main aspect can be found in Altvater's position,[40] though he is not representative in the sense that he pays only scant regard to the categories of political economy and the logical derivation of the state from these.[41] Instead he begins by positing the necessity of the capitalist state for the successful continuation of capitalist production.[42] He argues that there are certain basic and essential functions that the units of private capital were unable to perform because their concerns were too 'narrow' and limited by the unremitting need to make a profit. It was these functions which were performed by the state with their cost spread across the whole of society. These necessary functions performed by the capitalist state are divided into two groups, those concerned with the basic, infrastructural processes, which also included unprofitable but important industries such as coal mining, and those concerned with the extended reproduction of the social relations that were basic to the mode of production.

The capital-logic approach was criticised by others working on the same problem. The best of these criticisms were made by Hirsch in his article 'The State Apparatus and Social Reproduction' where he sought to describe the achievements and limitations of 'form analysis'.[43] Hirsch starts with a summary of the shared and key assumptions of the debate, that the state is an historical product and that its character can be derived from the categories of a critique of political economy and the defined central contradictions of the capitalist mode of production.[44] Hirsch argues the basis for the derivation of the special character of the capitalist state in the following way:

The manner in which the social bond is established, in which social labour is distributed and the surplus product appropriated necessarily requires that the direct producers be deprived of control over the physical means of force and that the latter be localised in a social instance raised above the economic reproduction process: the creation of formal bourgeois freedom and equality and the establishment of a state monopoly of force. Bourgeois class rule is essentially and fundamentally characterised by the fact that the ruling class must concede to the force which secures its domination an existence formally separated from it.[45]

This observation closely parallels the capital-logic approach. Hirsch's position is distinctive in his treatment of state functions, for it is in this context that he identifies the limits of claims based on a notion of logical derivation.

The attempt to derive from the development of the concept of capital analysed by Marx in *Capital*, those social functions objectively necessary for reproduction which can only be performed collectively outside the sphere of individual capitals, is undoubtedly an important component of a materialist theory of the state and one which on the whole has yet to be developed. But such an approach can only found the objective necessity of the state itself and its concrete mode of functioning.[46]

Extending that point, and indicating the limits of form analysis, he argues that:

Beyond these general determinations, nothing more can be said on this level of analysis about the functioning of the bourgeois state. To that extent, the general 'derivation of form' cannot go beyond trivialities. To go beyond this would require an analysis of the concrete historical developments of the capitalist reproduction process and of the changing conditions of capital valorisation and class relations.[47]

By rejecting some of the conclusions of the capital-logic position, Hirsch shows a way of linking empirical research with theoretical arguments, and the development of the state with the requirements of the accumulation process and the struggles of various political groups. The article does not go beyond making these suggestions.

On the basis of the state-derivation debate, and on the position of Hirsch in particular, Holloway and Picciotto have developed a version of the position that is related to the analysis of the British state.[48] They start from the 'historical materialist category of the capital relation', 'from the category of capital' and deduce the separation of politics (and the state) from the economic as moments in the reproduction process of capital.[49] On this basis they recognise the necessary (not relative) autonomy of the state 'It is thus necessary for the accumulation of capital (the reproduction of capitalist social relations) that the institutions controlling legitimate force should be separate from individual capitals' and the necessary range of state actions by the requirements, needs or imperatives of the accumulation process.[50] These include certain rather general ones like the maintenance of the conditions of commodity production (that is, labour as the commodity, labour power) and the socialisation of necessary, but unprofitable, areas of production. Holloway and Picciotto also deduce the necessary historical changes in the form of the state from the contradictions inherent in the category of capital as expressed in the changing forms of capitalist production. They do not give many details of how this is done, mainly illustrating it by reference to the increased part played by the state in the economy. Some of the elements of their position can be seen in this passage:

We see therefore that the forms of the state are reestablished, supplemented or reformed as part of the process of containment of the new contradictions created by the new stage of development of capital, to re-create or re-compose the capital relation in new forms. Equally, the *functions* of the state are also revised and supplemented, since they too are inflected by the dominant contradictions of each moment of capitalism.[51]

If Holloway and Picciotto differ from the rest of the practitioners of the capital-logic approach, it is in the emphasis which they give to the role of class struggle and the state as a fetishised form of capitalist social relations.[52]

Though the state-derivation debate has been very useful for focusing attention on the relationship between the state and the changes in, and the requirements of, the process of capital accumulation, there are some serious problems in this analysis. For instance, its exponents assume that, in having proved the necessity of the state, they have identified the reasons for it being a capitalist state. Rather this raises the problem: how is it that the state comes to fulfil those functions defined as necessary for capitalist production? The capital-logic approach side-steps the question of the mechanism by which the state comes to recognise the interests of capital, or the changed needs of the accumulation process, and implements corresponding policies. The deductions used in the capital-logic approach also assume that the theoretically identified institution to perform these necessary tasks is the same as the state which acts in a given social formation. At the least, it requires an argument to show that this is the case. The problems faced by actual states in performing these necessary functions are important and need to be considered in any detailed assessment of the capitalist state.

A complete critique of the state-derivation approach is unnecessary but it is relevant to focus attention on the particular way in which its exponents conceptualise class interests. Given the form of their arguments, it is obvious that they will have a distinctive treatment of interests, one related to the categories and processes of capitalist production and accumulation. However, their position on this question is never made explicit. In Muller and Neususs, there is a reference to the contradiction between the collective interests of capital and the interests of individual capitals as it is expressed in attitudes to the actions of the state.[53] Hirsch mentions interests and relates them to the requirements of the valorisation process[54] but provides no details of how interests can be precisely defined or used in analysis. Altvater rarely refers to interests at all. Holloway and Picciotto are quite categorical on the subject though neither precise nor detailed in their remarks. In criticising a comment made by Gough in his article on state expenditure they maintain that:

It is surely wrong to talk of the 'economic' and 'political' interests of capital. Capital (and its bearers, the capitalist class) has only one single interest (although the realisation of this interest depends, as we have seen, on economic and political means): 'Accumulate, accumulate! That is Moses and the prophets!' Accumulation is neither an economic nor a political but a historical materialist category which embraces both the economic and the political. It is a contradictory process, involving both the accumulation of wealth and the reproduction of capitalist social relations.[55]

They also share the rather common view that the state represents 'the interests of capital in general' though they suggest no means to identify what these interests are and how they are related to the sectional interests of capital or units of capital, nor do they indicate what is the mechanism by which the state comes to recognise and represent these interests. The important thing about their position and that of capital-logic, is not the specific details, but the fact that it focuses the argument about interests on the accumulation process understood in broad and social terms. It also illustrates the point that, though the question of class interests is an important part of the analysis of the state, it is frequently poorly conceptualised.

Unlike capital-logic, Claus Offe has focused his attention precisely on the mechanics of interest representation in both the structure and the processes of the state.[56] In his article in *German Political Studies* he rejects the positions of both Miliband and Poulantzas, on the erroneous grounds that they concentrate on factors external to the state.[57] (Interestingly his *New German Critique* piece would also be vulnerable to such a charge.)[58] He then argues that what would make the state into a capitalist state, and not just a state in a capitalist society, would be some characteristics of its internal structure which would guarantee that the collective class interests of capital would be both implemented and advanced.[59] Importantly he distinguishes these collective class interests from sectional interests and the interests of fractions and individual units of capital. The article ends with no firm conclusions but argues that it is necessary to continue the search for this internal structure which would provide the guarantee. In a later article he reconsiders the question and argues that the internal processes of the state *cannot* be adequate to the task of generating policies that will guarantee the interest of capital and illustrates this with reference to three different forms of the policy formation process.[60] Though his method leaves a lot to be desired, the general arguments about the necessary difficulties faced by the state in its task are important.

These brief accounts of different arguments about the capitalist state reveal the ways in which class interests were treated. Even where explicit mention was made of class interest, there was little to suggest that the term had been fully considered or adequately conceptualised. When trying to prove a point, there is always the temptation to exaggerate the shortcomings of what has already been done, but in this case it would seem that the characterisation of class interests, though important for the analysis of the capitalist state, has been seriously neglected. Even Poulantzas, who recognised the importance of class interests for the analysis, did not provide a clearly argued account of what these interests were or how they were to be identified.

Class and class interests

On the whole, the question of class is adequately treated in contemporary state theory. Though there is a tendency to use rather loose formulations to describe class and subclass groupings, this does not normally affect the actual definition of what constitutes class under capitalism, nor the significance of class in the analysis of the state. While there are some aspects of the arguments about class which I would reject, such as Poulantzas's treatment of the new petty bourgeoisie and their political significance,[61] the main definitions follow Marx. Thus, class relations under capitalism are defined by their relationship to the means of production, with the bourgeoisie or the class of capital owning or having a dominant access to the means of production and the proletariat or the class of labour defined by their need to sell their labour power to capital in order to form a relationship with the means of production and so to live. Disputes about who fits into which class are not relevant, just the broad contours of the classes and their definitions. In this argument there is a logical, third class grouping of the petty bourgeoisie or the self-employed: that is, those who own their own means of production and who consume their own labour, which does not appear to them as the commodity labour power.

It is important to include the notion of class fraction and the other internal divisions of the major classes as an initial part of the definition and discussion of class. The class of capital has two basic sets of internal division, firstly into individual and competing units of capital and secondly into fractions. The term fraction does not refer to an arbitrary or self-defined section of the class, but to those sections of capital which are involved in the basic, different parts of the process of capitalist production, circulation and exchange. It is in this sense that industrial capital, commercial capital or money capital have their distinctive meanings. There are, of course, industry and plant divisions and the separation between large and small units, but these are of a different order to the distinction identified by the term fractions of capital, though they are no less significant for that. The existence of

fractions is not meant to suggest that the class of capital is a fragmented anarchic conglomeration of disparate entities, for these fractions are always fractions of capital, that is, subunits of the class of
capital. Further, they exist in combinations and have a certain structured unity. In the process of production and accumulation, these
fractions and competing units of capital are brought into relationships with each other, and the very process of commodity and capital
circulation presupposes and recreates unity. There are also the interconnections between them, expressed by interlocking directorates
and overlapping shareholdings. The fraction nature of capital is not
intended to imply that the class itself is an artificial construct; it has a
real existence with these subunits as constituent parts of that class. It
should be pointed out that the unity of the class is most evident in the
unconscious interconnections implicit in the process of capitalist
production and accumulation.

The important point about the above discussion of the structured
and combined unity of the class of capital is that it indicates areas of
tensions and complexities in the very character of the class which
need to be taken into account in the discussion of interests and the
assessment of the policies and actions of the state.

The attempt to deal with interests is fraught with far more difficulties than the discussion of class itself. Though there are studies which
deal with interests, these are most usually concerned with the question of whether there is a public or collective interest, and the
philosophical consequences of such a claim. These deliberations are
not relevant to the present discussion. The question has also been
raised by Lukes in his work on power, which has the virtue of placing
the consideration of interests at the heart of the assessment of power.
Unfortunately, the way in which he defines interests and the procedures which he suggests for identifying them are not applicable to
the analysis of capital. There is an article by Connolly which introduces similar 'moral' considerations to the question.[62] Isaac Balbus
has also tried to identify the core aspect of the marxist conception of
interests.[63] He reduces the meaning of the term to indicate that some
person or class is 'affected by' an action or policy initiated by others.
Westergaard and Resler in *Class in a Capitalist Society* discuss the
question of interests and argue that they are objective, rather than
psychological and subjective, states of preference, and located in the
structure of class relations. Though these positions are quite diverse,
if they are coupled with the observations made about interests by
Poulantzas and those involved in the state-derivation debate, it is
possible to construct a slightly more detailed account of what is

entailed by the notion of interests and how it affects the analysis of the capitalist state.

There are three elements which can be combined to indicate the pattern and attributes of class interests under capitalism. Firstly, there is the proposition that interest refers to the potential of being affected by a policy or an action. It is important to note that the pattern of the possible effect of that action is not something free-floating, but related to the circumstances in which the action occurs. This is the second point: classes and class fractions have interests, the possibility of being affected by policy and action in a particular way, because of the places they occupy in the structure of class relations. It is in that sense that they are objective and it is this location in the structure which shapes the way in which different class groupings *can* be affected. Thirdly, given that classes exist within and as part of a process of capital accumulation, their interests will be defined in reference to this. It is built into the very nature of the definition of class outlined above, that the interests of capital will not be simple, necessarily direct or capable of a consistent expression in policy.

If we start with the question of the class interests of capital, that is, the interests which all the individual and subclass units will have as a consequence of being part of the class of capital, each of these units and the class as a whole will have an interest in remaining in existence as part of capital and will, as a consequence, have an interest in two sets of conditions. Firstly, they will have an interest in the reproduction of the social relations of production which make capital accumulation possible. In its basic form this will mean the maintenance of the conditions under which labour will take the form of the commodity labour power, which can be consumed in the process of capitalist production. In a crucial sense, this is what the maintenance of the hegemony of capital is all about. Equally it implies that all capital will have a general interest in the protection and guarantee of the rights of private appropriation and accumulation such that the continuity and expansion of capitalist production can be assured. Similarly, capital and each unit of capital will have an interest in ensuring that the other commodities which it requires for its operation will be available in the appropriate quantities and at the appropriate price. This remains true, even if the private unit of capital is involved in the production of raw materials and means of production. These then are the general, class interests of capital and they have a dual character; those that refer to the social hegemony of capital and those which concern the maintenance of the material basis of capitalist production.

As well as these general class interests of capital, each of the individual units and fractions have interests which pertain to their particular areas of operation. These may be considered as their particular or sectional interests and may be abstractly defined as securing the conditions which will permit their continued and profitable operations. The content of these interests cannot be theoretically prescribed and depend upon the nature of their operations and the place within the accumulation process as a whole, and the problems which they face. The content of these interests is, however, constructed on the framework of that concern. The important thing about these sectional, particular or fractional interests of capital is that they will not automatically, that is, of their very nature, harmonise with other sectional, particular or fractional interests or with the interests of the class as a whole.

Here it is important to recall that this pattern or framework of interests exists at the level of the structure of class relations. There is nothing in the argument about interests to suggest that they will be adequately embodied in policies advocated by that section of capital or the class as a whole, or that the state will similarly recognise them in their complexity and effect an appropriate compromise. There is an intervening stage between the identification of the framework of interests and the analysis of the mechanism and actions of the state. For interests to have pertinent consequences on politics and the actions of the state, there need to be institutions and procedures that will seek to *organise* the various class and subclass groupings of capital and to provide a relatively coherent expression of the relevant interests in the forms of policies. This role of organisation, and the necessary part that power must play, is crucial, for it is only through organisation and representation that interests appear in the deliberations and actions of the state. Furthermore, it cannot be assumed that policies advocated or implemented are accurate in their expression of the underpinning interests. The fractured and combined character of capital as a class necessarily complicates the character of the interests which need to be represented and analysed when considering, not only the character, but also the actions of the state.

The interests which are being generated into policies, then, are complicated by the class and sectional interests of capital and the particular and general forms which these take, and also by the consideration of long- and short-term perspectives. Emphasis is placed on the complex character of interests so that state theory can take a further account of the particular way interests are transformed into policies and the complications and tensions which must necessarily be present in such a task. In the subsequent analysis of the significance of government action and the changes in the status of ownership in the steel industry, the phrase 'the class interests of capital' or 'the interests of capital as a whole' has been used. The purpose has been to indicate the way in which policies that favour the interest of a section of the class of capital may not coincide with the interests of the whole class. Given the lack of some internal, class-wide system of organisation that can generate comprehensive policies for future development, the phrases refer to an abstraction and not to some actual expression or embodiment of the collective interests of the class. In the circumstances that prevail, all claims to act on behalf of the class or attempts to solve the problems faced by the class are necessarily contestable. Many groups of people, sections of capital or governments, may make the attempt to do so, but none has a secure basis for knowing what can be done or for ensuring that policies will be both implemented and effective.

Given the subject of the argument, power in the relations between government and private capital, the discussion of interests has been exclusively concerned with the class of capital. The class interests of labour are also relevant to the conflicts surrounding the nationalisation of steel as the move was introduced by a Labour Government which purported to speak and act on behalf of the working class. Using the same framework as that proposed above, it is possible to consider the general aspects of the class interests of labour. In a similar manner to those of capital, the class interests of labour are conditioned by the place of the class in the process of capitalist production. As a result of its subordinate position in that process and in the class structure, the interests of the class of labour are fundamentally divided. Labour has class interests both within and against the confines of capitalist class relations. Within capitalism it has an interest in protecting the condition and value of its unique commodity, labour power. It is on the basis of such an interest that concern with employment, conditions of work, welfare and health provisions are constructed. This can be described as the class's defensive or reformist interest since it relates to the protection and improvement of the class's conditions of life. Labour also has an interest in the abolition of class relations and capitalist society. Given the character of class relations under capitalism, it is the subordination of labour which governs the conditions of its life and also provides the basis for all the culture, progress and achievement of capitalist society. With its existence shaped by the fact of subordination, the class has an interest in the abolition of that subjugation.

Since it is a class in capitalist society, and it is defined by its relationship with both capital and the means of production, the revolutionary or transformative interest is contained in the need to abolish the commodity status of labour. In other words, the working class has an interest, as a consequence of its place in capitalist production, in abolishing the class relations upon which that social process is based. It has a class interest in organising society in such a way that labour no longer exists as a commodity and in which those who work dominate the shape, form and goals of social life, including the economic and political processes. Some people have tried to link the notion of 'the interests of the working class' exclusively with the revolutionary or transformative project. The view expressed here provides a way to analyse the two projects of labour under capitalism, reformist and revolutionary, on a division in the very framework of interests upon which such policies are constructed.

Not only are the class interests of labour fundamentally divided as a result of their place in capitalist class relations, but the class also has a complex internal structure which includes many divisions parallel to those in the class of capital. The division of capital into fractions and other subsections is related to divisions in the class of labour. The situation is further complicated as the class of labour is also divided by factory, plant, craft and skill loyalties. Consequently, the unity of the class and the harmonisation of the concerns of the various sections of labour need to be organised. Though there do exist institutions and procedures within the class, that seek to perform such a task, it is important to consider the implications of the various ways in which such organisation is attempted. It is especially important to consider this matter when assessing the policies suggested or introduced by institutions, like the Labour Party and the Trades Union Congress, which seek both to speak and to act on behalf of the working class. The process by which groups attempt to organise the unity of the class and to articulate its interests into collective policies relevant to the class, is as important when examining the actions of labour as it is for the analysis of those of capital. Any investigation is complicated both by the complex internal structure of the class of labour and by the fundamentally divided character of its class interests.

Implications for the analysis of interests and power

On the basis of the above discussion of state theory and the question of class interests, and the previous examination of approaches to the study of power, it is possible to outline the way in which the analysis of the various conflicts over the nationalisation of steel can proceed. In considering these disputes, it has been necessary to consider closely what the interests of the different interacting parties were and also the ways in which these have been represented as policies. The institutions and procedures by which these policies have been generated need to be identified. Given the comments made about the complicated internal structure of capital, it is revealing to consider the part that different governments may have played in either articulating these class or sectional interests or in organising the unity of the class of capital. Most importantly, the framework for the consideration of interests provides a basis for identifying the effect that various government actions have on the interest of the interacting or relevant parties. It also provides a basis for analysing the possible ways in which these interests may be affected by the programmes either suggested or implemented by other social institutions, or classes. On the basis of such an identified pattern of the different consequences for the interests of the various parties involved, it is possible to construct an argument about the purpose, character and forms of power evident in the interaction between a section of private capital and a succession of governments. It is always important to note that the complexity of the structure of class and class interests, and the relationship between these and sectional interests, means that the analysis is not a simple explication of direct links between actions, interests and consequences. Given the nature of the process and relations being examined, there are very few direct connections. These relationships need to be reconstructed and argued.

3

The steel industry 1919–1945

Between the end of World War One and the end of World War Two, there occurred a number of significant and relevant developments in the organisation and structure of the iron and steel industry. In considering these changes, it is not just a matter of providing interesting background information, but of establishing those factors that conditioned the situation in which the government and industry interacted in the period after 1945. As there are a number of histories of the iron and steel industry which deal adequately with the events, it is unnecessary to give a detailed account of what happened.[1] The main features considered in this chapter include all the various changes in the internal organisation of the industry as attempts were made to develop a unified, self-governing structure. These changes were part of attempts to develop institutions and procedures adequate to the task of generating policies which expressed the collective interests of the industry. The parameters within which government and industry interacted are also important as they provide a reference point for the analysis of subsequent developments. In this period the banks were uniquely involved in shaping the character of the industry and the form of these relations provides a similarly useful reference point. For the purpose of the examination in this chapter, it is useful to divide the period into three parts; from 1919 to 1931, from 1932 to 1938 and from 1939 to 1945. The logic of such a division will be made obvious in the text.

1919–1931

Though the British iron and steel industry had dominated the world scene in the nineteenth century, its position had been significantly undermined by the United States and Germany in the period before World War One.[2] The change in fortunes came about partly as a result of the improvement in the scale of production possible for newcomers to iron and steel production and partly because important technical changes were not eagerly implemented in Britain.[3] Such a relative decline set the framework within which the wartime arguments about reconstruction were conducted. As a contribution to the more general investigation by Lord Balfour,[4] an Iron and Steel Trades Committee was set up in 1916, chaired by a Mr Scoby-Smith.[5] The Committee was almost wholly manned by either masters or trade unionists from the industry and its observations can be used as a rough guide to the opinions then current.[6] It was asked to investigate 'the position of the Iron and Steel Trades after the War, especially in relation to international competition, and to report what measures, if any, are necessary or desirable in order to safeguard that position'.[7]

In its report, the Committee recommended various punitive measures to prevent the recovery of the German industry and its domination of the British market.[8] Certain restrictions were to be imposed on imperial trade. The British industry was vulnerable to competition from efficient and well-organised foreign cartels as it was dominated by too many small, inefficient and technically backward plants. Further, the 'individualism' of the many steel masters was such that it prevented the development of any effective form of co-operation between them.[9] Though the Committee's recommendations were rather mild, they do show that the representatives of the industry knew what was wrong and did have plans for improvement. There were a number of proposals for strengthening the internal organisation of the industry. Private merchants were criticised for allowing foreign competition to weaken the industry.[10] It was proposed that an export association, dominated by the largest manufacturers and divided into three product groups, should be set up as a voluntary association but supported by government encouragement and a measure of financial assistance.[11] There was also a call for a degree of tariff protection for the initial period of reconstruction.

It should be noted that the Committee's recommendation for the planned expansion and modernisation of the industry represented a significant departure from past practices. Though they wanted the expansion to be planned by the industry itself, they argued that 'the companies formed to build and work these plants should, if necessary, receive financial aid from the government, especially in view of the high costs of laying down large plants today'.[12] The Committee was not opposed to accepting financial assistance but it did not want the government interfering with the plans or organisation of the industry. It is worthwhile citing in full the Committee's view on the appropriate relationship between government and industry, as it neatly expressed the terms in which that relationship developed. They argued that:

the measures which should be taken to ensure the development and expansion of the British iron and steel industry should proceed upon the principle of combination within the industries themselves. The Committee feel that while government sympathy and assistance may be necessary in some degree, the development of the industries can best be achieved by the stimulation of manufacturing enterprise rather than by the creation of a great state industry. The function of the government will be the creation of conditions favourable to the industry rather than the internal regulation of the industry itself.[13]

The report did not become the blueprint for the reconstruction of the iron and steel industry although a number of the measures which it recommended were adopted in modified forms. On the whole the Scoby-Smith document was much too optimistic about future developments even though it had accurately understood the problems. It certainly underestimated the great amount of effort, by both government and the Bank of England, that would be necessary to achieve even some measure of the goals set out in the report.

Several important changes were wrought during the course of the war. There was strong government supervision of the industry and when the individualism of the steel masters hampered the creation of a central body to deal with the government on behalf of the industry, the relevant Minister threatened to appoint one himself.[14] Eventually a General Standing Committee headed by Mr Scoby-Smith was set up, though its position within the industry was not assured.[15] War demand stimulated the iron and steel industry and encouraged a significant expansion of capacity.[16] Without systematic planning, the expansion was quite haphazard and was not linked with any attempt to phase out small-scale and inefficient plants. Expansion continued for a short time after the war and was largely financed by loans from the banks.[17] At the end of World War One, little had been improved; internal organisation was weak, efficiency was low, capacity was large and the problem of international competition had not been resolved. A short but dramatic boom immediately after the war weakened the call for tariffs and strengthened the call for government decontrol of the industry.[18] When the boom collapsed the need for internal reorganisation and rationalisation was more urgent than ever.

In 1918, the General Standing Committee was replaced by a new body, the National Federation of Iron and Steel Manufacturers (NFISM).[19] Now, at least there was a formally constituted central body for the government of the industry though it lacked real authority and did little more than its prewar equivalent.[20] The slump conditions undermined the various attempts made by the new body to regulate production, plan reconstruction or to arrange some form of pricing policy. Industry-wide co-ordination was thwarted by the need of each firm to sell as much as possible, at whatever prices, without regard to the consequences.[21] It was the slump conditions, however, that paved the way for the important series of bank-initiated amalgamations and plans for reconstruction.

Traditionally there had not been a close relationship between the banks and industry, and the banks had not used their financial position to play a guiding role in industrial development.[22] In this, the British banks differed from their American and German counterparts. The conditions of the slump were such that there was a change in the attitudes of some bankers. It cannot be argued that the bankers realised that they had a responsibility for ensuring the planned rationalisation and reconstruction of British industry. Only gradually and grudgingly did the banks come to play any part at all, and then the major direction came from the Bank of England and its Governor, Sir Montagu Norman.[23] Norman had a particularly sanguine view of British industry and industrialists and this made him reluctant to make any special arrangements for industrial finance.[24] It also prompted him, once involved, to attempt a full-scale reconstruction and rationalisation of the steel industry.[25] After an *ad hoc* involvement with one of the armaments firms, Norman commissioned an important plan for the British industry, which recommended a substantial degree of amalgamation coupled with product and regional specialisation.[26] It was on this basis that the Bank of England provided financial assistance to carefully selected firms. To facilitate its industrial objectives, the Bank of England set up two related institutions, the Securities Management Trust and the Bankers' Industrial Development Company.[27] The first of these bodies was responsible for managing the Bank's industrial holdings and examining plans submitted for the rationalisation of particular industries. The second was the institution through which the various private and public banks could finance projects approved by the Securities Management Trust.

In this way the Bank of England attempted to rationalise the structure of the iron and steel industry. It used its credit facilities to impose its desired arrangements on particular firms. Duncan Burn has described the process in caustic terms: 'put quite bluntly, the policy advocated here was that the industry should be forced to reconstruction by extensive bankruptcy which would allow reform to be imposed by financial groups'.[28]

It is certainly true that the Bank used its resources to change the financial structure of the industry by promoting amalgamations and placing directors on the boards of the firms to which they granted assistance. These actions by the Bank gave the industry the basic firm structure that it had until nationalisation.[29] Though there is not much detail easily available about the way in which the Bank used its shares, it does seem that they were only held for short periods of time and eventually resold to realise modest profits.[30] There is a good deal of cynicism in the literature as to the achievements of the Bank's policies. Skidelsky and Boyle both note the small amount of money actually disposed of and the limited number of schemes approved.[31] Burn argues that it would be wrong to equate financial restructuring with an improvement in the level of technical efficiency and, further, that the emphasis on firms may have damaged the move towards rationalisation.[32]

There are two further points to be noted. First, the various changes induced by the banks did nothing to strengthen the internal organisation of the industry. Indeed, Burn argues that they might have had a weakening effect because the firms that gained financial assistance were often among those who broke quota and price agreements.[33] Secondly, there was another side to the Bank's involvement in that, as Clay observed, the Bank often acted to avoid the need for more government interference with the conduct of industry.[34] All in all, the period of active concern by the banks for the rationalisation of British industry was short-lived and not particularly successful in achieving its stated objectives.

1932–1938

1932 is significant as it was the year in which the industry was granted a large measure of tariff protection.[35] As mentioned in the preceding section, the Scoby-Smith Report had recommended a degree of tariff protection as far back as 1918, but the postwar boom weakened such calls and the industry was divided, since those firms which relied on the import of semi-finished products were in favour of free trade.[36] As the slump deepened, the demand for tariff protection increased and it was seen as the essential prerequisite for the survival of the industry.[37] The firms argued that the tariff was necessary for the survival of the industry and must precede any improvement in structure or efficiency. They were opposed by the orthodox free-trade thinking of government and bankers who argued that the internal changes were necessary before a tariff could be justified.[38] In the end, the disastrous state of the industry convinced the government that it would have to grant a tariff despite the fact that no new strong central body had been established in the industry and there had been no great improvement in technical efficiency.[39] The Import Duties Advisory Committee (IDAC) which recommended the tariff also argued that protection could be used to pressure the industry into making the desired changes.[40] Under the arrangements for the tariff, the IDAC was made responsible for supervising the conduct of the industry and encouraging the changes which it had recommended. This was the start of the industry's so called era of 'public supervision'.

The IDAC had a measure of success. It encouraged the setting up of a new, more comprehensive, governing body, though the change took a number of years.[41] The new body, the British Iron and Steel Federation tried to overcome some of the sectional squabbles that had been a problem for its predecessor. To help in this task the Federation was headed by an appointed independent chairman, Sir Andrew Duncan.[42] Duncan was acquainted with the industry and its problems, as he had been involved with Sir Montagu Norman and the Bank of England's rationalisation schemes.[43] As the basis for any improvement in the health of the British industry, the IDAC was concerned to get an agreement with the International Steel Cartel.[44] Once a series of import/export quotas had been established, it was possible for the Federation, encouraged by the IDAC, to develop a cartel structure for itself. Thus the most important achievement of the BISF was the setting up of a scheme for regulating the quantities, prices and profits for heavy steel products.[45] Though there had been attempts to make such arrangements in the past, they had always been undermined by the 'individualism' inherent in the firm structure of the industry.[46] The new arrangement sought to do what all cartel and monopoly arrangements do, and that is, to regulate and guarantee the rate of profit for slump periods as well as booms. As described by Burn, the price scheme was designed to produce monopoly losses during booms and monopoly profits during slumps.[47] One important consequence of the price scheme was the preservation of the existing mix of high-cost and low-efficiency plants as these were guaranteed access to the market and a share of the profit.[48] Both the IDAC and Duncan wanted to see a low stable price for steel which was nevertheless adequate to ensure a high output.[49] The Federation did not have the power to regulate prices as this was the task of the various product associations. They did, however, set up consultation procedures with these associations to discuss intended price rises. A Federation accountant was used to assess the changes in costs which had made the price increase necessary. Acting as a public watch-dog, the IDAC either approved or disallowed such rises. At a later stage, the IDAC prompted the Federation to investigate the price and cost structure for the industry as a whole. There were several other arrangements which proved to be important later. A special fund, financed by a levy on production, was set up by the Federation in 1936 to offset the increased price of raw materials.[50] There had also been plans for a special 'central fund' financed by a levy, 'whose function would be to assist exports, keep prices stable by subsidising high cost works whose continued existence was necessary in the national interest, eliminate redundant plant and assist market research',[51] and these were reactivated. It was not finally agreed to until 1939.

From the outset, the Committee had been concerned that the industry should develop some procedures for regulating its own orderly expansion and modernisation, and eventually consultative and vetting procedures were established.[52] Individual firms had to submit their expansion plans to a committee of the Federation chaired by Sir Andrew Duncan. If these were felt to be consistent with the objectives of Federation/IDAC policy, and not against the interests of the industry as a whole, then they were approved. There was a crucial problem in that the arrangements could never produce cohesive, industry-wide plans, since they relied on the initiative (and veto) of individual firms. Expansion must necessarily be an *ad hoc* process where the autonomy of individual firms is respected.

It was in relation to plans for modernisation that the disciplinary powers of the new governing body were best displayed. There were two instances of Federation disapproval, that of Jarrow and Ebbw Vale. Jarrow is the most widely known case, publicised as it was by the hunger marches during the depression.[53] Here a consortium had planned to build an integrated and modern plant which would, incidentally, have provided employment in an extremely depressed area. The plan was vetted and rejected by the Federation on the grounds that it would be 'uneconomic' in the context of other plans for the area. In its 1937 report, discussed below, the IDAC vindicated the Federation's behaviour over the scheme. The other example concerned the attempt to introduce a fully modernised steel complex at Ebbw Vale.[54] If operated at capacity, the only way to ensure its profitability, this plant would have severely undermined the Federation's quota arrangements. The setting up of such a complex was necessarily expensive and needed a lot of credit. The Bank of England became involved and gradually the board operating the plant had its membership changed so that it would conform to the Federation's objectives.[55] In both these cases the Federation, by means of a policy of persuasion and financial pressure, was able to prevent the operation of schemes that threatened its objectives. Hence the Federation was able to exert some discipline on the conduct of constituent firms and outsiders. It is revealing that both these instances involved opposing attempts to use modern techniques and integrated plants. On the matter of orderly modernisation and expansion, both the Federation and the Committee placed most emphasis on the 'orderly' part.

As a result of the Jarrow incident, there was a call for a public enquiry into the state of the iron and steel industry. Ironically, the government chose the IDAC to produce the report, which it did in 1937.[56] In considering events since the granting of the tariff in 1932, the report endorsed the Committee's policy and listed the industry's many achievements. It revealed that the Committee had wanted a particular form of reorganisation, described in these terms:

the central feature of the reorganisation which the committee had in mind was the creation of machinery which would bring about and maintain co-ordination of the various sections of the industry and co-operation with the constituent concerns, and facilitate such adjustments in productive capacity and prices as would place the industry on a reasonable profit earning basis and make possible that technical development and re-equipment which was becoming so urgently needed.[57]

The setting up of the BISF, the agreement with the International Steel Cartel, the arrangements for price stabilisation, and a scheme for vetting plans for expansion were seen as fulfilling these needs. Furthermore, the danger of subsidising high-cost and low-efficiency plants was also noted. There were no major criticisms of the industry's conduct in the period. Its main recommendation was that the government ought to set up a public supervisory body, something like itself, to ensure that the industry did not act against the national interest. The report also rejected a more active role for government or the public supervisory body.

From 1936 onwards, the demand for iron and steel products increased with preparations for the approaching European war. Such improved conditions strained the price-fixing arrangements but they were still intact when war was declared.[58] It is useful to stop at this point and consider the changes that had been made. Certainly the fortunes and organisation of the industry had changed considerably since the end of World War One. There was tariff protection and a central governing body which was cohesive and included the most important personalities of the industry. Price and profit stabilising arrangements had been introduced in the heavy sections and plans were being drawn up to extend these to other branches. The profit level in the industry had improved, and though this may have been partly a consequence of the improved financial structure of the industry, and the Federation's price scheme, it also owed a lot to the threat of approaching war. Furthermore, the central governing body of the industry had managed to discipline errant members who had attempted to modernise or rationalise in ways which would have endangered its cartel arrangements.

In certain other areas the changes had been far less dramatic. There had been no significant improvement in the level of technical efficiency and there were still too many high-cost, small-scale plants in existence.[59] There was still a large amount of over capacity which, if it had been eliminated, would only have intensified unemployment. Thus it is true to say that the industry had been reorganised in the period following the tariff and it was once again profitable, but it had not been rationalised as had been intended when the tariff was granted. The position of the Federation had been strengthened but it had never overcome the conflict between the collective interest of the industry and the private interests of the constituent firms. Despite consultative arrangements, its attempts to plan the orderly expansion of the industry foundered on the fact that the plans themselves were formulated, submitted and vetted by representatives of particular firms.[60] Though discipline over errant members had been effective in a number of cases, there was no guarantee that this would always be the case and though several schemes had been discussed to strengthen the authority of the Federation, none had been introduced. The suggestion that the BISF should be backed by statutory powers was rejected, as the industry preferred to be free of that degree of government involvement.

While the industry, governments and banks were devising various schemes for the future of the industry, the steel workers were also deciding what their position should be. The Iron and Steel Trades Confederation, the main union in the steel industry, both commented on the condition of the industry and made proposals for the future.[61] Problems in the industry were as obvious to the steelworkers as they were to the owners, managers and the financiers. In their arguments, the weakness of the industry, its poor competitive position and lack of co-ordination or planning were all noted. As Burn commented, the Confederation was also concerned to strengthen the cartel structure of the industry, and many of the proposals were similar to those in the unpublished Sankey Report.[62] The Confederation was suspicious of the capabilities and intentions of the steel owners and so they suggested the setting up of a public corporation to direct the affairs of the industry.[63] It is clear that they had in mind a body that would do more than supervise the operations of private managers and owners. Subsequently, they clarified what was meant by a public corporation in a call for the nationalisation of the industry which was endorsed by the 1934 Conference of the Trades Union Congress.[64]

On the basis of this move, steel nationalisation was incorporated into the Labour Party's official programme.[65] Though no detailed schemes were compiled for the conduct of a publicly owned steel industry, the embryonic form of these existed in both the Confederation's proposals and a book called *The Socialisation of Iron and Steel*.[66]

The position of the Confederation would have been sufficient to ensure that steel nationalisation remained on the political agenda. There were a number of other people working on Labour policy at that time who either proposed the nationalisation of steel, or whose suggestions were strengthened by such a call. For example, Hugh Dalton and Douglas Jay were both writing on the problems of economic planning and the measures needed to give governments the resources to control, not only the level of economic activity, but also the balance of economic activity.[67] Steel nationalisation fitted their schemes, as it was a basic industry and state control of basic industries would provide the appropriate power base for effective national planning. There were also those socialists who were concerned with extending the scope of democracy. In their terms, nationalisation was the only way to solve the problem posed by the concentration of power in the hands of a privately owned and increasingly cartelised steel industry.[68] Such concentrations of power were a threat to democracy, not just because they provided a base to resist the actions of a democratically elected government, but because they were irresponsible in the sense of not being subject to some form of democratic control. As can be seen, the subsequent conflict over the ownership and control of the steel industry had its roots in the contrasting positions developed in the 1930s.

1939–1945

The period of the Second World War was one of continued and assured prosperity for the iron and steel industry. During this time the organs of its self-regulation were consolidated and strengthened by close co-operation with the wartime government. A number of different structures for the administration of industry in the event of war had been prepared during the twenties and thirties.[69] Such plans had been finalised by the time war appeared imminent. Industries, including iron and steel, were to be run by special Controls responsible to the Minister of Supply.[70] These Controls were to be headed by people who were prominent in their field and who had been informally consulted on the arrangements. For the iron and steel industry that person was the chairman of the BISF, Sir Andrew Duncan.[71] The appointment presaged a close relationship between the Federation and the Iron and Steel Control who would be responsible for the conduct of the industry for the duration of the war.[72] Such a close relationship was confirmed by the agreement between the skeletal Federation, left in existence, and the Iron and Steel Control, on the secondment of a significant number of BISF personnel to man the Control;[73] and the interesting fact that, for a period, the Federation, and the industry by means of a levy arrangement, paid the salaries of those so seconded.[74] Even where Federation people were not involved in the administration of the Iron and Steel Control, it was still manned by prominent members of the industry.[75] A prima facie case could be made about a conflict of interests between the industry and the Control, and the matter was considered by several bodies.[76] They concluded that the problem of 'dual control' could be solved by arranging for the seconded Federation members to be classed as temporary civil servants and to be paid by the government.[77]

There were some quibbles about the close relationship that existed between the industry and the Control, and it is instructive to consider a few cases in which the government sought to impose conditions on the industry. In the early days of the war, there were a few conflicts between the British Purchasing Commission and the Control over the source, placement and payment for foreign supplies of iron and steel.[78] The Control, acting as the embodiment of the industry, wanted to use the old procedures and to represent itself. It was only after a significant degree of negotiation that the matter was resolved by appointing a member of the Control to the Purchasing Commission. At a later stage the Control wanted to protect the industry's supply of labour but the Ministry of Supply was reluctant to grant it an order unless there were dramatic improvements in the wages and conditions of those employed. In the end, the seriousness of the situation was such that special arrangements were made.[79] The preceding incidents, though they do involve conflict between the government and the industry as represented by the Control, do not suggest that the Control was doing anything untoward. There was the more interesting case where the Control sought compensation from the Government for the investment used to expand the industry's capacity.[80] It should be noted that the industry was not eager to expand as it did not wish to repeat the experience of the First World War. Though there was a degree of circumspection in the government's reply, a small grant was made to assist in the provision of capital equipment.[81] Despite several attempts to alter the structure and balance of the iron and steel industry, no great changes occurred. Most of the sectional interests were well able to protect themselves from the effects of schemes which they thought would be harmful.[82] In all the cases it would seem that the Control acted as a representative of the collective interests of the iron and steel industry in a manner similar to that of the BISF in the period before the war. Whether there was a conflict of interests depends upon an assessment of whether there was a divergence between the interests of the industry and the war effort.

The pattern of pre-war government/industry relations also affected the wartime arrangements for the operation of the price stabilisation scheme.[83] Essentially, the wartime procedures did not upset the peacetime pricing policy of the Federation. If anything, the policy was strengthened by being administered by an official government body, the Iron and Steel Control. The peacetime policy of an output-based levy to offset irregular increases in basic costs was continued, in order to compensate for the higher costs of production that inevitably followed the industry's increased reliance on imported raw materials.[84] Though the scheme was designed to regulate prices and to modify any rises, the price of steel rose dramatically until the end of 1940 when the government decided to freeze it.[85] The levy fund was then used to support the broad profit structure of the industry, guaranteeing certain levels of profit calculated against a standard year, 1936–7.[86] These arrangements were often criticised but the various investigators were satisfied that the industry's profits had not been unduly inflated during the war.[87] It is important to note that the base year for determining the standard rate of profit was one of the best years for the industry since the end of World War One.[88] The assessment of the justness of the profit earned during the war depends on the adequacy of the profit level in the base year used for wartime calculations.[89] On the whole, the continuation of the pre-war pricing policy guaranteed that there could be no undue increase in profits if they were compared with the base year.[90] As one of the historians remarked:

The initial maximum price schedule was merely the pre-war price schedule frozen and sanctioned by the Ministry. This was regarded as a temporary expedient which was bound to guarantee monopoly and cartel producers the advantages of their existing monopolistic profits, at least for the time being.[91]

There was some criticism of the profits earned in the light steel sections of the industry which were much higher than even their high pre-war levels.[92] It was this section that was largely outside the Federation's pre-war arrangements. Some attempts were made at regulation by means of a voluntary rebate scheme[93] but this was not overwhelmingly successful.[94]

In general terms, it is possible to conclude that the industry ended the war in a strengthened and profitable state. The internal organisation was strong and effective and the price/profit arrangements were working well. Indeed the industry had enjoyed its longest burst of prosperity in the twentieth century. It was certainly well equipped for the postwar struggle over nationalisation.

Power in the shaping of the 1945 situation

It is not intended to give a detailed account of the power evident in the developments surrounding the steel industry prior to 1945, as these were not central to the dispute over nationalisation. Matters discussed in the previous sections of the chapter are relevant to the analysis of the struggles over the ownership of the steel industry which emerged in the period after the end of the Second World War. The chapter's description of the state of the industry, its problems, and the various suggested solutions provide a reference point against which the subsequent pattern of changes can be assessed. The period included three features that deserve further consideration. Firstly, there was the setting up of the BISF as the industry's self-governing body or trade association. Of significance were the ways in which the Federation sought to unify the industry and to provide it with an organisation capable of reconciling the claims of the different producers and sections of the industry. During these years, the Federation attempted both to generate an industry-wide perspective and to secure the interests of the whole industry in its relationship with governments, with the body responsible for watching over its conduct, the IDAC, and with other industries and parts of capital. It was in this period that the steel industry came to have the particular organisational character which it retained until the Federation was dissolved after final nationalisation in 1967. Secondly, there was the part played by the government in supporting moves within the industry and in suggesting others. It was the accepted limits of government action which were most revealing. Thirdly, there was the distinctive part played by the banks, particularly the Bank of England, in seeking to rationalise the structure of the industry and to promote improvements in its technology. The combination of these three factors formed the background to the conflicts after World War Two and effectively shaped the environment within which various attempts would be made to alter the shape and fortunes of the steel industry.

Self-government of the iron and steel industry

The Scoby-Smith Report and the industry's response to it revealed that leading figures in the industry were aware of the problems and the need to develop policies capable of overcoming them. As they saw it, there were two main tasks. First, it was necessary for the industry to overcome its fragmentation by the development of an effective central organisation that could govern its collective affairs. In the context of the industry's past history, such an organisation would have to be based on a voluntary association of the various firms. On the basis of such a central body, it was hoped that the iron and steel industry would be able to move away from a situation in which the fortunes of the industry and the individual companies were the result of unregulated market forces. It would then be possible to encourage the orderly modernisation of the industry's structure and its technical efficiency. The second task, the rationalisation and the introduction of new technology, was of less importance than the first and was to be tackled on the basis of a successfully established form of industrial self-government. This order of priorities was evident in the position taken by the industry over the granting of the tariff and the eventual progress in the setting up of the Federation if contrasted with the limited improvements in technical efficiency.

In terms of the analysis outlined previously, that is, of a concern with the institutions and procedures that exist to articulate basic interests into complicated policies relevant to the situation faced by the industry, the changes in the internal organisation of the industry are most important. The initial creation of the NFISM, under pressure from the government during World War One, and its supersession by the BISF after the end of that war, represent stages in the evolution of such institutions and procedures. The first body, the NFISM, had been both weak and unable to speak on behalf of large sections of the industry. It was easily ignored by those producers who wished to do so and it was not adequate to the task. The second body, the BISF, which was also set up under pressure from various governments, was much more representative and more comprehensive in its scope. As an institution for the generation of policies relevant to its interests it was not without its problems. Given the circumstances in which it had to operate, the Federation had to try to formulate plans that matched the collective needs of the industry, but the procedures by which this was done had to respect the autonomy and commercial judgment of the individual firms. Any plan or policy had to be implemented by the firms on a voluntary basis. Under the Federation's arrangements matters were further complicated as sectional associations, such as those for heavy producers or the re-rollers, retained the right to fix prices for their members.

There were two factors which combined to enhance the strength and significance of the Federation: pressure from governments and the banks, and the prospect of setting up an effective cartel structure. Indeed the gradual development of industrial self-regulation can be viewed as a significant part of an attempt to create a disciplined cartel, protected by a tariff, that could assure reasonable returns to all firms, regardless of their basic efficiency. It was noticeable that all the instances in which the central committee of the Federation was able successfully to discipline errant firms or sections, concerned proposals which threatened the working of cartel arrangements.

Though there was a gradual, uneven strengthening of the industry's internal organisation, the Federation lacked procedures which made it fully competent for its task. The main weakness was revealed in the difficulties of formulating industry-wide development plans. The Federation could not initiate such plans; it could only vet those that were submitted by the constituent firms. At best, it could try to achieve some form of compromise that would prevent the wasteful duplication of proposed schemes. Under such arrangements, planning could only be an *ad hoc* affair and the central organisation could only play a limited role. Though the leading figures in the industry and a large number of firms agreed that there was a need for a more comprehensive central organisation of the industry, such feelings were not enough to bring about the required changes. All the internal arrangements that were set up depended on the support, encouragement and, occasionally, the coercion of the banks or the government. The actions of these external bodies were important but the industry, through the Federation, remained in charge of its own development. The important thing to note about the period was that the iron and steel industry had, by the end of the Second World War, effective and agreed arrangements for its own self-government. Despite the problems, the BISF was operating competently to provide collective services for its constituent firms and representing them in relations with the government. The Federation's organisational character and its apparent significance within the industry set it apart from other trade associations and attempts to set up cartels. It was the fact of having some organisational procedures which could generate collective policies for the industry and represent it in its relations with other industries and outside bodies that was significant.

The role of the government

Throughout the twenties and the thirties, the part played by the government was quite restricted. It accepted in action the relationship as defined by the Scoby-Smith Report; to encourage the plans developed by the industry itself. Its acceptance of such a role was not the result of any power exerted by the industry over the government. It was rather the consequence of the governments themselves accepting orthodox thinking about the proper sphere for government action. Changes in the party-political character of government were almost wholly without significance for this subject, as all governments accepted the same orthodox position. The nature of government initiative can be seen in the way in which tariff protection was granted and in the part played by the IDAC in supervising the industry's development. In that the IDAC's influence was only backed by the increasingly improbable threat of a removal of the tariff, its significance was very limited. Though the IDAC was formally charged with the responsibility of ensuring that the tariff was not abused and that the industry modernised its techniques and rationalised its structure, the Committee did little more than endorse changes proposed by the industry. Nevertheless, its actions were not without significance as it continually encouraged the setting up of a comprehensive governing body and sought to strengthen the part that this played in the conduct of the industry. In trying to increase the importance of the BISF, much of the IDAC's effort was centred on the strengthening of the cartel structure of the industry, an unusual task for a government-backed supervisory body.

The Committee's 1937 report on the state of the industry endorsed the Federation's view of itself and supported the argument that the government should play a passive supporting role. The Report did conclude that a specific public body should be set up to supervise the industry, along the general lines of the IDAC, and it was recognised that this would confer legitimacy on the internal government of the industry. A distinctive feature of the period was the limited extent to which various governments sought to interfere with or direct the plans of the industry. However, it did give the industry a secure economic environment, granting the tariff, and it increased the strength of the industry's domestic and international trading position by encouraging the setting up of a cartel structure.

The role of the banks

The part played by the banks, and particularly the Bank of England, was one of the distinctive features of the period. The banks generally complemented the actions of the government though there were some matters on which they exercised more initiative. They were far less concerned with the development of centralised organisation in the industry than with the rationalisation of its financial structure and the modernisation of its techniques. Theories of finance capital have always suggested such a role for the banks at a certain stage in capitalist development.[95] Basically, it is argued that, with the increased size of capitalist concerns and an increased reliance on credit, the banks are in a position to act as an embodiment of the collective consciousness of the class of capital. As a consequence of their financial dealings, they have connections with all the leading sectors of production and are aware of the problems faced by each. Their credit powers ensure that they are capable of planning the future development of the capitalist economy. As such, they are uniquely placed both to work out a plan for the whole of the system and to have it implemented, even against the wishes of some sections of capital or particular firms. The plans generated by the banks would respond to the overall needs of the class and would be concerned with the rationalisation and modernisation of the structure of capitalist production. This view of how the banks operate could be applied to the actions of the Bank of England and its relationship with the steel industry.

The steel industry was a problem for both capital as a whole and for the banks in three ways. First, steel was a basic industry, supplying essential raw materials to the manufacturing sector upon which the health of the capitalist economy depended. Secondly, the level of unemployment in the industry was high. It should be noted that although the Bank of England regarded the unemployment situation as one that prompted a change in its relations with industry, its actions and plans were never tempered by a consideration of the consequences for employment. Many of the schemes proposed would have had the effect of further increasing unemployment. Thirdly, the unrationalised structure of the steel industry was a serious drain on limited financial resources. Whatever its motivation, the Bank of England did try to impose a comprehensive plan on the development of the steel industry and it had a measure of success in consolidating the financial and firm structure of the industry by a series of sponsored amalgamations. It was not successful in its attempt to promote improvements in technology and modernisation. There was never a thorough commitment to either industry in general or to steel in particular, and this was most clearly shown by the Bank's short-term holding of industrial shares and the limited funds made available for rationalisation. In the long term, the Bank's initiative was unsuccessful, largely because it lacked adequate machinery for determining and implementing collective policies for the class. Its overriding perspective was financial prosperity and this limited the kinds of changes it could encourage. The actions of the Bank in this period provide an example of the previously identified possibility that some section of capital could, given the internal character of the class, seek to organise its unity and to impose a plan of development on it. In Britain, the Bank of England was uniquely placed to make such an attempt but its efforts were not successful. However, the actions of the Bank form a background pattern against which later moves by Conservative and Labour Governments can be assessed.

The parameters of power

In considering the pattern of power in the interactions between the government and the iron and steel industry for this period, it is difficult to be precise, though several useful points can be made. These can be formulated as the conditions for success in the attempt by the government to influence the industry. For example, when the government sought to impose its wishes on the industry, it only succeeded when there already existed a significant body of opinion within the industry which agreed on the policy and was working in that direction. Strengthening the internal organisation of the industry was a case in point. When the government sought to impose priorities that were not backed by a measure of agreement in the industry, it was either unwilling or unable to exert sufficient pressure to be effective. An example of this was the dispute over the granting of tariff protection and the necessity for rationalisation and modernisation. The failure of the government to have these priorities accepted was not the consequence of the industry imposing its position by an exercise of power. To a large extent it was the government's definition of its legitimate tasks and responsibilities that led it to acquiesce. The consequence was the same as if a significant degree of power had been exerted: the industry's priorities were realised by a change in government policy. There were further instances in which agreement between the industry and government was not enough to guarantee that the shared objectives could be realised. More than anything else, both agreed on the need for the industry to become profitable again but this took a long time. When it did come, the improvement was as much a consequence of the increased demand which accompanied the threat of another European war as it was the consequence of the policies of either the government or the industry. The parameters of the power interactions between industry and the government were set by an agreed definition of the appropriate role for government action.

4

The first nationalisation of steel: conflicting proposals

The past history of the steel industry's relations with various governments and government agencies, coupled with the industry's condition at the end of the Second World War, suggested the general possibility of a political controversy over its future. As the result of a government decision, capital expenditure in the industry had been kept low throughout the course of the war. Consequently there was a great deal of equipment which needed to be replaced or repaired. It also meant that the basic structure of the industry was unchanged. Steel production was still carried out in a large number of small, outdated, technologically inefficient and economically wasteful plants. The location of these plants was still unrelated to economic criteria. Though the structure and efficiency of the industry had not been improved by the war, the relationship between the industry and the Iron and Steel Control meant that the BISF, as the central organisation of the industry, was more significant and more competent than it had been before. The effective operation of the price policy had provided the industry with a secure financial base to carry out the needed modernisation. Under some circumstances the condition of the industry would have resulted in a variety of problems, but two factors had a mitigating effect. First, there was a high level of domestic demand in the period of reconstruction. Steel would be needed in vast quantities, both to re-equip industry for peacetime production and for the making of consumer goods to meet the demands which had been restrained during the war. Secondly, the industry's main competitors had been badly affected by bombing and occupation. Only the U.S. industry was in an undamaged condition. However, the high level of domestic demand would have the effect of reducing the significance of international competition as imports would supplement rather than undermine the production of the British steel industry.

Though the history and the condition of the steel industry made its future a likely political issue, the election of a Labour Government with a secure majority guaranteed that it would be. The Labour

Government of 1945–51 has been studied quite extensively. No matter how radical its election programme may have seemed in 1945, it is now clear that the Government was not involved in an attempt to transform capitalism into socialism.[1] Instead it was involved in a complicated social project that included both the setting up of a comprehensive welfare programme and the creation of a mixed economy.[2] It is only with this second aspect that this work is concerned. Though Rogow, in his study of the Attlee Government's policies towards business, was able to discern the parameters of a theory of the mixed economy in the Government's actions, it should be remembered that at the time the Party had no clearly theorised position on the question.[3] It is true that a number of texts had been produced on the problems of economic planning in a period of Labour Government, but none of these was fully accepted by the Party;[4] nor did these studies provide a logical examination of the character and shape of the mixed economy. To the extent that the Government did succeed in creating the basis of the mixed economy it did so for a number of reasons, including a desire to reduce the prospect of unemployment and to honour long-standing political commitments. Its actions were more a product of the logic of the political process than the implementation of a detailed blueprint for the construction of a mixed economy. The place that the nationalisation of steel had in such a process, and the consequences of the more or less *ad hoc* manner in which the Government constructed the base of the mixed economy, will be considered in greater detail below. The significance of the Government's action, and the implications that this has for the analysis of power in the relationship between government and private capital, depends crucially on the connection between the nationalisation of steel and the building of the mixed economy.

Steel was not the only industry that the 1945 Government was pledged to nationalise. For a variety of reasons the Bank of England, the electricity and gas supply industries, the rail and road transport systems and coal mining were all part of the nationalisation programme.[5] There was a sense in which this diverse collection of business and industries were linked in the construction of the public base of the mixed economy. The Bank of England was nationalised for a number of reasons, including its behaviour over the gold standard during the depression, but it provided the government with a means of controlling the financial affairs of the nation.[6] The extent to which it used that control should not conceal the fact that nationalisation granted that formal capability. All the other industries were similar in that they provided essential inputs for the manufacturing industries in the shape of energy or transport. As such, they have been described as the intra-structural aspects of the production process. Their other common feature was that they were either already municipalised, as in the case of electricity and gas, or they were not very profitable for their private owners. Compensation was, of course, paid for all the industries nationalised. It is significant that the Conservative Party were not very vehement in their opposition to these nationalisation proposals though they did argue that the compensation terms were unfair. On the whole, the Conservative Opposition gave the impression that they were willing to acquiesce in most aspects of those nationalisations. Steel was the exception.

Before outlining what actually happened in the course of the dispute between the steel industry and the Labour Government, it is possible to summarise what these other nationalisations reveal about the Labour Government's social project. As the nationalisation programme was implemented, it became increasingly clear, if it had not been at the outset, that nationalisation was not intended to provide a social challenge to capital.[7] Nationalisation was not to be justified on general socialist grounds; it was a policy to be applied in only a limited number of cases and in certain, imprecisely defined, circumstances.[8] It was most relevant where private ownership had proved itself to be incompetent to run an industry for its own benefit, or the benefit of the community.[9] The payment of compensation, often on quite generous terms, was justified on the grounds of equity.[10] It would be unfair to confiscate some areas of capitalist property if others were being left untouched. The payment of compensation defused the social challenge of nationalisation and also bound the nationalised industries with debts to the private sector.[11] The newly nationalised industries were organised along lines which further emphasised the lack of social challenge in Labour's nationalisation programme. Despite a good deal of opposition from the trade unions and sections of the Party, Morrison's invention, the public corporation, was the favoured arrangement.[12] The setting up of public corporations insulated the nationalised industries from political control. It also provided the basis for the re-establishment of capitalist management within the state-owned industries. Most significantly of all, nationalisation did not alter the status of workers in the enterprise: they were still excluded from control of the production process.[13] Indeed, the workers were to have hardly any more say in the management of the nationalised industries than when they were privately owned and managed. It is within such a programme and against such a background that the dispute about ownership and organisation of the steel industry was fought out.

As the European war was coming to a close, the Federation began to consider plans for the period of reconstruction.[14] The caretaker government, which operated between the ending of the wartime coalition and the 1945 election, asked the industry to draw up a development plan for its future expansion.[15] This was submitted to the newly elected Labour Government in December 1945 and contained a five year programme of new works, and amalgamations to be completed in seven years.[16]

Meanwhile, the Government was considering what to do with the industry in the long term as it had a clear manifesto commitment to nationalisation even though this had been included only after a dispute within the drafting committee.[17] As there were no detailed plans for steel nationalisation, and there were other nationalisation schemes with priority, no action was scheduled for the first parliamentary session.[18]

As a prelude, the Minister for Supply, Mr Wilmot, announced both the intention to nationalise and an acceptance of the industry's development plan.[19] An Iron and Steel Board was set up to supervise the conduct of the industry in the interim and to give advice on the plans for nationalisation.[20] The Federation refused to nominate or suggest members to serve on the Board if it was expected to play any part in the preparations for nationalisation.[21] After a brief period of dispute, the Government backed down and removed the offending clause from the Board's brief.[22] The Iron and Steel Board then functioned with members drawn from the industry, trade unions and consumers.[23]

In the period before the Bill was actually placed before the House of Commons, there was some attempt to produce a hybrid measure that would provide strengthened public supervision and avoid the need for nationalisation.[24] This proposal was sponsored and negotiated by Morrison who had never been more than tepid in his enthusiasm for steel nationalisation. Though he secured the agreement of the BISF, it was rejected by the Cabinet. There were many other quibbles and disagreements in the negotiations between the Federation and the Government.

When the plans for nationalisation were quite advanced and the introduction of the Bill was imminent, the Federation's members refused to accept re-appointment to the Board.[25] In fact, only the trade union representatives made themselves available. Supervision of the industry returned to the Ministry of Supply, but because of the BISF's attitude to co-operation, there were two separate sections within the Ministry working on steel; one concerned with the day to day conduct of the industry and the other with the preparation of the nationalisation plans.[26]

When the Iron and Steel Act was introduced and debated,[27] it was strongly opposed by the Conservatives, who were fed points, facts and arguments by the Federation,[28] which also conducted a strong publicity campaign against the Bill.[29] The ubiquitous Mr Cube, prepared by Aims for Industry for Tate and Lyle, added his efforts.[30] The parliamentary struggle was complicated by procedural and constitutional matters and the Bill was held up while the delaying powers of the House of Lords were reduced.[31] There was a conflict over the proposed vesting date as the Government wanted it to be before the general election but later agreed that it should be postponed.[32]

The Government was returned with a much reduced majority. However, the transfer of the industry to public ownership was made. The Federation continued its refusal to co-operate with nationalisation by securing agreement that none of its members would serve on the new British Iron and Steel Corporation's board.[33] As a result it was difficult to find someone with knowledge and experience of the industry either to chair the new body or to serve on it. Almost all relations between the Federation and the Corporation were complicated by dissension and this included the question of representation on the executive of the Federation and the conduct of the various subsidiaries that provided collective services to the steel industry.[34] In the end, the Government's intention that the Corporation should take over collective arrangements such as the bulk purchase of imported raw materials was given up. A liaison committee of leading members of the Federation was set up to communicate with the Iron and Steel Corporation, but not to smooth its operations.[35] The actual nationalisation did little more than transfer from private hands the largest concerns in the industry.[36] The Iron and Steel Corporation left the old management structures intact and its only initiative was to remove a few directors whose presence on the boards of nationalised companies may have involved a conflict of interests.[37]

It is not a simple matter to discuss the conflict over the nationalisation of steel in such a way that the different aspects of what was at stake will be clearly revealed. Most of the numerous complications arise from the general problem of deciding what is at stake in any conflict once it has been accepted that the obvious pattern of opposition may not accurately indicate either what the contending parties were after or what was achieved by the outcome. In the dispute over steel, the problems come when trying to show what the support for nationalisation or its alternative the public supervisory board, signified for the ongoing development of the mixed economy. The procedure in this chapter will be as follows; first, to identify the main aspects of the two opposing plans for the steel industry, and then to analyse what these implied for the pattern of social development.

Before discussing the industry's plans and arguments it is useful to set out, schematically, what I think the conflict was about and the way in which the conflict was, in effect, layered. First, the conflict was about the obvious question of whether the steel industry should continue to be run by private enterprise or whether it was to be nationalised and owned by the state. Secondly, it was about the status of the industry's proposals for its own conduct, the notion of a public supervisory board regulating the conduct of an essentially self-governing industry. At this level the conflict concerned the form of the general relationship between government and industry in the new period ushered in by the Labour Party's nationalisation programme. Thirdly, the conflict was over the shape and conduct of the mixed economy. In arguing whether the steel industry should be nationalised, the various parties were also arguing about the size of the public sector and how it should act in its relations with the larger privately owned sector. Fourthly, it was about the form of the industry's relations with the consumers of steel products. This aspect was most evident in the debate on the procedures by which profit levels were fixed, the arrangements to guarantee that the public interest was not being infringed and the institutional forms to secure an adequate representation of the consumer's interest.

The industry's proposals

It is difficult to describe the positive content of the industry's proposals since they were largely formulated as the defence of arrangements introduced by the same government as the one that wanted to nationalise the industry. The enthusiasm of the industry for a publicly appointed board to supervise its conduct, and the improvements it advocated, suggests that these were the arrangements that they actually preferred. Indeed, such was their enthusiasm that they believed similar arrangements would be the solution to the general problem of relations between privately owned industry and the government.[38] The BISF had grown up with such a body and had been encouraged by the IDAC, so it is not surprising that they would view a

supervisory board as an appropriate solution to their problems. Wartime experience of the Iron and Steel Control would have strengthened the impression. As such, the industry's support for its conduct to
be overseen by a publicly appointed Iron and Steel Board was not just
an *ad hoc* defence of the status quo.

Though the arguments for the self-government of the industry
under the supervision of a government appointed board were often
distorted by the polemical forms in which they were expressed, the
main elements were clear. For the purposes of analysis all the Federation's references to a golden age of competition and efficiency will be
ignored as they were nothing more than rhetorical gloss. In outline,
the Federation's case was opposition to nationalisation of steel combined with a defence of their role in the conduct of the industry to
justify the retention of the experiment of public supervision. The
positive case for the Board was only argued explicitly in a few places,
usually by the Federation's President, Mr Hunter.[39] More normally,
the idea of a Board was defended on the grounds of the success of the
First Development Plan and the general harmony between the Board
and the industry over its implementation.[40]

The argument against nationalisation

One thing that is immediately striking about the case made by the
Federation is the absence of any theoretical or general defence of
private ownership *as such*. There was no sense in which the Federation argued a philosophical case against the abolition of private
ownership. Nor was the Federation concerned to argue against
nationalisation in principle. It was not opposed to previous nationalisations even though the steel owners had often been owners of coal
mines as well. When private ownership was defended, it was almost
always in terms of the flexibility it allowed in the organisation of a
complex industry like steel. Furthermore, these observations were
most emphatically based on notions of managerial responsibility and
prerogatives. Thus, when arguing against a single state-owned corporation, they maintained that it would result in the unhealthy unification of ownership and control.[41] Indeed, they went so far as to argue
that it would create the very monopoly the industry was charged as
having under the leadership of the Federation.[42] They also argued that
if the industry was owned by the state, the government would no
longer be able to look after the national interest as it would have a
sectional interest in steel which would cloud its otherwise clear-
sighted vision.[43] Time and time again the Federation stressed that

nationalisation would undermine the initiative and responsibility of managers. The following passage states the position explicitly:

The present flexible organisation of the industry aims successfully at the maximum degree of decentralisation consistent with the co-ordination of effort necessary in an economy subject to more conscious planning than before the war. Within the framework of the present State supervision, the various units in the industry provide their own machinery for common services in the form of the British Iron and Steel Federation. . . . This represents a remarkable development in industrial co-operation, achieved without limiting in any restrictive way the real responsibility of management for the successful operation of their companies. The transfer to a single Corporation of the ownership of all the companies to be taken over will necessarily tend to over centralisation, uniformity and rigidity, and will weaken in managements their feelings of personal responsibility for the works which they direct. Since it is on the opposite of these tendencies that efficiency and progress depend, the industry may be expected under the Bill to become inefficient, to lower its productivity and to prove unreceptive to new ideas.

The individual manager's sense of personal responsibility will be further weakened by the consideration that, under the Bill, he has no security of tenure and may at any time be removed from his appointment by the sole shareholder – the Corporation. He cannot then find alternative work within the nationalised sector of the industry. Since much of the craftsmanship and many of the technical developments on which it has been built up have originated in men of individuality and initiative whom a bureaucratic Corporation might find 'difficult' it is hardly to be expected that the Bill will encourage the production of new ideas.[44]

This passage is not unique and similar complaints abound in all the Federation's documents.[45] Opposition to nationalisation as a threat to the right of ownership was combined with nationalisation as a threat to the right of managers. The organisational structure of the Federation was dominated by the 'leading personalities of the industry' who owed their influence to their roles as managers and directors of the largest firms.[46] This coloured their perception of both the threat of nationalisation and the way it was to be countered. The Federation argued the rights of ownership through the spectacles of managerial prerogatives and nationalisation was opposed in those terms.

The Federation and the First Development Plan

In the various pamphlets published by the Federation, it portrayed itself as a voluntary association providing common services for the benefit of the industry and the community.[47] It stressed the voluntary character of membership as part of an attempt to prove that it was not the monopolistic and restrictive body alleged by the industry's critics.[48]

The Federation claimed that it was unable to compel the constituent bodies and member firms to do anything, and in that sense could not be the instrument of an unhealthy monopoly.[49] As the account of the development of the Federation given in Chapter 3 indicated, this was not completely true: there were instances when the Federation was able, on important matters, to impose a collective policy on errant members. The most important role of the Federation's self-defence was the argument over the role of competition preserved within the industry's collective organisation.

The industry's critics openly condemned the Federation's pricing policy. It was argued that the price was set at such a level that even inefficient producers were rewarded and that the industry was conducted in a restrictive manner.[50] Not surprisingly, in its propaganda, the Federation ignored the history of its determination of prices and profits with the assistance of the IDAC. For the postwar period, the Federation claimed that the price levels were determined by the government in a manner external to the industry or the various firms.[51] Such a defence is ingenious and distorts the reality of the price policy. It is true that the government, through the Iron and Steel Board, had the right to declare a statutory price level for the sale of steel products. It is also true that the Board had its own accountants and technical advisers to determine the cost structure of the firms producing particular products. The calculations of cost were done on the basis of procedures developed and introduced by the Federation.[52] Furthermore, the principles of cost accounting had been approved by the Public Accounts Committee during the war. All these points were stressed by the Federation in their account.[53] Unfortunately, these three points do not prove that the price for steel was determined by the Iron and Steel Board in a manner *external* to the firms and the industry, which was essential to their refutation of the charge of monopoly.[54] The formal mechanism granted the power of price determination to the Iron and Steel Board as a continuation of the wartime arrangement when that power had been vested in the Iron and Steel Control. The exercise of that power had been based on close co-operation between the Federation and the Control and later the Iron and Steel Board.

The matter of prices was of great interest to the Federation and to the various product Conferences. Indeed, as regards prices, it was a matter of the Federation making 'recommendations' or 'applications' for price changes which were either ratified or not by the Board. Such a process can not properly be construed as external to the industry. Furthermore, there was the question of the adequate return on capital which was a prominent part of the Board's evaluation of proposed price rises.[55] The matter had not been fully considered at the outset of the war and afterwards the process was one of a technical adjustment of prices within the broad movement of costs. Even the Federation's evidence revealed that almost all firms in the industry made a profit, even if a particular section was working at a loss, a situation that would have been unlikely if competition prevailed or if prices had been determined in a manner similar to free market forces.

Nevertheless the Federation believed that, in a situation where a common price was set for the sale of steel products, the beneficial effects of competition were retained. They argued that the only way for firms to prosper under such conditions was to improve their efficiency, expand their share of the market and improve the proportion of profit within that selling price.[56] This was meant to guarantee good service to the consumers of steel products.[57] On this point, it is revealing to note that Burn, not considered a critic of the industry, maintained that the Federation's price policy and the Industry Fund effectively sheltered the high-cost producers from their inefficiencies. As he noted when commenting upon a later description of the Industry Fund, 'who except someone with intimate knowledge would have supposed from this that here was an arrangement which consistently for years had transferred large sums running into millions of pounds from low cost to high cost producers'.[58] Thus it would seem that there were other ways to profit than by improving either technical or market efficiency.

The Federation also believed that the industry, through its policies, had managed to supplement the forces of competition and described what the critics saw as its cartel structure as a form of 'constructive co-ordination'.[59] Unrestricted and blind competition had two main disadvantages; first, it led to dramatic fluctuations in prices and secondly, investments could prove wasteful. The first problem was cured by the price policy[60] the second by the 'common services' provided by the Federation.[61] As they argued the case:

In regard to co-ordination between firms, the vital new element introduced here is the increasing recognition that the decisions of individual firms can, with advantage, be taken within a framework of knowledge and not as a result of what is very often almost a blind assessment of the position taken (when the units in industry were smaller) on a trial and error basis. The primary function of the British Iron and Steel Federation, which is the central organisation on the management side of the steel industry, has therefore been to provide a body of knowledge regarding the industry as a whole which was valuable to all the constituent firms, as well as to the community at large. Beyond the provision of greater knowledge, so that competition ceases to work in the dark, the Federation has also been concerned to ensure the provision of co-operative service in any field where the efforts of individual firms can be assisted by advice or collective action of a constructive character.[62]

The common services to harness the power of competition included statistics for production, projected levels of demand for the various steel products, schemes for pooling the costs of the use of imported raw materials, particularly important in the postwar situation,[63] and schemes for equalising the costs of transport between the various sites and the users of steel products. Most significant was the part the Federation played in the co-ordination of the development projects of the individual firms.

The background to the Federation's attempt to develop adequate co-operation between firms on the matter of development has already been given. These procedures were taken to a new level in the postwar period and provided one of the key points in the Federation's case against nationalisation. It has already been mentioned that the Federation prepared a development plan for the industry which was accepted by the Government as 'broadly right'. It is now necessary to turn to the details of that planning process and the way in which the Federation highlighted its virtues. At the outset it should be noted that there were very few details available on how the plan was devised, how the priorities were established or how the Federation convinced various firms and sections to accept the projects finally allocated to them.[64]

The Federation has published an account of the general arrangements for the Plan, based, of course, on the voluntary participation of the constituent firms and Conferences. In their terms, the First Development Plan was compiled in the following way. All firms were requested to give the Development Committee details of the expansions and modernisations that they intended to make. These were scrutinised by the Committee and its technical experts, not drawn from any of the steel firms, for possible duplication, waste or unnecessary projects.[65] These were set against the projected level of future demand (a point of dispute between the industry and its critics, though not relevant to the argument here)[66] and the intended projects were adjusted accordingly. The details were published in a government White Paper.[67] On paper the Plan was a combination of modernisation and technical improvement with a phasing out of excess and high-cost or inefficient plant.[68] The BISF praised a number of aspects of its planning process. For a start it was voluntary and entered into by the various firms as 'responsible bodies'. In other words, the firms who were going to build and fund the new plant had a say in the planning process as independent units and not just as the servants of some central planning body.[69] As a consequence, the Plan was closely linked to what was possible and had benefited from the criticism of those with practical experience and tested commercial judgment. As they argued the case:

The value of its (the Federation's) planning derives essentially from the fact that the firms making up the industry, and contributing to the formulation of the plan, are responsible units and not mere delegates to the central organisation. They do not, therefore, carry out a centrally dictated plan but contribute their own, often very strongly held views, on the commercial and technical soundness of schemes. The plan is, therefore, thrashed out between responsible people and, when agreed, has been through the severe test of commercial practicability.[70]

The main importance of the First Development Plan was to prove that the industry was co-operating with the government, serving the nation, modernising; that it was progressive and doing everything that could be asked of it. The progress of the Plan was continually monitored and cited in the Federation's publications. The fact that the industry was producing 'record' amounts was used to show that there was no need to nationalise the industry.[71]

It is necessary to make a few comments on the reality and achievement of the First Plan and the criteria used by the Federation to pronounce it a success. Success was always measured in terms of the industry's output and not in terms of the modernisation achieved or the inefficient or outdated plant scrapped, and this fundamentally distorted the picture of long-term achievement.[72] The industry had never been short of capacity, even when the development programmes were suspended during the war. Its capacity was easily capable of producing fourteen million tons before the war and the initial estimate of the Development Plan was for a capacity of around sixteen million tons.[73] This meant that the main emphasis of the Plan was on replacement of obsolete plant and the figures given by the Federation on the percentages of new plant confirm this.[74] If it was possible for the industry to increase its capacity *without* a large-scale replacement programme, as envisaged in the initial plan, then output achieved could not be an adequate measure of the Plan's success. In fact that is what happened. There was a programme of new building but very few old plants were actually scrapped.[75] The increase in output over pre-war production was achieved as a result of other

changes. Firstly, the industry went over to a system of continuous
working which increased output without modernisation.[76] Secondly,
there was a conversion to oil-fired furnaces, a technical improvement
which increased production but did not lead to the scrapping of old
plant.[77] Thirdly, there was the retention of plant that had been
intended for scrapping.[78] It was argued that the increase in the cost of
building new capacity had made many of these old plants economically viable. There is an unstated corollary to this, that new plant was
a luxury and not immediately economically viable in the industry's
eyes. Finally, those new plants which were built generally exceeded
the capacity indicated in the Plan.[79] These were the reasons why the
industry was able to boast record performances and meet a revised
forecast of demand without devising new development schemes.[80]
Against such a background the oft-cited figures for the parts of the
Plan completed and projects authorised do not look so impressive.
Certainly there was modernisation and technical improvement but
this was not accompanied by the wholesale scrapping programme
envisaged in the original document.

The Iron and Steel Board

The Federation, having established the benefits of the internal organisation of the industry, justified the prices charged and the profits
made, then considered the supplementary part that could be played
by an independent Public Supervisory Board. The remarks on the
appropriate, and from the perspective of the industry legitimate, role
of the Iron and Steel Board were both explicit and revealing. The most
significant reason for having such a body was to legitimise the collective organisation and action of the industry both to the consumers of
steel products and to the public at large. As they argued the case:

the industry fully recognises the many benefits which can result from
cooperative action in the field of supplies, information, planning and so on.
This cooperation, however, may arouse suspicion that concerted action
might be taken to raise prices artificially or to act in some other monopolistic
way. It therefore seemed reasonable to the industry to accept at the outset the
fixing of prices by a public board as there was certainly no intention of
adopting any price policy which would exploit the consumer.[81]

Or, as a more general recommendation for industry, especially with
the development of strong 'positive' trade associations, 'an independent authority capable of judging fairly as between producer and
consumer, fixing price levels on the basis of full information at a level
corresponding to long term marginal costs'.[82] The independent

authority could even play an important role in legitimising the collective actions of the industry to aggrieved firms. Thus when commenting on the drawing up of a development plan it was stated: 'It ...
seemed quite appropriate to the industry that any plan drawn up
should be submitted to a public body for criticism, not only in regard
to the programme as a whole, but in order that any individual firm
who may feel aggrieved by some aspect of it should have access to a
broadly based public body.'[83] There were other supplementary
reasons why the supervision of the Iron and Steel Board was accepted.
These ranged from the recognition that there were social issues
involved that might demand solutions beyond the perspective (or the
responsibility) of the steel firms to the rather vague benefits of having
an outside body to watch over and encourage new developments.[84]

Before analysing what such comments and justifications reveal
about the steel industry, it is useful to consider the actual character
and performance of the Iron and Steel Board set up to supervise the
conduct of the industry in the period prior to nationalisation. At the
outset it should be stated that the formation of self-governing trade
associations supervised by publicly appointed boards was a crucial
part of the Labour Party's strategy for the privately owned sector of the
economy.[85] It should also be stated that they had very little success in
getting such arrangements accepted. On this matter the Government
and the steel industry agreed that, in general, the public board was an
appropriate way to regulate privately owned industries. They did not
agree on its appropriateness for the steel industry. Obviously the
Federation was able to claim that the Government was undermining
its own programme by threatening to nationalise the one working
example of such a procedure.[86] The interim Iron and Steel Board was
set up with the following tasks:

1. To review and produce programmes of development needed for the modernisation of the iron and steel industry and to watch over the execution of
   approved schemes in such programmes.
2. To supervise as necessary the industry in current matters, including the
   provisions of its raw material requirements, and the administration, under
   power delegated by the Minister, of such continued direction over the
   production, distribution and import of iron and steel products.
3. To advise on general price policy for the industry and on the fixing of
   prices for controlled products.[87]

The members of the Board were chosen to represent the following
interested parties: the owners and managers (through Federation-
approved appointees), the workers (through trade union representatives), the consumers of steel products, and the civil service through

the appointment of a treasury official.[88] Though the Board was everywhere fulsomely praised by the Federation for its contributions during the period of its office, Burn's long analysis of its actions reveals
quite clearly that it was, on the whole, unadventurous and insignificant.[89] This in no way affects the importance of the Board for the
Federation's arguments, as it stood as a symbol of an alternative to
nationalisation that could ensure public supervision without attack-
ing ownership, management prerogatives and the reward of profit.

The tasks set for the Board were significant as they all touch on the
matter of the relationship between the industry and its consumers;
that is one area in which the imbalance between the highly organised
character of the steel industry and the unorganised character of capital as a class could have serious consequences, and in which there
were no effective mechanisms for resolving any emerging conflict.
The impression that the Board was not adequately organised for its
task was reinforced by the numerous recommendations that the Federation proposed to strengthen the Board and which were consolidated in the drafting of the denationalisation proposals.[90] The Board
was also significant in the rhetoric of the Federation's opposition to
nationalisation as proof that the industry did co-operate with the
Government and that nationalisation was not necessary to ensure that
steel, or any other industry, would serve the national interest. To
prove this the Federation could point to the lack of conflict between
the industry and the Iron and Steel Board.[91] The Public Supervisory
Board represented the ideological solution to two problems, first, the
relations between government and industry in a period when most of
the economy would remain in private hands[92] and, secondly, the
harmonisation of relations between different sectors of capitalist production, expressed in BISF literature as the problem of ensuring that
the interests of steel users were neither prejudiced nor endangered by
the collective organisation of the industry.

On the basis of the preceding schematic view of the industry's
response to nationalisation and its positive proposals for the future
organisation of the industry and its relationship with government, it
is possible to advance a number of observations about the character of
the steel industry and its proposals. At the outset it can be shown that
the steel industry represented a progressive or liberal section of capital.[93] That is, the Federation did not argue its case in terms of a
backward vision or dogmatic exposition of the virtues of competition,
private ownership and free enterprise as did some vocal business
bodies during this period. The contrast with the rhetoric of Tate and
Lyle most clearly illustrates this. It had a vision of how relations

between government and industry should be organised in the period
of the 'mixed economy'. Here they were decisively in advance of their
class. This was particularly evident in the arguments about nationalisation, acceptable in certain cases, and government regulation,
which was seen as having positive benefits for the steel industry and
the class as a whole. Ironically, it was in agreement with large sections of the Labour Government's proposals for industry as, in a sense,
they shared the same vision of future problems and solutions.
Furthermore, the industry had sharp views on the limits to the expansion of the state-owned sector of the economy. Nationalisation should
stop before it reached steel but the general grounds upon which the
Federation agreed with nationalisation were never made explicit. Not
only did they have views about the size of the publicly owned sector,
they also suggested certain guidelines for the conduct of the mixed
economy. These were most usually expressed in the Federation's
criticisms of the unfair way in which state-owned industries could act
against their privately owned competitors and consumers.[94]

All in all, the steel industry, via the British Iron and Steel Federation, had a well-developed and fairly comprehensive conception of
how the problems inherent in the structure of a 'mixed economy'
could best be handled, from the point of view of itself, as a subunit of
capital, and of capital as a whole. Such visions were not unpre-
cedented, and the fact that its proposals existed did not guarantee that
they would be successful. What they do indicate is an awareness of
the problem. Whether the steel industry came to express these progressive attitudes as a result of some profound change in the character
of the industrialists prominent in the industry, bearing in mind that in
the 1920s they had a reputation for being obstinate individualists, or
as a considered and skilful response to the threat of nationalisation, is
almost completely irrelevant.

The Government's proposals

Nationalisation of steel was the political issue of the 1945–51 period.
It was a test both of the character and resolve of the Labour administration and of the British political system. More significantly, the dispute over steel nationalisation was crucial in determining the size
of the publicly owned share of the mixed economy that was then in
the first stages of construction. The Labour Government lacked any
well-thought-out criteria for fixing the extent of the state-owned
sector, and the dispute served to set limits which remained effective
for almost two decades. The dispute within the Party over the priority

for steel nationalisation and the character of the industry's post-nationalisation organisation reflected the difficulties involved in finding an easy solution to the problem. It also reflected the objective tensions inherent in the creation of a new form of organisation for the capitalist economy and social system without the existence of any procedures adequate to the expression of the interests of the capitalist class as a whole. Without such arrangements, conflict between a particular industry and a reforming government was the only appropriate adjustment mechanism. In these circumstances, the Government's indecision over how quickly steel should be nationalised and the disjointed character of the arguments advanced, can be understood. The lack of consistency was noted by most commentators though few of them attempted to put it in its proper perspective.[95] These signs should not be treated as revealing fundamental flaws in the Government's case, as the BISF proclaimed; rather they show the real problems that the nationalisation of steel posed for the Government's social and political project. They certainly do not show that the Federation's case was correct.

The general grounds used by the Labour Party to justify nationalisation have already been discussed and all of these were called in to service the demand for the nationalisation of steel. But the arguments were not advanced in a ritualistic manner. Though the Government did not produce a full-scale critique of the industry, there were several available, written by left-wing socialists within or closely related to the Labour Party.[96] These provide sufficient evidence to analyse two important aspects of the nationalisation case, first, the grounds for the rejection of the Public Supervisory Board and, secondly, the positive grounds for nationalisation. Labour critics of the steel industry did not lack ammunition for their rejection of the Federation's proposals. They could cite the whole history of IDAC/Federation relations to show that in that exercise of public supervision all major initiative resided with the Federation, especially in the areas of prices and profits.[97] The wartime arrangements and the difficulty that the Public Accounts Committee and other official bodies had in finding out the details of the price arrangements in the industry, did nothing to lessen their suspicions. All in all, the Government's and the industry's critics were cynical about the reality of public supervision in the past and doubtful whether it could work for an industry as well organised as steel. The critics did not believe that an Iron and Steel Board would have sufficient positive powers of direction or action to ensure that desirable developments occurred.[98] Indeed, the consequences of private ownership and of each firm seeking its own profitability and security could not be eliminated by more supervision. The problem needed to be tackled at its roots: progressive development would only be possible under state ownership. These critics were also dubious about the planning policies of the Federation, again with good cause.[99] Thus they noted the ease with which the Federation changed the cost and shape of its plans and the lack of detail in the ways in which these were drawn up and how compromises were effected between the various firms. All these points had been made by other, non-labour, commentators on the industry. The net effect of this accumulated suspicion was to destroy belief in the claims that the industry had reformed itself and had abandoned its bad habits of the inter-war years. Any change in behaviour was attributed to the prospect of nationalisation which made the industry eager to please.

The positive case for nationalisation was built upon this suspicion. It was also based on a consideration of the technical character of steel production and the organisational problems facing the industry. For instance, Cole, Fienberg and Evely, and Owen all treated the existence of a monopoly form of organisation as a consequence of the technology of the steel industry; monopoly was the necessary outcome of the industry's production process.[100] Monopoly and the consequences of monopoly were, then, the cornerstone of the nationalisation case. The industry, with the Federation as the overseeing power, followed monopolistic practices in the determination of prices and the level of production.[101] What, for the industry, was a response to recession after World War One was, to the critics, evidence of the industry's monopoly practices. Monopoly was further manifested in the industry's inability to implement a wholesale reconstruction and modernisation programme.[102] As far as the critics were concerned, the industry showed an unhealthy tendency to prefer the maintenance of outdated and technically inefficient plants to modernisation that would not substantially improve the level of returned profit, but which would eliminate waste and inefficiency.[103] Thus all the strands of the Labour Party's general case for nationalisation were united in the analysis of the steel industry and its organisation.

Though it was possible to argue that, on the grounds of technological improvement alone, nationalisation was justified, most of the critics saw in the monopoly organisation of the steel industry a threat to democracy in Britain. It was argued that the scale of monopoly organisation not only conferred commercial advantages on the industry but also gave them an unduly significant concentration of power.[104] The steel industry was portrayed as the basic industry of the modern economy as its products were used in almost every facet of manufacturing. If such an industry was organised along monopoly lines, it gave a small number of people the basis for very significant power which could be exercised against the programmes of a legitimately elected government. Such power could be exercised to undermine a reforming government's economic policies or to pressure the government into changing its programmes. Even the internal decisions of the industry were of such social consequence that they ought not to be taken by a small group of owners and managers responsible only to their commercial judgment. Hence the argument became one about power and the need for the steel industry to be run in a manner consistent with the democratically determined government programme. The position was accurately summarised like this:

The case for nationalisation, simply stated and divorced from the many subsidiary supporting arguments is as follows: Steel is basic to our mechanised civilisation. As a result of fundamental factors affecting the industry, it has drifted into monopoly. In this industry monopoly is inevitable. It cannot be de-monopolised. The problem, then, is to nominate someone to run the monopoly. The power of steel is such that it should not be left in the hands of private individuals answerable to sectional interests. Indeed the power of steel must be vested in the nation if we are to take positive steps to restore the economy. There is no satisfactory method of controlling in the public interest the decisions and activities of a private monopoly. Therefore steel should be nationalised. This will ensure that the power of steel is used to serve the people, to give them control over their economic destinies.[105]

There is an overstatement in the argument on the importance of the steel industry in the capitalist economy. Frequently steel is portrayed as the basic industry for capitalist production and the move to nationalise steel as a direct blow against capitalism.[106] The overstressing of the importance of steel may be explained by the tactical needs of those within the Labour Party who wished to prevent their less-committed colleagues from wavering. But the error is more significant than that. Steel is a product of great importance in the manufacturing of physical commodities and as such it has a lot in common with the other infra-structural processes already nationalised, such as coal, gas, electricity, water and rail transport. This does not mean that it was either the commanding heights of capitalism, or the basic industry for *capitalist* production. The distinctive thing about a capitalist economy is that physical, and other, goods are produced as commodities that can be circulated so as to realise a portion of the surplus value embodied in them as profit and capital. In that sense, no single industry is the basis of capitalist society. Instead, one sector is basic: that in which commodities are produced and surplus value generated. The image of 'commanding heights' was inappropriate as it was the basic separation of the labourer from the means of production, and the class's subordination to capital that made the production of commodities possible. It is the assault upon the basic capital/labour relationship which is important in nationalisation and not just the encroachment upon areas of production. In the Labour Party argument, this matter remained concealed and was only approached indirectly through a concern with industrial democracy in the nationalised enterprise.[107]

The largest divergence was between the arguments advanced to support nationalisation and the actual proposals made for the nationalised industry. The actual proposals were severely constricted by tactical considerations, mainly the anticipated need to defuse BISF opposition, and a very strange conception of ownership. Further, the proposals show the way in which the Labour Government was aware of the problems involved in the construction of the mixed economy. This was revealed in the 1949 Iron and Steel Act when the duties of the Corporation, the body in whom the ownership rights would reside after nationalisation, were listed. The first of these stated that the Corporation should act

To promote the efficient and economical supply of the products ... and to secure that these products are available at such prices as may seem to the Corporation best calculated to satisfy the reasonable demands of the persons who use these products for manufacturing purposes and to further the public interest in all respects.[108]

Hence the Corporation would be concerned with the harmonisation of relations between the industry and its consumers, the manufacturers. That is, the Corporation would be concerned with smoothing relations between the state-owned sector and manufacturing, but privately owned, industry. The second listed duty was designed to ensure that the nationalised steel industry could not use its powers to discriminate amongst its consumers on other than commercial grounds. The reference to public interest in this clause was a matter of ritual as, in the Act, public interest meant the interests of manufacturing industry which used steel products. This can be seen in the provisions for the protection of the consumer's interests, which referred, not to the general public, but to the manufacturers.[109] The attempt to define and facilitate relations between the publicly owned and privately owned sectors of the capitalist economy is also evident in many other sections of the Act and the nationalisation proposals.

The purpose of the 1949 Iron and Steel Act was to secure the transfer to public ownership of a number of firms whose output of steel products exceeded a legally designated limit. It sought to do nothing else. The Corporation was instructed to run the industry in such a way that the interests of the manufacturers were served. There was no attempt to change the structure of the industry, to define new principles of conduct or to set out the details of a new and different development plan. The only significant matter was that of ownership. Here the Labour Party was committed to a very ineffective view of managerialism. It was assumed that the transfer of ownership from private to public hands would alter the constraints that were imposed on management and that their perspective would, as a consequence, be changed. They believed that it would be a relatively simple task to detach managers from the owners of the firms and indeed appealed to the managers in those terms.[110] It was hoped that managers would now be concerned with efficient management, unfettered by the requirements to make a profit or the restrictions imposed by backward owners, and that social perspectives would replace or at the least complement commercial judgment. They believed that managers were professionals who would work for any owner, be it a private firm or the state. To this end, and to minimise the grounds for opposition, the Act did not include any change in the firm structure of the industry. Overall, it was a very pusillanimous and uninspired document, flawed and weakened by its desire to upset the managers of the existing steel firms as little as possible. The net effect of the appeasement policy was that nationalisation could have no direct or immediate effect upon the routine work experience of those employed in the steel industry.

The nationalised steel industry was to be unified only at the level of ownership and in the broad direction of policy. Decentralisation as a key feature of the industry was written into the duties of the Corporation.[111] As with the previous cases, nationalised steel was to be run as a public corporation with all the autonomy that that had come to imply. Nationalisation was not going to be used as a pretext for full-scale social control of the steel industry.[112] The relevant minister could give broad directions on matters of general policy but could not 'interfere' with the daily conduct of the industry. The Iron and Steel Corporation was to run the industry as an analogue of the Federation, foreshadowing obvious conflicts between the two bodies, since the statute made no directions on the relations between them. The Corporation was to regulate and co-ordinate the relations between the various nationalised steel firms and to set the price at which steel goods could be sold. It was also charged with making a profit as it had to cover costs, 'taking one year with the next', and to pay off the compensation debt of the initial nationalisation. The organisation and conduct of the nationalised steel industry would not represent a challenge to either the basic labour/capital relation of capitalist society or the industry's subordination to the overarching logic of capital accumulation that linked the publicly and privately owned sectors of the economy.

The clearest consequence of the minimal nationalisation proposals was the lack of detail on how technical efficiency would be improved or how the modernisation programme would be speeded up as a consequence of the change from private to public ownership.[113] This certainly undermined the pro-nationalisation criticisms of the development programmes prepared by the industry. It also meant that the argument had to rely upon rather general observations on how the unification of ownership would, in the future, facilitate more adequate development plans. In fact, when the industry was nationalised, the Corporation's only act to restructure the industry was the removal of directors and others from sitting on the boards of the various firms where there was a conflict of interests, not a particularly significant move.[114] At the most, there were a few rumours about a change in the shape of the industry by the promotion of regional concentration and centralisation, though nothing was done about it.[115] Nationalisation was designed to introduce no significant change in the steel industry other than the transfer of the formal rights of ownership to a public body. This had consequences for the financing of the steel industry and the pricing policies which it could follow. Government subsidies could spread the cost of a radical modernisation programme across the whole of capital and the whole of the working class in a way that privately owned industry could never do.

The move to nationalise steel was complicated by two factors: first, the fortunes of the industry changed after the war and, secondly, trade union enthusiasm diminished. These two factors are relevant to the consideration of interests. A combination of high demand for steel in the postwar period coupled with effective internal organisation suggested that the profitability of the industry was secure. The steel industry was no longer a problem for its owners, who could be expected to treat nationalisation as a threat and something to be opposed. Increased security also made a modernising development plan more feasible, especially as part of an anti-nationalisation campaign. The improvement in profitability did not automatically reduce the problems for the class of capital, as the steel industry still was a source of frustration and was frequently criticised for problems with quality, output and orderly delivery. The trade unions' reduced enthusiasm may be read as recognition that immediate benefits would not flow from nationalisation. If craft-based trade unions are sensitive to anything it is to the calculus of material reward. The trade union response to the pusillanimous nationalisation scheme was not to argue that it should be strengthened, but to cool their support for the measure; an understandable reaction.

It is now possible to summarise what was at stake in this particular dispute between a section of private capital and a reforming Labour Government. There were two alternative proposals, either national-isation and a public corporation or a privately owned industry co-ordinated through the British Iron and Steel Federation and super-vised by an Iron and Steel Board. Both proposals approached the problem of harmonising relations between the steel industry and manufacturing industry. This was evident in the provisions made to ensure that the 'rights' or 'interests' of the consumers were repre-sented or served. There were two alternative views on the size of the publicly owned sector of the mixed economy, including or excluding the steel industry, and the character of the mix in the mixed economy. The criteria for inclusion in the public sector, the limits to the public sector, were being fought over. Should the public sector include only industries that were not profitable in private hands? Should it include all industries that were basic for the manufacturing process? If a basic industry is profitable should it be nationalised as part of a scheme to make the public base of the mixed economy comprehensive? A further issue was the basis upon which the relations between the two sectors should be conducted. In part, these were resolved before the Iron and Steel Act by the organisation of nationalised industries as public corporations and by the inclusion of 'no discrimination' clauses in the charters of nationalised concerns. The relevance of industrial self-government was also being debated as a complement to the argument over the size of the public sector. These were the issues at stake in the conflict over the nationalisation of steel. They go beyond the question of who should own the steel industry and refer to the dilemmas faced in the construction of a mixed economy and the servicing of conflicting class interests under such conditions.

5

Steel nationalised and the role of power

There is no other incident in the development of British capitalism that is so obviously relevant to the analysis of power in the interaction between business and government as the conflict surrounding the initial nationalisation of steel. The details of the struggle and the outcome have been used to illustrate many different arguments; some about the character of power, some about the 'loyalty' of business to the norms of the democratic system, and some about the socialist commitment of the Labour Party. Not all these arguments are relevant to the issues being discussed here. Though the character of the Labour Party is not being studied, Brady,[1] Miliband[2] and Coates[3] have all used the timidity of the Labour Government in the face of business obstruction as evidence that the Labour Party either lacked a serious commitment to socialism or was not firmly resolved to win its more limited, social-democratic objectives. These views are unexceptional, but the grounds for the Government's 'timidity' need to be examined more closely.

Much more relevant are the debates about the character of power and the significance of business resistance. In this area, a group of authors have used the conflict over steel to support a number of related propositions: either that the government prevailed in conflict with business, or that business accepted the legitimacy of government action (signalled by the refusal to use illegal methods in their opposition to government policy), or that power was widely distributed within the political system and that policy was the consequence of inter-group competition resolved by a neutral government. The argument that business accepts government domination is clearly found in the work of Finer[4] and Castles.[5] Finer based his argument on the premise that there is nothing illegitimate about business trying to secure its own interest[6] and then shows that business opposition to the Labour Government of 1945–51 did not exceed the limits of legality. As he states it, 'the surprising feature about industry's relations to the Labour Government of 1945–50 is not that such sporadic and remediable resistance sometimes occurred but that so very much of so revolutionary a programme was accepted with such docility'.[7]

Over steel nationalisation Finer argues that, first, the industry could have offered more determined resistance than it did and, secondly, the industry's and the Government's attitudes were a product of the narrow Labour majority in the 1950 election.[8] Castles's position is slightly different. He has sought to show that the dispute over nationalisation severely strained business acceptance of government action. In his terms, it was the strength of a normative code which stopped business groups from stepping outside the limits of British political practice.[9] Both authors ignore the problem associated with the special character of government and their analyses suffer as a consequence. They are vague about the significance of the outcome and its consequences for social development. If Finer's exaggeration of the Labour Government's political programme is ignored, there is enough in his defence of business resistance to warrant a further discussion of his argument after the analysis of the actual passage of the dispute about steel nationalisation.

Though the 'A has power over B' reasoning underlies Finer's arguments, its use is more apparent in two recent articles by Hewitt.[10] In these he has not only used such a formulation, justified by arguments about the virtues of the decision-making approach, but has also sought to test what he describes as elite and pluralist hypotheses about the distribution of power. Much of his argument fails because of the weak formulation of these contending hypotheses. The general deficiencies of Hewitt's procedures have already been discussed (see p. 19), but his comments on the nationalisation of steel reveal further problems. He does not use the nationalisation of steel to prove that governments dominate the actions of business groups, as he knows that the industry was subsequently denationalised. Indeed, he recognises in denationalisation that the industry's resistance was effective. He fails to take up the implications that this has for his broad interpretation of the significance of government action. What is most striking about Hewitt's treatment is his almost total lack of concern with the significance of the incidents he is considering; the implications of developments and changes almost completely elude him. What is worse, he twists the shape of the interaction between business and government. He describes the conflict over steel as being between pro- and anti-nationalisation groups, which conceals the fact that it was the Labour Government which was pressing most strongly for the nationalisation of steel.[11] In this way, his conclusions about the role of government are written into the terminology of his account. Hewitt's perspective prevented him from recognising and analysing many of the important and revealing features of the conflict, and steel nationalisation, in his hands, becomes just another piece of hypothesis-testing fodder.

There were other uses of the conflict over the nationalisation of steel which were not trapped by the '*A* has power over *B*' formulation. Rogow, in his previously cited book on relations between the Labour Government and industry, argues a quite different case.[12] The effectiveness of the analysis is enhanced by the fact that he is not concerned to judge the actions of the Labour Government against some abstract notion of socialism. Instead, the actions of the Labour Government are measured against a model of the mixed economy which Rogow saw being constructed at that time. Naturally, the conflict over steel nationalisation is an important part of his analysis. He argues that the conflict over steel set the framework within which the tensions between government and industry could be resolved in the mixed economy. The implications that this has for the analysis of power were lost in a later discussion of the character of the society produced by the actions of the Labour Government. Rogow, looking back at the period, is concerned to emphasise the harmony which existed between the Party's theory and its actions as a government. The account presented in the previous chapter shares Rogow's general views on the relationship between the mixed economy and the nationalisation, though the basis of the argument is quite different.

The previous chapter dealt with the significance of the alternative proposals for the future of the steel industry. It is now necessary to consider how the actual conflict over steel was conducted. On that basis, it is possible to analyse all aspects of the dispute surrounding the initial nationalisation of steel and to see what can be revealed about the character and role of power in conflict between a section of capital and government. It is not necessary to give a detailed account of the various initiatives and responses in the conflict as Ross's book, *The Nationalisation of Steel*, provides one. The main incidents in the conflict have already been summarised and any further elaboration of what happened would not help the kind of analysis of power being developed. On the basis of the two chapters which dealt with the analysis of power and theories of the state, certain questions need to be taken up here. Firstly, it is necessary to examine the way in which the two main parties to the dispute conducted themselves, in order to see how they viewed their goals and fought for them. Their conduct can then be used to consider what was the character of power evident in the interaction between them. Secondly, it is necessary to consider the significance of the outcome, not just to assess who had triumphed but to see whose interests were secured by the nationalisation of steel in the form carried through by the Labour Government. Finally, it is possible to make some initial conclusions about the part played by power and conflict in the articulation of sectional, class and system interests in this particular example of conflict between government and an industry. In part these remarks must be as tentative as the resolution of the conflict. Consideration of the subsequent history of the interaction between various governments and the steel industry in the process of denationalisation and renationalisation is needed to complement and extend these initial, limited observations.

The conduct of the dispute

The Government

All the key incidents in the conflict show that the Government was determined to nationalise the steel industry but that it was not prepared to pursue that goal with all the resources and energy available to it. The restraint was self-imposed and aimed to minimise the significance of the rupture between itself and the business community over the issue. It was impossible to prevent some breach, as the Government was attempting to nationalise a profitable industry. Not only was steel profitable but it was more than a simple infra-structural industry like coal; the firms which made steel were also involved in the production of a wide range of manufactured goods.[13] Indeed, the very process of steel production included some processes which were very similar to those of manufacturing industry. Yet the steel industry was largely concerned with the production of a raw material to be used and processed by other manufacturers. In other words, the boundary which separated infra-structural and manufacturing processes ran through the steel industry. Given that a breach was unavoidable, the Government sought, by action and argument, to minimise its extent and seriousness. In the course of the dispute, and as its intensity became obvious, it became clear that the Government had little intention of seeking to nationalise any other manufacturing industry, regardless of what other sections of the Party might want. The very terms of the nationalisation proposals were designed to placate the rest of industry as much as to defuse the anticipated and obvious opposition of the BISF. Similarly the terms used to justify the nationalisation of steel made it unlikely that any other industry could even be considered for nationalisation.

In the actual conflict with the Federation, many things stand as evidence of excessive moderation in the pursuit of the Government's stated goals. The Government was everywhere and always conciliatory in the hope that it could gain the co-operation of the managers of the steel firms. Whenever a contentious question arose, the Government sought to circumvent possible opposition and never chose to meet the Federation head on. This produced some improbable consequences such as the existence of two separate and non-communicating sections of the Ministry of Supply, both dealing with the steel industry.[14] One was concerned with the day-to-day conduct of the industry and the other with the preparation of the plans for nationalisation. In a similar way, the Government accepted the Federation's opposition to the Iron and Steel Board playing any part in the preparation of the nationalisation plans. The conditions under which the first Board could function were effectively set by the Federation on the basis of the above objection and the refusal of those associated with the Federation to accept re-appointment of the Board once nationalisation appeared imminent.[15] Throughout the dispute the Government refused to see that any of the Federation's actions were a challenge to its authority. When there were differences, the Government most frequently changed its position. Whether such changes were significant or were the consequence of a successful exercise of power by the steel industry is considered later.

Partly as a response to the intensity of the Federation's opposition and partly for reasons that relate to the objective difficulties of what it was trying to do, the Government could not even remain united on the need to nationalise. From the outset, some members of the Government were unenthusiastic about the nationalisation of steel. This lack of enthusiasm did not diminish as the conflict intensified and the nationalisation plans were nearing completion. Morrison, with at least the tacit approval of Attlee, approached the Federation with a scheme to strengthen the Iron and Steel Board and avoid nationalisation.[16] Though there are few available details of the hybrid scheme, it would have represented a significant change in policy and would have accepted the positions expressed by the Federation in its opposition to nationalisation.[17] It would have ended the conflict between the Government and the Federation on grounds favourable to the Federation. If it had been accepted, the conflict would have been truncated and it would be necessary to ask whether the legislation passed by the Government, formulated as a consequence of its own initiative, stood as evidence of the successful exercise of power by the steel industry. The rejection of the hybrid proposal postpones the question until the analysis of denationalisation. Morrison's scheme was rejected as a result of the composition of the Cabinet. Dalton, Bevin and Cripps were sufficiently determined to dissuade Attlee from supporting Morrison, and the proposal lapsed.[18] The members of the Federation were bitter and felt that they had been betrayed.[19]

What does the timidity of the Labour Government's approach to the nationalisation of steel reveal? Not that it did not want steel nationalised; it did and steel was eventually nationalised, but there were real and severe tensions in its governmental project which were most sharply focused in the dispute over steel nationalisation. The arguments about the apparent weakness of the Government's case and the limited nature of the nationalisation proposals themselves also apply to the Government's timidity. The Government's attitude expressed the problems which it faced in completing the construction of the mixed economy while needing to establish and maintain harmonious relations between the public and private sectors of the economy, as seen in good relations between governments and business. The Labour Government was groping blindly and untheoretically to consolidate the mixed economy, and the nationalisation of steel was an important part of that task. It was not just that steel had to be nationalised to make the public base of the mixed economy comprehensive, but that the limits of the mixed economy and an appropriate form for the relations between the two sectors had to be agreed as well. The steel industry was the focus of these tensions because it lay at the boundary between infra-structural and manufacturing industries; it was profitable but needed substantial reconstruction and it advocated an adequate set of arrangements for the harmonising of government/industry relations in the conduct of the private sector. These factors explain the depth of the Government's timidity and set out an area which needs to be considered further in the investigation of the character of power.

The Federation

For the British Iron and Steel Federation, the issues were obvious and their actions were never constrained in the same way. Their intention was to stop the nationalisation of steel and, if that was not possible, to minimise the damage of nationalisation and to prepare the ground for eventual denationalisation.[20] The Federation believed that the industry would not be nationalised for long and this belief was strengthened by the vigour with which the Conservatives opposed the measure in Parliament. Co-operation between the Conservatives and the Federation in preparing the opposition left them with little doubt that denationalisation would occur quickly and in a form favourable to the owners and managers of the industry.[21] With clearly defined objectives and obvious incentives, the Federation pursued its policy with great enthusiasm and it was able to exploit the Government's timidity in a very effective manner.

The actions taken by the Federation can be seen as different combinations of passive non-co-operation and skilful propaganda. For example, the limits imposed on the duties and duration of the Iron and Steel Board and the denial of its accumulated technical expertise were instances of effective non-co-operation. Since personnel from the Federation had been so extensively involved in the wartime Control, there was only a small number of people with a close knowledge of the steel industry available to the Government.[22] This made passive resistance even more telling. After nationalisation, the Federation continued its hostile attitude, refusing co-operation and hindering the Government in the execution of its nationalisation plans. As mentioned earlier, this included discouraging leading figures in the industry from serving on the new Iron and Steel Corporation, minimising the amount of the Corporation's participation in the Federation's affairs and preventing the Corporation from taking over the collective import of raw materials.[23] In all these cases the Federation succeeded and won concessions that left the power and character of the Federation virtually unaltered. It certainly retained an effective base for operating should the industry be denationalised.

Though the Federation's actions were effective and often successful, they could not prevent the nationalisation of the industry. It is also true that the Federation did not resort to a crude policy of total opposition or seek to prevent the nationalisation of steel by illegal means. Finer emphasises this fact, though it is difficult to see what illegal means could have been more effective. A policy of complete non-co-operation by the managers of the nationalised steel companies was more likely to have promoted the unwanted restructuring of the industry than the policy of official passive resistance tempered by co-operation at the point of production. The scope for illegal opposition which would not have damaged the industry's prospects in the event of denationalisation was small. Indeed Finer makes too much of legality; the important fact was that the Federation did initiate an attempt to thwart the Government's programme and, though it failed to prevent nationalisation, it did create a very strong base for denationalisation. The extent of the conflict over steel weakened the Labour Party's resolve to stay in government and strengthened the coherence of the Conservative opposition.[24] Castles's argument that the actions of the Federation were constrained in that it accepted the legitimacy of the Government to make policy, is relevant. It would seem to be true that the Federation did accept the legitimacy of government to make policy and it directed its efforts to have either the policy or the government changed. The strength of its opposition helped to make the latter more probable. However, to stress that the Federation accepted the legitimacy of government and the rules of British democracy is to obscure the significance of the resistance it had organised and the success which it had achieved. What Finer and Castles observed was evidence that Britain was not in a period of revolutionary crisis and that the dispute over the nationalisation of steel was not such that it threatened the fabric of the existing political system or the domination of capital.

What does the Federation's resistance and its degree of success reveal? Unlike the Government it pursued its interests with vigour, convinced that it was also acting for the rest of the class. It used all the means at its disposal which were likely to prove effective in a strategy to minimise the damage caused by nationalisation. The techniques of its opposition are relatively unimportant to the assessment of the character and form of power involved. Nevertheless, it must be pointed out that the Federation was not just a pressure group like any other. Far better organised and with a much more secure financial base than groups demanding the abolition of hanging or an end to animal research, its capabilities for action were far greater. Its base in a strong, large and significant industry meant that it was always far more important than a mere pressure group clamouring to have its claim recognised amidst a roar of contending voices. Though the techniques used by the Federation may have looked something like the techniques used by a pressure group, the significance of it being an industry cannot be overestimated. The Federation did succeed in making the Government's task as difficult as possible whilst not succeeding in preventing nationalisation. It is the combination of efficient resistance without success with the creation of a strong base to encourage denationalisation that needs to be probed further in the analysis of the power involved in the conflict over the nationalisation of steel.

The significance of the outcome and the character of power

There are many difficulties involved in assessing the significance of the eventual nationalisation of steel, given that we know it was denationalised after a short period and that it was renationalised in the 1960s. It is necessary to be cautious in analysing what was in fact a very tentative outcome. Traditional analysis was very much concerned with instances of conflict, like the nationalisation of steel, and sought to use them to measure who had exercised power on the basis of who secured the outcome. If these procedures were used for the first nationalisation of steel, then the conclusion drawn would be that the Government triumphed and had power. Such an observation has been effectively undermined by the knowledge of subsequent developments and the previous discussion of power, class interests and the state.

The ability of the Government to nationalise steel indicates that it possessed the formal competence to enact legislation and that its opponents, both in parliament and outside, lacked that competence. There is nothing surprising here. Similarly, the legislation to enact the denationalisation of steel also reveals such a formal competence. Without further argument, the fact that a government passes a law cannot be used to show that it has power. It is here that the special character of the government is important. As argued earlier, the government is not like any other body in an *A/B* conflict: it is the institution authorised to make decisions about the direction of social development. Given its distinctive character, how is its power to be measured and how is the significance of its legislative victories to be assessed? In previous chapters I have argued that power and the exercise of power were the medium through which interests were articulated, advanced and secured. If that were true, then government is best viewed as a facilitating medium for the serving of the interests of classes, class fractions or other parts of the social whole. In this instance, the government was involved in a complicated interaction between labour and capital as well as a dispute with a part of capital and the class of capital as a whole.

In a real sense the nationalisation of steel was an ambiguous and incomplete resolution of the problems discussed in the previous chapter. One thing is clear, the nationalisation of steel in the form achieved by the Attlee Government did not substantially advance the interests of either the steel workers or the working class. Despite the fact that the initiative for nationalisation came from the working class and was processed by the institutions of the labour movement, the eventual outcome does not show that they either had, or successfully exercised, power in the conflict. The main interpretative problems arise in the need to unravel the complicated and even contradictory strands of interest between the steel industry, other fractions of capital and the class as a whole. The nationalisation of steel did not advance the interests of that portion of capital actually involved in the steel industry. Their opposition was real and based on an accurate assessment of the adverse effect which nationalisation would have on their positions as owners and managers. If the hybrid scheme, sponsored by Morrison, had been accepted then they would have won a considerable victory. It would have secured both their policy goals and their interests. When the hybrid proposal was rejected they lost the attempt to secure their most immediate interests. Then it became a struggle for the second best and here the Federation was able to minimise the changes to the firm structure and the pricing policy of the industry. From the perspective of the private capital involved in the industry, this was essential for any subsequent return to private ownership. In securing these conditions the Federation had exerted considerable and significant power.

In identifying the existence and exercise of power by the steel industry, it is necessary to point out that, in a large measure, the successful exercise of power was here facilitated by the Government itself. The internal divisions within the Cabinet, the tactics pursued by the Government and its genuine attempts to minimise the dislocation of the nationalisation proposals combined to make possible the success of the Federation's second-line strategy. None of this can obscure the fact that, at least temporarily, the Federation did not win the conflict about the organisation and ownership of the steel industry. Here both the 'A has power over B' formula and the analysis of power as the medium for advancing interests coincide in their diagnosis; the steel industry, represented by the Federation, did not have or exercise sufficient power to prevent nationalisation. It should not be forgotten that the same factors which secured their second-line goals were almost strong enough to secure their principal goal as well. The second approach does not make the mistake of assuming that the temporary defeat of the steel industry indicates either that government dominates the economic process or that the Government's success here shows that it is far more powerful than capital or private business.

The actual steel nationalisation legislation served, in an indecisive manner, the interests of the manufacturing sector of capital and the class of capital as a whole. The interests of the manufacturing sector, or industrial capital, were advanced through all the provisions that sought to attune the conduct of the steel industry to the requirements of the consumers of steel products. The interests of the class as a whole were advanced through all the proposals that sought to harmonise relations between the steel industry and the rest of industrial capital, to make the publicly owned base of the mixed economy comprehensive, and to make explicit the ways in which publicly owned industries would be operated to serve the needs of private capital without challenging either its profitability or the basic opposition between labour and capital. It should be noted that these class-wide interests were not advanced in a coherent or comprehensive manner. Part of the reason for the complications in the way in which class interests were advanced and protected lay in the fact that the policies were not conceived with that end in mind. Steel was not nationalised with the sole and exclusive intention of rationalising the structure of the mixed economy or to complete its publicly owned base. There were various motives behind the moves and these included an attempt to fulfil long-standing political promises, a concern to attack undemocratic concentrations of power and a desire to make the actions of private capital subject to national planning. This complex of motivations does not reduce the significance that the nationalisation of steel had for capital as a class or the processes of capitalist production. The Federation's proposals sought to secure a sectional advantage. However, the way in which they acted did not threaten the class interests of capital. The dispute between the Government and the Federation was over two different ways of advancing the interests of the capitalist class, one articulated by a subsection of capital which sought to advance its own interests in a way compatible with the interests of the rest of the class, and the other by a reforming Labour Government through the construction of the mixed economy.

There was also good reason why other sections of capital may not have been enthusiastic about having their interests served by the nationalisation of steel. The lack of adequate procedures for generating class-wide policies further complicated matters. The same reasons which made the steel industry a problem for the Government also explain the lack of enthusiasm of capital. Steel was profitable and, on the whole, capital shows a preference for the nationalisation of unprofitable or excessively expensive sections of industry. The mechanics of the mixed economy were not clearly established, nor could they be certain that the procedures to guarantee the interests of the manufacturing sector were indeed adequate or that they were more adequate than those proposed by the Federation. Furthermore, the wide range of industries that the new Corporation could operate was such that there was the possibility of having a government-backed competitor, even though the Government disclaimed any intention of using these as weapons in a struggle against private

enterprise. A nationalised steel industry would have concentrated
even more economic resources in the hands of the government and
these could have been used to further undermine the prerogatives of
the remaining sections of private capital. The nationalisation of steel
would have reduced the area in which capital could operate freely
and earn a profit. Given that steel was profitable, the move to nationalise it posed a symbolic threat. If the move were successful, then
nationalisation might appear to be a reasonable option for other
sections of profitable manufacturing industry.

In many ways, the time was wrong for the nationalisation of steel
and the consolidation of the mixed economy. The industry did not
look as much like a problem as it had in the period before the upturn
in demand associated with the approach of the Second World War.
War and the boom in the period of reconstruction made the technical
weaknesses of the industry less apparent, though there were still
problems with the supply of steel. In 1947 steel was described as the
major bottleneck handicapping reconstruction. Though the industry
blamed factors beyond their control, such as the use of steel as a
substitute for timber, problems in the supply of coke, or the import of
raw materials,[25] there were still indications that all was not well with
the steel industry. In other, changed, circumstances the basic problems of the steel industry could re-emerge and the policy of nationalisation would again become relevant. This would provide the opportunity to rationalise the public sector base of the mixed economy. But
after the war this was not obviously so. It would be wrong to assume
that the project of constructing the mixed economy was something
that had to be done in a very short time. Its coherence and the
principles of its operation had to be established through conflict in a
situation that lacked both the institutions and procedures adequate to
the task.

Having argued that the working class did not advance its interests
through the nationalisation of steel and that the steel owners and
managers were unsuccessful, it is necessary to consider the form,
meaning and character of power as revealed in the incident. As the
matter stands, I have argued that the interests of manufacturing or
industrial capital were protected by the form in which steel was
nationalised and that the class interests of capital were advanced. The
way in which these interests were affected may not have been supported by industrial capital or the class as a whole. It is the implication that this has for the analysis of power which must be explored
further.

Traditionally, analysis was designed to identify who had power through an assessment of whose will prevailed in a situation of conflict. For good reasons, it was not legitimate to argue that someone had or exercised power simply because they had gained something out of the conflict. It was particularly illegitimate if that someone had played no obvious part. Such a position would seem to be perfectly adequate for the field upon which the conception was based, the interaction between individuals, but any extension of that reasoning to interactions amongst socially significant groups in a class-structured situation would need to be carefully examined. It is true to say that a class or class fraction that had its interests advanced without having acted to secure that advance cannot be said to have exercised power. It does not mean that such a class or class fraction did not have power or that power was not relevant in securing a beneficial outcome. If this statement is correct, then the overt exercise of power cannot be the key to understanding either the distribution of power or the way in which interests are secured or advanced. Different arguments need to be constructed.

In the case of steel nationalisation, the Government exercised power, understood in traditional terms, as it was able to ensure that its will prevailed. The exercise of power was not the only significant thing. What mattered was that in exercising power, the Government advanced the interests of an important fraction of capital and the class as a whole. Government action worked to some other groups' advantage.

To answer the questions 'How was it possible for these interests to be advanced without action?' and 'Why did government action serve the interests of other groups?', it is necessary to reconsider the place of government and the state in the structures and processes of capitalist society. The policy to nationalise steel was not advocated to advance or protect the class interests of capital. The steel workers had wanted nationalisation to protect their positions. Some within the labour movement had called for the nationalisation of steel to break the undemocratic social power of capital or to make the economic system more susceptible to national or democratic planning. Regardless of these or other intentions, the meaning of the policy was changed so that it served contrary purposes. These changes were not simply imposed on the Labour Government by the power of the capitalist class or the strength of the steel masters' resistance. Resistance might have had some effect on the form of the nationalisation proposal but it was not decisive. The form of steel nationalisation was not all that dramatically different from previous, less contested nationalisations. The changed significance of the move to nationalise steel must have occurred in the process of policy formation. Somehow or other, the structure of the governmental process, or the context in which policies were produced and implemented, had the effect of altering the significance of the attempt to nationalise steel. To explain the outcome, there must have been something in the character of government and the forms of the capitalist state, or in the heavily determined structures of class society which meant that these fractions of capital, or the class as a whole, did not need to exercise power to have their interests advanced and protected. The problem is to find terms that can explain how this happens.

As a starting proposition, if a group, a class fraction or a whole class has its interests advanced or secured by the normal operation of the system and without direct or significant action, that group, class fraction or class can be said to have power. Since these interests are secured without action, the source of power, that is, the ability to secure an advantage, resides in the structural relations between classes or, if within a class, between the constituent fractions and other subunits. It is these relations which are the source of power and which define its character and limit its effective scope. These structural relations are not themselves power relations, though power may have been used to create, maintain or extend them. They do, however, provide the grounds upon which power operates. In certain circumstances it is possible that power may be exercised by, or expressed indirectly in the actions of, an intervening third group or institution. For the analysis of the example considered here, the important mediating institution is that of the government, a specialised body for the exercise of power. As a result of the complicated situation of class and government action, it must be stressed that it is rare for interests to be advanced in a direct, unequivocal or unambiguous manner. If power is being exercised by a mediating institution, that exercise must be facilitated by the various classes in a dual sense. On the one hand, there must be a process of authorisation whereby the institution is empowered to act. This may be evident in the structural location, the character or relations formed by the institution and the various social classes. On the other hand, there must be a process of recognition such that the actions of the mediating institutions are accepted as legitimate. If government is considered as such a mediating institution, then the classes upon which it acts must grant the Government a scope within which it can be effective and not oppose its general actions. The term 'grant' is used here in a figurative sense for these arrangements are not made consciously. The Government gains its scope for action in its relations with capital on the basis of the internal divisions and complications faced by the class. It gains its influence from the situation of tension which exists between capital and labour. Nevertheless, government action must be generally accepted as legitimate or the authorisation process breaks down and the classes assert their own conceptions of how social development should be organised.

These positions are necessarily incomplete and focus only on what is needed to explain how interests can be advanced without an overt exercise of power by those who benefit from a particular action or situation. They have the effect of suggesting certain areas that need to be discussed further if the character of power in interactions, such as those that resulted in the nationalisation of steel, is to be clarified. For example, the process by which governments are authorised to act raises many questions about what happens when there is a conflict between the class that authorises the general exercise of power and the institution so authorised. What does such a conflict reveal about the character and limits of power? The dispute over the nationalisation of steel is a relevant example of such a conflict. On the basis of the propositions outlined above, it can be seen that the dispute was partly about the boundaries of the Government's legitimate use of power and that the actual conflict was an important part of the authorisation process itself. It was not a dispute about the general right of the Government to act but about the timing, area and character of its actions. In the circumstances both the steel industry and the Government were attempting to serve the interests of the class of capital in different ways and, for a short while, the Government's proposals were implemented. The Government was not supported by the rest of the capitalist class and its actions pushed at the boundaries of authorised action. Without the active support of the rest of capital, or at least its willing acquiescence, the Government's position was weak and the extent and character of the conflict increased the possibility that there would be a change in the government. In this way, it can be seen that the struggles over nationalisation of steel was also about the scope and character of legitimate government action. The positions listed above make it more possible to recognise the significance of that particular conflict than the traditional use of the 'A has power over B' formula.

What then was the role of power in the conflict, given the various ways in which the outcome was significant for social development? At one level, power was an important part of the process by which policies relevant to the collective interests of capital as a class were generated. The conflict with the Government was a significant factor conditioning the way in which the steel industry sought to develop policies which would advance its sectional interests in a manner compatible with harmonising relations with the rest of the class. The extent of the conflict also affected the character of the Government's proposals for nationalisation and set the limits to the size of the publicly owned sector of the mixed economy. Another feature of the conflict was the way in which it led to the clarification of the principles on which the public sector would be run and the way in which the mixed economy would serve the interests of private capital. Given the lack of any explicit or adequate theorising about the limits and character of the mixed economy this was a most significant consequence. Furthermore, the conflict served to elaborate the criteria which would justify the transfer of an industry from private ownership. In these ways power and conflict were central elements of the process by which policies were generated to serve the class interests of capital. It was through neither the existence of capital as an economic class nor the existence of the state as a necessary institution of capitalist society that this was achieved. It was only through the conflict between government, as the active principle of the state, and a part of capital, the steel industry, that these policies were generated. As capital lacked effective procedures for the generation of class-wide policies and the state lacked internal arrangements to guarantee that its actions worked to advance the interests of capital, conflict between sections of capital and sections of the state was the only way in which the direction of social development could be established and policies roughly harmonised with the class interests of capital. It was conflict of this kind which solved the problem of the lack of effective organisation of the capitalist class and provided the framework within which the Government could act to secure the collective interests of capital.

6

The denationalisation of steel

In contrast to the drama which had surrounded the move to nationalise steel, the return of the industry to private ownership was a much
quieter affair. Though both the Labour Party and the Trades Union
Congress opposed denationalisation they were not able to wage a
significant campaign against either the Conservative Government or
the industry as represented by the BISF. Apart from passing a few
resolutions condemning the intention to denationalise, their most
significant act of opposition was to refuse to sit on consultative bodies
before the Government had declared its proposals.[1] This had far less
impact than the Federation's policy of limited co-operation in their
fight against nationalisation. That the steel union's enthusiasm for
nationalisation had waned can be seen in the fact that one of their
leading figures, Lincoln Evans, with the approval of his union,
accepted appointment to the new Iron and Steel Board.[2] Such a
change in the character of the conflict does have repercussions for the
analysis of power especially with the focus on the relationship between private capital and government action.

Denationalisation can properly be viewed as an end to the previous
conflict between the steel industry and the Labour Government. It
was ended, not because the industry succeeded in its campaign, but
because the Labour Government was replaced by a Conservative
Government which had the consequence of altering the balance between the contending forces. One of the earliest acts of the new
Government was to issue a standstill directive to the nationalised
Corporation to prevent it from making any changes which would
handicap the transfer back to private ownership.[3] Despite the initial
move, denationalisation was not prominent amongst the Conservative legislative priorities and it was not until June 1953 that the
Nationalisation Act was effectively repealed. Not only was there
legislative delay but the actual form of denationalisation was not a
simple matter. There were complex technical details to be decided on
the particular form that denationalisation would take. Wilson, in his
account, suggests that the Conservative Government quickly agreed

103

to the Federation's request to denationalise the industry.[4] Others disagree on the willingness of the Conservatives to denationalise.[5] Certainly, the period of delay needs to be explained. There were obvious problems involved in the attempt to sell the industry back to private owners and several alternative schemes were considered.[6]

Some doubts were raised about the worth of denationalisation. Indeed, a commentator in *The Economist*, argued that it was better to let the industry remain nationalised than to set up some compromise scheme of private ownership and public investment, or to sell the industry back in the unrationalised shape it had before.[7] In the end, the Government decided to denationalise the industry in a form which would put it back into the pre-nationalisation position under the Iron and Steel Board. There was one complication: the industry was not to be returned to its previous owners but sold by a specially appointed agency. Hence there was a delay in the actual return of the industry to private ownership in a way which complicates the analysis of denationalisation.

Given the importance of the fact and form of denationalisation, it is necessary to consider the way in which these arrangements affected the interests of the various relevant parties. It is also necessary to consider the important question of the relationship between the class of capital as a whole and the particular part of capital which was involved in the steel industry. Did the particular form of denationalisation advance both the interests of capital in the steel industry and those of capital as a whole? This question is given a special importance by the type of analysis used to explain the significance of the strategies advanced in the preceding struggle over nationalisation. In a sense, the fact of denationalisation questions the efficacy of the previous explanation of what was involved in the conflict; it certainly raises doubts about the adequacy and relevance of the Labour Government's proposals. The fact that it was a government of a different political character which denationalised the industry introduces many questions about the importance of the succession of governments for the different strategies for capitalist development which are implemented. Indeed it moves emphasis away from the broad generalisations about the character of the capitalist state to the actual mechanisms by which the state comes to implement specific policies and to adjust its programmes to the interests of capital.

Given the particular needs of the analysis of denationalisation in terms of power and interests, the chapter is divided into the following sections. The first deals with the details of the particular form of denationalisation and considers the various ways in which the interests of capital and other groups were affected by it. The second section takes these arguments and considers the implications for the analysis of power. The main questions are 'How was the industry returned to private ownership and what effects did this have on its organisation?', 'How were the interests of the various parties affected by the particular form of denationalisation and in what way?' and 'What was the character of power involved in this interaction between private capital and government action?'

The form of denationalisation

In the course of the election campaign, the Conservative Party and the British Iron and Steel Federation gave the impression that the denationalisation of steel would be a relatively easy matter. The Nationalisation Act would be cancelled and the industry would be transferred back to its previous owners. Since nationalisation had done nothing to disturb either the managerial or financial structure of the industry, the return to private ownership ought not to have been very complicated. Sandys's standstill memorandum, referred to above, carried the implication that the Government intended to hand the industry back to its former owners. That was the rationale for stopping changes being made before denationalisation legislation could be prepared.[8] But denationalisation was not to be so simple or uncomplicated. Preparing and drafting the proposals took a long time and it was not until July 1952 that a White Paper outlining the Government's intentions was published.[9] In this document it was revealed that the industry was not to be returned to its previous owners but would be sold at prices, and in a manner, to be determined by the Iron and Steel Holding and Realisation Agency (ISHRA), the body designated to replace the nationalised concern.

This new procedure raises the question 'Why was steel not compulsorily returned to its previous owners in exchange for the compensation stock which had been issued when the industry was nationalised?' For an answer, there are a number of factors which combine to explain both the delay and the changed form of denationalisation. The compensation stock was, of course, saleable like all other stock and some of the previous owners had already disposed of theirs. Furthermore, the value of the stock along with similar issues had fallen in value since the time it was issued.[10] It was unclear what the connection between the value of the physical assets of the industry and the compensation stock was at this stage. Though the Federation had complained that the rate of compensation had undervalued the

assets of the industry, there was no attempt to take this into account.
There was another complication as some of the former owners would
not have been pleased to be saddled once again with what were, for
them, cumbersome assets. When the Labour Party threatened to
renationalise at the earliest opportunity, and at rates that gave no
more benefits to owners than if it had remained nationalised, defen-
ders of the industry claimed that this would complicate matters as
former owners would be reluctant to want their firms back on such a
tentative and punitive basis.[11] In the White Paper all that remained of
the original intention was the statement that, in selling the industry
back to private ownership, preference would be given to the previous
shareholders.[12] Though there was no reference to a policy like this in
the denationalisation legislation, the Iron and Steel Holding and
Realisation Agency did make provisions to give a preference to
previous owners.[13]

The details of the denationalisation proposals introduced by
the Conservatives harked back to the hybrid proposals rejected by the
Labour Cabinet in 1947. This fact was thrown up as a taunt by the
Minister of Supply, Duncan Sandys, and the BISF.[14] In the hybrid
scheme, nationalisation was to be avoided by leaving the industry
privately owned but with its conduct supervised by a stronger version
of the Iron and Steel Board, one supported by positive powers. The
hybrid scheme had nothing to say about the problems of denationalisation but this was the main problem faced by the Conservative
Government. Any problem that existed was solved by dividing the
Act into two parts one of which dealt with the return of the industry to
private ownership and the other with the form of public supervision
of the whole industry, regardless of ownership.

The period of nationalisation was defined as coming to an end with
the dissolution of the Iron and Steel Corporation. All its assets were to
pass to the new Iron and Steel Holding and Realisation Agency which
would perform all the functions of normal shareholders whilst
arranging for their sale back to the public.[15] The Agency was to be
staffed by a small number of professionally competent people who
were free to make the best of the opportunities to sell the firms.[16]
Resale could be spaced out over a period of time and there were no
specific deadlines. Treasury permission was needed for the various
deals that they made.[17] There were several other important clauses
governing the actions of the Agency. It would be free to regroup the
firms under its control so that they would make more viable financial
and commercial concerns and hence be more attractive to potential
buyers.[18] Such arrangements would have to be referred to the new

Iron and Steel Board.[19] In making such changes the Agency would be
continuing the work done by the Bank of England when it had attempted to strengthen the financial structure of the industry. As it was
not anticipated that the resale of the industry would be achieved
quickly, the Act made provision for the Agency to raise money
through the Treasury for the modernisation and re-equipment of the
plant of the companies which it still 'owned'.[20] In one sense the
sections of the industry whose shares remained with the Agency
would still be nationalised, gaining their funds from either the Government or from internal sources, but they would be managed by their
old managements and supervised by the new Iron and Steel Board.

Though these were the formal terms in which nationalisation
would be brought to an end, denationalisation would not actually
occur until the firms were once again privately owned and so it is
necessary to consider the way in which the Agency managed its sale
policy. Duncan Burn, in *The Steel Industry*, gives a comprehensive
account of how the sales were arranged.[21] The Agency worked
through a group of merchant bankers and had some assistance from
the City. Sales were of two kinds, either by private treaty, to former
owners or new ones, or by public offer.[22] The sale of the major firms by
public offer started with United Steel in November 1953 and proceeded gradually, with some caution at the time of the 1955 election,
concluding with the sale of the Steel Company of Wales in March
1957.[23] Three of the remaining firms, which were unattractive public
offerings, were eventually sold to a consortium of leading steel firms
acting as Iron and Steel Investments in 1963.[24] Richard Thomas and
Baldwins was never sold, partly because it was involved in a very
large investment and expansion programme.[25] This listing of major
sales by the Agency exaggerates the significance of the denationalisation programme as do figures that show 'by January 1955 steel companies accounting for some 50% of steel output had been disposed of
by the ISHRA. Two years later, with the sale of the Steel Company of
Wales, the proportion had risen to 86%.'[26]

Such statements conceal the extent to which the state, through the
Agency, remained a major shareholder and creditor to the denationalised companies. As Burn argued, it would have been very difficult to
sell off all the assets at their value and, as a result, the important thing
for the Agency was to sell off the equity shares, for with these went
control.[27] One consequence was that the Agency was left with a large
number of 'prior charge' shares in the denationalised firms and their
subsidiaries.[28] As Vaizey indicated, 'by the Autumn of 1957, ISHRA
held £125 million of debentures in denationalised companies'.[29]

This was not the only significant connection between the state and industry. The Agency had also been crucial in raising the necessary investment for these companies both before and after their sale to the public and often at terms which were extremely favourable, given the state of the money market.[30] Thus Burn described the general pattern of the resale policy like this: 'the line adopted was in general to canalise all the funds which "the market" would provide into the purchase of the equities of firms; the Agency remained the provider of money at fixed interest, often with the promise of additional funds to meet the cost of committed future capital investment as it arose'.[31]

As time went on, the rest of the shares were slowly sold to the public and the loans arranged by the Agency were repaid.[32] Though the Agency made a substantial contribution to the financial health of the industry through its investment policy, this diminished until it was almost solely responsible for the major expansion projects of Richard Thomas and Baldwins, for which it advanced more than £100 million.[33]

Another consequence of the Agency's resale policy was to spread the ownership of shares far more broadly in steel than in other comparable industries.[34] Such a dispersal did not mean that control or the significance of ownership had changed in any way. Though the Agency had the formal power to rationalise the company structure of the industry, Vaizey noted that it did very little in this direction.[35] Its main concern was to create attractive, saleable packages. The resale policy pursued by the Agency had little or no consequence for the boards or management of the steel companies, for, as Burn described it, 'Most of the boards of the companies went straight on – into and out of nationalisation.'[36] These details about the actual form of denationalisation and the resale of the industry to private ownership are essential for the subsequent assessment of how and whose interests were affected by denationalisation.

The other side of the denationalisation legislation was the setting up of a new Iron and Steel Board which was supposed to have been based on the long history of supervision in the industry and to have incorporated the lessons learnt from the first Iron and Steel Board.[37] It was this aspect of the Bill which has been seen as the crowning achievement of Sir Ellis Hunter, the then president of the BISF, as it incorporated his arguments for a stronger Board.[38] The new Board was to be different in that it would have statutory powers and could enforce its decisions by legal means.[39] This was meant to give it a positive capacity for direction which its predecessor had lacked. However, the powers of the Board were defined in such a way that there was very little scope for the exercise of any positive direction. The 1953 Act set up the Board to supervise the whole industry defined in terms of the basic processes of iron and steel production.[40] The Board was to be staffed by an independent chairman and representatives from both sides of the industry, and the consumers of steel products.[41] It had three main tasks; to supervise plans for development, to fix maximum prices for steel products where it thought these were necessary and to supplement various industry arrangements for the supply of imported raw materials, research and training facilities and the collection and publication of statistics for the industry.[42] Though the White Paper had given some observers the impression that the Board would have too much say over policy matters, the final draft of the Bill made it clear that the main initiative would reside with the steel firms themselves.[43] The Board's powers over development were limited to major projects and could only reject a company's submitted expansion scheme if it could show that such a scheme would threaten the ordered and efficient development of the industry.[44] Aggrieved firms could appeal to the Minister. If the industry failed to come up with plans that the Board thought necessary, it could not compel any firm to do anything, nor could it take any action itself. Necessary additional projects would have to be undertaken by the Ministry of Supply, either directly or through some agent.[45] Such projects would still come under the supervision of the Board. On the matter of prices, the brief for the new Board endorsed the old price policy operated by the Federation.[46] The Industry Fund and its levy arrangements were to remain and delivery charges would still be included as costs in the determination of maximum selling prices.

Even *The Times* noted that there would be difficulties in the relations between the new ISB and the Federation.[47] It was obvious that this would be the case as the Board was empowered to fulfil many of the tasks which had previously been performed by the Federation. For example, under the first Board it had been the Federation which had been responsible for co-ordinating and vetting intended development plans submitted by the individual companies. Under the new arrangements this task was to be performed by the Board. Though the Act included many references to the industry's own arrangements, presumably those organised and run by the Federation, and to representative bodies in the industry, which presumably included the Federation and its constituent assemblies, there were no direct references to the Federation or the part that it was to play in relation to the Board. Therefore, whatever else happened, these areas of potential difficulty would have to be resolved in practice.

It is a simple matter to see how this situation came about. Initially the Federation had wanted its internal organisation and practices to be supervised and given legitimacy by a publicly appointed body akin to the Import Duties Advisory Committee. The first Iron and Steel Board did just that. In the process of warding off nationalisation it had been necessary to respond to those critics who claimed that the Board lacked adequate powers of direction and that it was, as a consequence, the creature of the Federation. It was for these reasons that Ellis Hunter began to argue for a stronger Board.[48] In working out the details of what such a body would look like, the Federation's activities were used as a model. Thus, the strengthened Board came to be seen as an amalgamation of two things: the old-style supervisory body whose powers were merely to supplement areas of Federation activity on such matters as research, training, statistics and the import of raw materials; and the functions of the Federation projected into the constitution of the Board itself as, for example, with development. Indeed, the terms in which the Board's responsibility for development planning were stated were almost identical with the Federation's previous description of its own procedures. The relationship between the Board and the Federation would have to be clarified. The ways in which the two bodies resolved these differences, and the character and efficacy of the public supervision introduced by the 1953 Act, will be analysed in the next chapter.

Interests and denationalisation

To determine the significance of the form in which denationalisation was arranged it is again necessary to focus attention on the ways in which various interests were affected by it. At the outset, it can be stated that the resale policy of the ISHRA had little or no effect upon the interests of the iron and steel workers or the working class as a whole. Gradually they were returned to a situation where they again worked for private owners but the conditions of work, safety or wages were not altered. The rate of technical change was not increased by the formal change of ownership, given that most development was still financed by resources provided by the Treasury and channelled through the Agency. As a result their jobs were no more threatened by the prospect of modernisation and rationalisation than they had been under nationalisation. Rather, like the managements and the Boards, their position had not been altered by nationalisation or denationalisation.

The same is not so obviously true for the previous owners of the steel firms. Nationalisation and the rates of compensation had only served the interests of some of those involved. Was the same true of denationalisation? Those whose investments had been locked in the less attractive propositions, because they either needed or intended large-scale modernisation programmes which would have meant very limited returns on the invested capital, were advantaged by the particular form in which the industry was denationalised. Their commercial interests, that is, their concern to have their funds invested where they could earn adequate returns, did not suffer because they were not forced to give up their compensation for such a potentially unremunerative burden. In many ways the interests of the previous owners who wanted to buy back their old concerns were also advanced by the resale policy. The Agency's policy of diversifying share ownership in the industry meant that they needed fewer shares to dominate and control the re-bought firms. To a certain extent the Agency's restructuring of the share capital to ease the sale of equity reinforced this tendency, as the value of the physical assets over which this gave control was greater than the cost of the shares. Furthermore, the way in which the Agency negotiated fixed-interest loans for capital expansion and modernisation, further reduced the problems associated with ownership in the steel industry. In another way, the Agency's resale policy worked to the advantage of other sections of the capitalist class who wanted to buy into the steel industry to supplement their manufacturing activities or for some other purpose. Under the old conditions of private ownership this would have been very difficult, if not impossible. Under the denationalisation programme it happened.[49] In all these ways the resale policy of the Iron and Steel Holding and Realisation Agency worked in the interests of the former owners and others who wanted a stake in a privately owned steel industry.

In the preceding analysis of the conflict surrounding nationalisation it was shown that the pattern of opposition was crucially shaped by the part played by the senior managers and directors in the councils of the Federation. In what ways did the denationalisation policy affect their interests? Unlike that section of capital who were involved in the industry only as owners, the managers and directors were the only group whose interests were positively advanced by the delay in the resale of the steel firms. The initial standstill order issued by Duncan Sandys secured their prerogatives from the interference and influence of the Iron and Steel Corporation. When the nominal functions of the shareholders were taken over by the Agency more than eighteen months later their position was not weakened in any way. The gradual and uneventful resale of the individual firms had no bad consequences for the senior managers or the boards of these firms. Whatever separate influence private ownership had over management in the period before nationalisation, nationalisation and denationalisation did much to insulate further management boards from such pressures. These observations are not intended to lend credence to the notion of a managerial revolution, which is an argument based upon a weak understanding of the character of capitalism.[50]

The identification between the managements, the industry and the Federation was intensified by the experience of nationalisation, the standstill directive and the gradual resale of firms back to private owners.[51]

The denationalisation of steel was not only significant for serving the immediate interests of managers and owners, it also had profound consequences for the shape and operation of the mixed economy. Much of the argument in the preceding section on the way in which the general interests of capital as a whole could be advanced by the nationalisation of steel centred on its importance for the construction of the mixed economy. If that argument was correct, then the denationalisation of steel did not automatically serve the class interests of capital in a comprehensive manner as it effectively ruptured the coherent base of the mixed economy. Given this consequence, it is not correct to assert categorically that denationalisation, because it returned the industry to private ownership, necessarily advanced the class interests of capital. At the end of the last chapter I argued that the conflict between the Federation and the Labour Government concerned two different strategies for advancing the long-term interests of capital. The denationalisation of steel put the Federation's strategy to the test. If the overall class interests of capital were to be advanced by denationalisation, it would be necessary for the particular form of denationalisation to assure a number of things. Firstly, that there would be an adequate supply of steel for the consumer industries and that this could be supplied at as low a price as possible. Secondly, that the technical and financial structure of the industry would be modernised to ensure that a disproportionate amount of capital and labour would not be consumed in the making of steel. In these ways the relations between the industry and the consumers of its products and the whole of the class would be harmonised. Thus the extent to which the denationalisation of steel advanced the interests of the rest of the class of capital would be conditional upon the effective operation of the Iron and Steel Board. Such efficacy cannot be judged from the formal proposals for the regulation of the steel industry contained in the Iron and Steel Act of 1953. At this stage it is worth noting that, just as there was nothing in the nationalisation legislation that contained obvious implications for the modernisation and rationalisation of the industry, the denationalisation law was similarly silent. Furthermore, should the Federation and Conservative Government's arrangements fail, there was always the threat of renationalisation carried in the pledge of the Labour Party.

Implications for the assessment of power

The particular form of denationalisation, and the complex way in which interests were involved, raises many questions about the character of power evident in this interaction between private capital and government action. As a first point, it is useful to consider the reasons for the denationalisation of steel itself. When the Conservative Government assumed its duties it did not automatically denationalise all the industries taken into public ownership by its Labour predecessor. For various reasons it allowed the nationalisation of the railways, coal mining, and the supply of gas and electricity to stand. Nor did it try to alter the conditions of the pseudo-nationalisation of the Bank of England. There were only two pieces of Labour's nationalisation programme which it wanted to reverse, steel nationalisation and road transport. It is necessary to consider both the arguments put forward for these particular acts of denationalisation and the reasons behind the Conservatives' decision to act on these two cases. There is not much similarity between steel and road transport but they do stand out from the other industries left nationalised for a number of reasons.[52]

The basis for the Conservative denationalisation of the road transport system can be found in the contrast between it and the railways. Labour's reasons for the nationalisation of all road haulage had been based on the need for a comprehensive and co-ordinated transport system, one which would combine both rail and road services. The Conservatives stressed the difference between the conditions of the railways and of road transport. Where railways were in decline, road transport was growing in significance. Furthermore, road transport was flexible and, as far as it was possible to measure these things, efficient. There was neither a monopolistic owner nor a cartel structure dominating the business of road transport. Importantly the business was profitable and likely to remain so. Thus, though both the rail and road systems were part of the transport infra-structure of capitalist production, the Conservative Party recognised the profitable character of road haulage and wanted it denationalised. Unlike steel, the administrative problems involved in the denationalisation of road transport have been discussed in several articles.[53]

As indicated in the previous discussion of nationalisation, steel was quite a distinctive case and only partly fitted the category of an infra-structural process. It did supply crucial raw materials for the rest of manufacturing industry but it stood on the border line between infra-structure and manufacturing. It is in this ambiguous character that the reasons behind the move to denationalise are to be found. The industry was not clearly infra-structural and, despite all its technical and structural problems, it was profitable. Though it is very hard to make comparisons about profit levels, those figures which do exist suggest that steel, under its central organisation and supervised by the Iron and Steel Board, was at least as profitable as other areas of manufacturing industry. It would also seem that some sections of it were a good deal more profitable. Even when the companies were operating as part of the nationalised Iron and Steel Corporations their profits were suitably large to be an embarrassment to the Corporation who tried to explain them away as the consequence of exceptional circumstances. Furthermore, though the industry was technically inefficient and backward, this did not reveal itself as an obvious inability to produce the required volume of steel, though there were delays and complaints about quality. Thus, apart from any of the previously mentioned reasons, the Conservative case for denationalisation could be based on the industry's profitability and performance.

While arguments about profitability and its place in the process of capitalist production may provide the background to Conservative arguments over steel denationalisation, and indeed some of the industry's vigour in opposing nationalisation, they do not explain why the Conservative Government actually decided to denationalise steel. It is here that questions about the character and analysis of power become relevant; was the steel industry denationalised because of an exercise of power by the industry over the government? For, if we take the analysis that saw in the nationalisation of steel proof of the power of government, would it also see in the successful denationalisation of steel proof of the power of the industry, or of private capital, in its exercise over the government? Though there is something in the denationalisation of steel which reveals aspects of the power of private capital, and some of the problems which the class faces in the exercise of power in action, the question cannot be approached in such a simple manner. The traditional approach would founder on the obvious fact that the political character of the government had changed and as such it could not be treated as a fixed element in the assessment of the power of either private capital or of government. This is a problem that is never directly faced by those who try to find proof that the government has the power (real as opposed to formal) to regulate and dominate the economic process. No amount of government action is enough to prove that point; it is the character, not the fact, of action which has to be established. If the example is translated back into a situation where the character of the government remained fixed then the point will be clear. For instance, if the Federation had organised and pursued its struggle against the Labour Government in such a way that it decided to denationalise, then we would have a case in which it could be shown that the steel industry (and through it the class of capital?) had and exercised power against the government. But that is not the situation which has to be analysed. Here the act of denationalisation is undertaken because the government has changed. A Conservative Government has come to office and it wants to denationalise the steel industry; the interaction between private capital and government has been substantially transformed and the problem has become more complicated.

In the changed situation, the question of whether the act of denationalisation was the consequence of an exercise of power by the steel industry remains, though the answer cannot be presented in the same terms, nor will it have the same implications. As a consequence of a number of factors such as the past co-operation between the Federation and the Conservative Party in opposition in preparing the case against steel nationalisation, and the general ideological disposition of the Conservative Party in favour of private property (especially profitable private property) and against state ownership,[54] the Conservative Party and the Federation agreed on the need to denationalise steel. The exercise of power by the Federation against the Conservative Government was unnecessary. That is not to argue that the situation in which denationalisation occurred was not seriously affected by the power of the Federation or that some of the power of private capital is not revealed by it but that there is no need to use either the 'A has power over B' formula (which is inappropriate and unable to deal with situations without conflict) or the direct exercise of power by the steel industry to explain what happened. If anything, the fact of denationalisation and the circumstances in which it occurred strengthen the view of government as a medium for the facilitation of interests as a result of conflicts between classes and within the dominant class.

If the incident is to be understood in terms of who triumphed, who was defeated, and the part played by the exercise of power, the whole conflict needs to be conceived in other terms. The conflict over the nationalisation of steel was a conflict between labour and a section of private capital which became transformed, through the process of government policy generation (to use Claus Offe's term), into a struggle over two different ways in which class interests of capital could be advanced. It was the interests of labour which were defeated in all aspects of the conflict. Both the form of nationalisation and the eventual denationalisation defeated attempts to advance the class interests of labour. In the conflict over nationalisation the Labour Government was successful, for a short time, in trying to advance the interests of capital through a strategy based on a comprehensive mixed economy. In the struggle over the two strategies, the private owners in the steel industry lost and their strategy was defeated. The form in which the industry was nationalised was such that as little damage was done to their interests as possible. After the Conservative Government came to office, it reversed the previous policy and acted not only to advance the interests of private capital in the steel industry but also to implement the strategy proposed by the industry for advancing the interests of capital as a class. On all levels then, the denationalisation of steel was a triumph for that section of private capital involved in the production of steel and its success was facilitated by the actions of the Conservative Government. It is the implications of this situation which need to be considered.

If the character of power revealed by denationalisation is approached in the same way as in the case of nationalisation, the success of the steel industry reveals that it had power, not because it exercised it directly to secure the outcome, but because its interests were advanced by the particular action taken by the government. On this basis, it could be argued that the power exercised by the Conservative Government to denationalise steel was power exercised on behalf of that section of capital involved in the steel industry and whose interests were advanced by denationalisation. Such a proposition contains two related areas of difficulty. The first concerns the way in which the relationship between the private capital involved in steel and the government (or state) is conceptualised, and the second concerns the relationship between that section of private capital and the rest of the class with all the tensions implicit in that relationship.

As part of a discussion of the first problem, the relationship be-

tween the steel industry and the government, it is necessary to consider the adequacy of those views, in some ways quite close to the
argument being put forward here, which treats the state as an instrument of capital or a fraction of capital. This includes neither those
positions which see the state as being instrumental for private capital
or sections of it nor those which see the state acting to secure the
interests of private capital but rather those views which describe the
state as if it were the creature of either private capital or some fraction
of it. In these views the state acts to secure the interests of a section of
capital because of the particular way in which the state and that
fraction of capital are related. The state is seen as doing the bidding of
capital. It is necessary to consider the adequacy of these views now
since it is possible to construct an account of steel denationalisation
in a way which almost perfectly illustrates their case. With such an
approach, the fact that steel was denationalised and that the form of
denationalisation secured the interests of private capital involved in
the steel industry, can easily be explained. In this context the state
was the instrument of that section of capital and did its bidding.

Though such a proposition can embrace all the facts of denationalisation, its treatment is fraught with conceptual and empirical difficulties. These affect not only the treatment and characterisation of
government but also the question of its relationship to the class of
capital as a whole, that is, as something more than the summation of
its disparate elements. For instance, to explain denationalisation in
terms of this approach, it would be necessary to search for the connection between the industry and the government which would have the
effect of turning the latter into the creature of the former. But there are
no direct connections which can go anywhere near explaining how
such a relationship could have been established. Without such a
direct connection it is necessary to look for indirect links to explain
the actions of the government. If the causal connection is an indirect
one, then the view of the state as an instrument of some particular
section of private capital must be undermined. The view of the state as
an instrument is inadequate because it depends on being able to
establish a direct connection between who benefits from state action
and the government, which in most cases of government action does
not exist. Even if it did exist for the steel industry there would still be
major difficulties involved in such a formulation. How would the
other actions and concerns of the government be explained? Would
the denationalisation of road transport need to be analysed in terms of
a similar direct connection between that part of capital and the government? What of the government's actions on welfare or defence –

what kind of connection, and with whom, could explain these kinds of concerns? In all these ways the view of the state as an instrument fails because it focuses attention on a fruitless search for a direct connection. Even if a direct connection was found it would not solve the problems in the explanation but would raise instead a whole series of complications.

The other problem involved in the opening proposition about the character of power revealed through denationalisation, that which concerns the relationship between the capital involved in the steel industry and the class as a whole, is another area where the 'instrument' approach is completely ineffective. The Conservative Government, in this particular context, chose to implement a particular strategy with potentially significant consequences for the overall class of capital and the process of capitalist development. The content of the choice has been examined earlier but the consequences for the analysis of power were left unexplored. It is now necessary to consider the implications which the form of denationalisation, and the impact which this had on capital as a class, had for the characterisation of power. Importantly, it raises the question of power in the relations between the various subunits of capital and the class as a whole. In what terms are these relations to be conceived and how are they fought out, adjusted and harmonised in the normal course of capitalist development? What effect did the form of denationalisation have on the relations between the steel industry and other sections of the class of capital?

Here it is necessary to distinguish between two levels of areas in the constitution of the overall social formation, between the economic and the political. Within the economic processes of capital accumulation and capitalist development, the unity of the class of capital is affected as an unconscious by-product of the necessary interconnections involved in the very process of accumulation. In other words, for accumulation to occur, it is necessary for the various capitals to exchange commodities and money, and through these exchanges and the competition between individual capitals, the unity of the class is forged. It is not the intended consequence of the actions of the individual units of capital but the product of the structured context in which they operate. At the economic level, the well-being of the class as a whole is achieved by the movement of capital from one sphere of production to another in the pursuit of profitable accumulation. It is this which leads to the improvements in techniques and revolutionises the various areas of the class's economic activities. Leaving aside arguments about the viability of laissez faire, capitalism or capitalist production without the complementary existence of non-capital units, it is clear that the class of capital as a whole will face problems if, for whatever reasons, an area of useful production (that is, one which supplies raw materials or necessary commodities to other industries) becomes either backward or derelict. How is that deficiency to be overcome? In the absence of any other institutions it would mean that the class would have to develop a more conscious unity and the ability to plan and co-ordinate its development. In Chapter 3 there was the example of bank capital unsuccessfully trying to act in such a way on behalf of the class as a whole. In the section on nationalisation, there was the case of a reforming Labour Government trying to fulfil such a task with the construction of an adequate public sector to serve the needs of private capital accumulation in a comprehensive mixed economy. With denationalisation, the Conservative Government decisively interrupted that process of construction and sought another solution to the harmony of the class in the relations between the steel producers and manufacturing industry which used steel as a raw material in its production processes.

What then are the implications of the Conservative Government's action to reduce the size and alter the character of the public base of the mixed economy? Firstly, the form of public supervision established in the 1953 Iron and Steel Act was only a conditional solution to the problem of harmonising class interests. There were no clauses or procedures established which would guarantee that the industry would now be run in such a way that it would adequately fulfil its place in the process of capitalist production. That adequacy would be tested in action and will be assessed in the following chapter. The consequences for the mixed economy strategy were far more definite. It ended the dispute about the limits of government action and the character of the mixed economy for almost fifteen years. It should not be forgotten that those fifteen years turned out to be decisive for the long-term health of Britain's capitalist economy. Was the change in the structure of the mixed economy decisive? For the initial period it would seem not. All the previous arguments used to explain why steel had ceased to be an obvious problem for capital in the period after the Second World War also suggest why the changed shape of the mixed economy would have had little consequence for the overall development of the capitalist economy. The long-term consequences are not so obvious. Once again it would depend upon the efficacy of the public supervision introduced by the Conservative Government. If public supervision worked then there would be no adverse long-term consequences, if it failed . . .

What then are the consequences of these two problems for the earlier statement about the character of power revealed in the process of denationalisation? Crucially they serve to modify the extent to which denationalisation indicates the isolated power of that section of private capital involved in the steel industry. It is not a particular direct connection which can explain the fact or form of denationalisation, though the co-operation between the Federation and the Conservative Party in opposition did play an important part. Denationalisation of steel was an important element in the Conservative Government's strategy for the process of capitalist development and an expression of its general attitude to property and the private appropriation of profit. As a strategy it was to be tested in the circumstances of public supervision of the steel industry.

The denationalisation of steel also had important implications for other sections of private capital and for the class as a whole. It was this which made the solution introduced by the Conservative Government and the steel industry a conditional one. The question of whose interests were served by steel denationalisation rightly indicates that the steel industry had power, but it is necessary to consider the relationship between the industry and the class as a whole to understand the full character of the power revealed in the incident. Though the use of the 'A has power over B' formula, with suitable modifications to take account of the changed political character of the government, would have indicated the power of the steel industry, it would not have been able to reveal as much as the consideration of power through the perspective of interests.

7

Power in the period of public supervision

It is far harder to analyse the operation of the steel industry under private ownership and public supervision than either the process of nationalisation or denationalisation. The period of public supervision has not been studied previously for the character of power contained in the apparent co-operation between the steel industry and a government agency. There is very little overt or significant conflict that could be compared with that of the struggle over nationalisation. If conflict was used as either the prime or the sole guide to the existence, distribution or character of power, the assessment of what happened would suffer because the significance of any disagreements would be exaggerated. The 'A has power over B' formula is not applicable to the analysis of public supervision. Nevertheless, Rose, a most sophisticated pluralist, has commented on both the process of business regulation and the problems of interpreting co-operation between government and business.[1] Rose claims that there is nothing significant in such co-operation and sees it as something inevitable in a 'rational society'.[2] This states rather than solves a problem. Capitalist society is rational and the concurrence of business and government may indeed express that rationality, but it still needs to be analysed for what it reveals about the character of power. Rose's statement, that the fact of co-operation between government and a section of capital cannot be used to show anything about power, is unnecessarily cautious, though there are many problems in the analysis of such co-operation.

Rose's comments on the power relations involved in 'independent regulation' are a useful starting point for the discussion of the relationship between the steel industry and the government in this period. He argues that, in the process of independent regulation, the only group with both the resources and a desire to influence the process of regulation, is the business group itself. Outcomes which favour this group are not surprising. They reflect the special concern of business groups with their own legitimate sphere of society, the economy. It is not only Rose who has noted the distinctive relation-

ship between independent commissions and the industries they regulate. Wilcox and Shepherd, in their standard textbook on the policies
of government towards private business, indicate the main features
and problems involved in the relationship.[3] In the United States,
independent regulation was designed to protect the public or consumers from the consequences of monopoly, while guaranteeing the
monopoly a 'fair' return on its capital. Since the commissions are
neither expert nor well staffed and financed, and the rate of profit
depends on the decisions of the commissions, regulated businesses
have every incentive to try and influence their policies. In practice,
the commissions identify with the firms they are to regulate and this
reduces both their critical perception and their independence. Consequently, the regulated monopoly may gain considerable benefits
from its 'protected' status. The impetus to efficiency may also be
dulled. Rose, and Wilcox and Shepherd, are writing on the American
situation, as are most of the works on the relationship between business and government referred to in this book.[4] The British situation is
not the same. Regulation, or supervision as the Federation preferred
to see it, was not intended to be independent. The ISB was to be
manned by interested parties and chaired by an independent person.
There is no British equivalent to regulation in the United States. The
steel industry was not the same kind of business as those being
regulated in the U.S.A.

The analysis of public supervision faces more problems than just
those of method. The period itself is full of complications. First,
public supervision lasted from 1953 until 1967, and included a
change of government in 1964. Many of the issues raised by developments between 1964 and 1967 are considered in the next chapter on
renationalisation. Within the period, the fortunes of the steel industry
changed dramatically. From 1953 until 1960 the industry was
expanding and profitable. After 1960, there was a serious recession
from 1961 to 1963, and then a succession of swift changes from good
years to bad, in which its profits were considerably reduced. Though
fluctuations in the fortunes of the industry complicate the exposition,
the fifteen-year period included the end of the postwar boom and the
start of the now familiar problems characteristic of the declining
British economy. It will be necessary to consider the relationship
between developments in the steel industry and the fate of the rest of
the economy.

The analysis is complicated by the criteria that can be used to judge
the success or failure of the process of public supervision, the problem defined in the conclusions to the previous chapter on denational-

isation. On the basis of the analysis of interests in the struggles over nationalisation and denationalisation, there would seem to be a number of areas in which developments need to be assessed for the implications which they have for the character of power in the interaction between government action and private capital. For one thing, it is necessary to consider the relationship between the Iron and Steel Board and the Federation. What were the Board's relations with the Government? How solidly did or could the Board pursue an independent course in its supervision of the industry? To what extent did the Federation remain in charge of the industry and to what extent did its judgments govern those of the Board? If its judgments prevailed, would that constitute proof that the industry, via the Federation, was exercising power over the Government or the Iron and Steel Board? If these questions are to be answered, the process of public supervision needs to be considered for its effects on, first, prices and profits and, secondly, expansion and modernisation. Under these two headings, it is possible to assemble all the evidence needed to assess how the interests of the various parties were affected by the process of public supervision.

Though the arguments about renationalisation are examined in the next chapter, it is useful to consider the end result of public supervision. It seems very unlikely that it could, from the perspective of the iron and steel industry, be described as a success. Even without the threat of renationalisation, the industry entered the period after 1964 in a very weakened condition. During the long postwar boom, its output, investment and profits had been expanded, but by 1964 its situation seemed insecure. The industry faced a resurgence of international competition that it was ill-equipped to meet. The price policy which had ensured the earlier balance between profitability and investment had been undermined by a court decision and a change in the industry's market circumstances. The stability and regularity which steel had needed to be successful and to work in harmony with the other sectors of capitalist production seemed to have gone. The operation of private ownership under public supervision had, effectively, brought the future status of the industry into question.

The question of development

The formal duties of the Iron and Steel Board, as specified in the Iron and Steel Act, 1953, have already been described. Most importantly, the Act made the Iron and Steel Board responsible for overseeing the industry's course and pattern of development.[5] It was charged with the task of 'independently' assessing the future pattern of demand and ensuring that the developments intended by the industry were broadly in line with those requirements. To this end, the Board conducted a number of investigations which it published as a series of Special Reports on development in the industry.[6] These had the shape of general five-year targets, mainly emphasising the amount of steel-making capacity which would be needed to meet projected demand.[7] They also included comments on the importance of improving productivity, technical efficiency and the organisational structure of the industry.[8] In line with its statutory duties, it considered all plans for expansion over a certain specified cost, £100,000, and judged whether these accorded with their assessments of the industry's needs.[9] Each annual report contained a list of the projects approved in that year and the projected cost of their installation.[10] It also recorded, though no precise details were given, those occasions when the Board rejected a company's proposal or was negotiating with it over specific matters.[11] All in all, it could have seemed that the Board were adequately supervising development.

Even if the problems which appeared after 1960 are ignored, there were grounds for doubting the validity of such a judgment. In reading the Board's annual comments on the companies' submitted development plans, it is surprising that there is so little disagreement. Only a few projects were ever delayed and even fewer were rejected completely.[12] The details given in these instances are singularly unhelpful for any evaluation of the efficacy of the Board's supervision. If attention is shifted from the listing of projects approved to the accounts of 'planning', the doubts about the Board's role must be increased. The first report on development, issued in 1955, revealed a very spasmodic, *ad hoc* approach to the question and a situation in which the initiatives of the individual companies were the main factor.[13]

The Board is silent about the part played by the Federation in the generation of the industry's development schemes. As such, the Federation is only a ghostly presence in the Board's reports which occasionally refer to its technical judgments.[14] The role of the Federation needs to be considered further. The past significance of the Federation in the co-ordination of company developments was too great for it just to have ended with the setting up of the Iron and Steel Board.

The Federation's account of the planning process is, in many ways, more revealing than even the Board's special reports, though, ironically, in their literature it is the Board which makes the rare guest appearance and whose significance appears slight. The Board made reference in its reports to the part played by the companies in the Federation in the following terms:

Normal proposals for development come from within the industry, the initiative resting in the main with individual producers who are responsible for the detailed planning, financing and implementing of individual projects. Additionally, in the case of the wide field covered by the British Iron and Steel Federation there are arrangements under which schemes are submitted by its member firms to the Federation at the same time as they are submitted to the Board. The Federation examine them and express their view on the schemes from the technical and industrial aspects as well as in relation to the broad development of industry.[15]

The implications of those arrangements and the duplication which they revealed were never commented upon by the Board. The Federation presents the same basic facts but with a different emphasis. As the President explained at the Annual General Meeting of the Federation in 1961:

The arrangements for forward planning in the steel industry are often misunderstood. It is therefore worthwhile repeating that the primary responsibility rests squarely on the individual companies, reacting as they see fit to their assessment of market trends and taking full financial responsibility for the success or failure of their judgments. It is the companies who are the prime movers in the development field.

That position does not preclude other influences from coming to bear, of which two deserve special mention. Firstly, the company plans are influenced by their joint review of the longer term position, made through the Federation . . . Secondly, of course, the companies' plans are also influenced by the independent review made from outside the Industry by the Iron and Steel Board. But when such influences have been fully allowed for, it remains the individual companies who bear the primary responsibility in the development field.[16]

A more comprehensive account of the Federation's view of its relationship with the Board is given in a pamphlet describing its own work. Here it states that:

At the industry level, co-operative planning proceeds through the machinery of the Federation which acts as the industry's spokesman and as the focal point of this work. The Board make their influence felt continuously on all matters of public concern and act as a stimulus to the industry's efficiency and, if necessary as a corrective to its plans and policies.[17]

or

Financial and executive responsibility for the industry's development

rests with the individual companies. The Federation undertakes the co-
ordination and planning of the programme on an industry-wide basis
subject to the statutory responsibilities and powers of the Iron and Steel
Board.[18]

In this pamphlet it was also claimed that the Federation was responsible for ensuring that the individual projects formed 'a well balanced
programme as a whole, adequate to meet the expected trend of
demand'. The Federation also prepared estimates of projected demand and disputed the growth targets with the Board.[19] Certainly, in
the Federation's eyes, the Board's role on development was quite a
muted one. The formidable nature of the Board's powers was only to
be emphasised when the industry felt the need to ward off a threat of
nationalisation.[20] At all other times the leading role was played by the
Federation and its constituent firms, and the Board's task was the less
significant one of supervision, a process which legitimised the Industry's actions to outsiders. If these views are anywhere near correct,
and it is necessary to bear in mind the Federation's tendency to
exaggerate its own usefulness, then the whole character of the
development process would need to be reassessed. In no sense would
it be correct to see the Iron and Steel Board as planning the future
developments in the steel industry. At best there was an attempt to
impose the Board's vision of need onto the Federation's intentions. If
that were the case, it would be necessary to consider whether the
Board's powers were adequate to the task.

In various studies, the role of the Board was critically assessed,
even in the period prior to 1960. Burn concluded a long discussion on
the Board's policies by highlighting their conservatism, their attach-
ment to the traditional thinking of the industry and a singular lack of
vigour and freshness.[21] In commenting on the relationship between
the Board and the Federation, he remarked that he felt the balance had
been tipped in favour of the Board.[22] The main reason for this judgment was a comparison between the Federation under the Chairmanship of Sir Andrew Duncan and its later, lacklustre character. He also
noted the movement of Shone and Aubrey Jones from the Federation
to either the Board or the Government. Keeling and Wright's account
of the industry, commissioned by the Federation, portrayed the relationship between the Federation and the Board in the normal way,
stressing the significance of the Board's part in the development of
the industry.[23] They did differ from the Federation in that they
emphasised the illusory quality of the Board's, so called, positive
powers of direction.[24] As a final comment on the relationship between
the Federation and the Board at this time, it is useful to cite the

assessment of *The Economist*: 'All these matters [demand and capacity] lie within the responsibility of the Iron and Steel Board, but the board were indeed concerned in all of these, but in none, last year, did it quite hold the initiative.'[25] Here we have a picture of mildly troubled relations between the Board and the Federation in which some insignificant differences occur. The conflict between the two bodies on the matter of development was within a shared frame of reference and a shared view of possible policies.

The character of the problems faced by the industry and the Board in the sixties can best be understood by considering the general pattern of expansion endorsed by the Board, and the difficulties which arose when they tried to change it. In the period after the war, the industry committed itself to a programme of expansion which relied as much on modifying existing plants as it did on the construction of completely new ones. As a result of numerous modifications and revisions, the planning process of the industry was of slight significance, though the industry always managed to exceed its planned production targets. In the early fifties there was a report published on the productivity of the British steel industry that highlighted the small size of the production units and the consequences which this had for technical efficiency.[26] Though the document set clear priorities for the industry, there is very little evidence to suggest that the Board attempted to use its powers to increase the size of production units or to increase the amount of comprehensive modernisation.[27] The development plans of the industry were costly but capacity expanded, despite differences between the Board and the Federation on the target that should be aimed for and a minor recession in the fifties.[28]

Finally the Board realised, perhaps with the help of a recession and obvious over-capacity, that the character of development in the sixties would have to give more emphasis to improved efficiency and less to a simple increase in capacity.[29] As a result, it stressed the need for more money to be spent on research which the industry needed.[30] The Board did not force substantial restructuring of the industry or a significant increase in plant size.[31] As the sixties went on, it became increasingly clear that, at some time, this would have to be done.

Part of the attempt to improve the technical efficiency of the industry was the move to have old and obsolete capacity taken out of service, but the Board had no power to act on this matter.[32] Though it could recommend and persuade, the initiative had to be taken by the individual companies. Recession proved to be more effective than any recommendation by the Board.[33] The industry showed a considerable reluctance, for which there are several explanations, not least their profitability under the Board's initial price policy,[34] to recognise either the significance or existence of outdated plants.[35] As the figures produced by the Board show, a large proportion of output came from plants which were old if not outdated and obsolete.[36] For most of the period, obsolescence was defined in economic terms which did not coincide with those of technical efficiency.[37]

When compared with Britain's international competitors, the number of modern plants was extremely small.[38] The Federation, more noticeably than the Board, proclaimed that the industry was at the forefront of technological development and cited as proof the rate of conversion to the use of oxygen and the use of computers.[39] Since these claims figure prominently in the dispute over renationalisation, their significance will be considered in the next chapter. At this stage it is only necessary to point out that there were very few completely new plants and the most important were in the works of the still state-owned Richard Thomas and Baldwins.[40]

On the question of output, the main problem faced by the Board and the industry in the early sixties was that of a world surplus capacity and the problems of international competition.[41] This revealed itself as an imbalance between imports and exports; British imports were up but the value of her exports decreased.[42] This revived fears of a trade war between the major steel-producing nations and a collapse in the industry's orderly internal price structure.[43] The Federation and the Board both argued that the problem of world surplus capacity should be solved by international negotiation and an agreed pricing policy for steel exports.[44] When it became obvious that this was not going to happen, the Government imposed an import surcharge on certain products and the situation was slightly eased.[45] The general problem of a world surplus steel capacity remained and it seemed possible that problems similar to those that had existed before the introduction of tariff duties in 1932 would return.

Though relations between the Board and the Federation were generally harmonious during the fifties there was one noticeable dispute over development policy and that concerned the need for and the location of additional strip-mill facilities. The Federation was once again more cautious than the Board on the need to expand capacity.[46] In the end, the Conservative Government played the decisive role by deciding that there would be two new strip mills and, for political reasons, one would be in Scotland and the other in Wales.[47] The Cabinet negotiated a deal with Colvilles which completely bypassed the planning processes of both the Federation and the Board.[48] The Board subsequently endorsed the two projects and the Government pledged £120 million to the two companies for the expansion project. The ISHRA agreed to give an additional £110 million to Richard Thomas and Baldwins for their part in the scheme.[49] Colvilles eventually ran into severe financial troubles,[50] and the incident undermined the Federation's defence of its planning procedures.[51]

Throughout the period there were a number of differences between the Board and the Federation over some aspects of development policy. The Board wanted more development on home ore sites, while the Federation preferred to rely on cheap imports and felt itself vindicated when the price of imported ore gradually dropped.[52] They disagreed on the size of necessary capacity, the closing of obsolete plants and the need for a greater effort to improve technical efficiency. Yet for most of the period the facade of effective public supervision was maintained by both parties. This apparent agreement was only broken when the Board, in its final Annual Report, outlined the areas in which its powers and policies had been ineffective.[53] In this Report, the Board showed how limited its powers were. It is not just that its formal powers were inadequate but that the Board often did not recognise what policies were needed, as it was effectively trapped in the traditions of the steel industry. It was these traditions that had led the industry into the difficult circumstances of the sixties. What was the situation like? The industry had sufficient capacity to supply basic home demand but its structure and efficiency were not such that industry could compete in the world steel trade.[54] Its fortunes were linked to the health of the domestic economy and the nature of the Government's credit policy. There was a guaranteed succession of boom years and recessions, fatefully reminiscent of the situation in the twenties and thirties.

Prices and profits

The statutory power of the Board to fix the maximum selling prices for the major classes of steel prices was undisputed. It was not the formal competence of the Board that was important but the principles which governed the policy towards prices and profits and the consequences that the policy had for both the producers and the consumers. At the start of its term of office, the Iron and Steel Board made its general criteria explicit. In its first Annual Report, the Board stated its intention to fix the price for all relevant products and that it would use the established procedure of calculating the price on the basis of average cost plus a reasonable margin for profit.[55] The Federation's Industry Fund was endorsed by the close supervision of the Board and its costs were built into the price policy.[56] In justifying an acceptance of the existing procedures, the Board stated the rationale succinctly.

They [the Board] adopted the general principle of basing prices on costs of production. They accepted that in such event the maximum price laid down for a product should be sufficient to enable a maker of reasonable efficiency to cover his costs, including an adequate allowance for depreciation and obsolescence of fixed assets, and to obtain a reasonable margin of profit.[57]

There were two major problems: how to calculate costs and how to calculate the margin of profit, and the Board gave some details of their procedures. As regards costs, the Board chose to use 'the average of the current costs of each product' but they excluded certain unspecified high-cost producers from the assessment. On the question of profit margins

the Board decided that this should be assessed by reference to the capital which it was estimated would be employed in the manufacture of the relevant products by those producers whose costs were taken in arriving at the constituent of the price. . . . The allowance for profit for each type of product was then determined as a rate of return on the relevant capital which had regard *inter alia* to the nature of the industry, current interest rates and what might be expected to be a normal level of working in relation to capacity over an extended period of time.[58]

It is important to note that the Board never published the rate of profit used in their calculations. The level of prices also took into account the need for the industry to finance the expansion programme sanctioned by the Board. After a year, the Board commented that, on the basis of the statistics supplied to it, 'so far as these iron and steel products subject to the Board's price control are concerned, the evidence before the Board has satisfied them that the earnings on sales in the home market are no more than is reasonable'.[59]

At various stages in the periodic supervision, the Board adjusted the maximum price to accommodate changes in the structure of costs.[60] Prices were not always increased; occasionally there were reductions either for products or for steel prices in general.[61] When there were price rises, these did not always fully compensate for the increase in costs. The Board sometimes left a margin to be filled by an improvement in efficiency.[62] As well as adjusting the level of prices, the Board altered the way in which they were calculated. There were minor changes in the depreciation allowance and the rate at which plants were assumed to be working.[63] At one stage, the whole basis for the assessment of costs was changed. In 1956, the Board investigated the hypothetical costs and returns for a fully modern and technically efficient green site (that is, new) plant, and used this to determine the appropriate level of prices.[64] It was hoped that the change would reinforce the Board's development programme and encourage modernisation. Prices based on the new calculation would generate even higher rates of profit to finance the needed development programme.[65] These changes in the calculation of costs did not affect the terms in which monopoly prices were justified. They were still thought to create conditions in which development would occur and other forms of competition would force firms to improve their efficiency.

The Federation's role in the price policy was not as incidental as the above account may make it seem. Since there was a direct connection between the Board's price determinations and the profits of its constituent firms, the Federation had a real incentive to monitor the operation of the price policy. It is clear from an examination of both the Board's and the Federation's account of what happened that the Federation took a keen interest in not only the technical basis upon which prices were calculated but also the final level of prices. For example, when the Board did its assessment of the costs at a green field site, the Federation disagreed with their conclusions and after a period of discussion the Board revised its estimates.[66] This was important for constituent firms who could be profitable, without a high level of output or technical efficiency.[67]

In the period of expansion in the fifties, the disputes between the Federation and the Board over prices were hardly serious. After recession began to appear as an ever-present possibility, the Federation became more determined in their attitude to the price policy. Hence, after the 1961 cost review which led to a one per cent price increase, the Federation issued a public statement deploring the rise as 'totally inadequate'.[68] Though the Board did not agree to an immediate upward revision they brought forward the major cost review which normally took place every two years.[69] As a result there was a very large price increase. Another major review and price increase followed in 1965.[70]

The Federation continually complained that the price policy, as administered by the Board, was eroding the profit margins essential to attract and service the high volume of investment needed in the steel industry.[71] It is interesting to note that the level of investment in steel dropped sharply as the profit margins fell. A similar argument to that expressed by the Federation had been used by the Board in the fifties to justify the profit margins then awarded the steel companies.[72] What were the levels of profits earned by the steel industry during the period of the Board's responsibility? When dealing with profit figures there are always difficulties in assembling a set of statistics which will reveal the ways in which the earnings of the leading steel companies varied. There is a problem in choosing the figures which most usefully indicate profit levels, those calculated taking earnings before or after taxes, with or without depreciation, with inflation taken into account or not. Similarly there is the question of deciding against what figure the mass of earnings will be considered: the amount of capital invested in the industry or company, the total volume of costs in the year the profits were earned, the turnover of the firm, or some other basis. In discussing the steel industry there is an added complication in that most of the major steel firms were also involved in various manufacturing and engineering processes.

Despite these difficulties, it is possible to show the general trend of changes in the rate of profit without being committed to particular figures. The reason for considering profit levels is to see the way in which they changed between the period of expansion in the fifties and the problem years of the sixties. There are several sets of figures for the period from the end of the war up until the early fifties. These suggest that the rate of profit was somewhere in the region of six per cent.[73] Those figures that exist for the late fifties, near the record year of 1959–60, suggest that earnings were somewhere in the region of fifteen to twenty per cent.[74] It is the drop from this peak that is important. All the calculations agree that there was a decline in the rate of profit from that level to one below five per cent in 1963 and, after a slight improvement, by 1966 it had dropped below two per cent.[75] The Federation noted the decline and its significance when they argued that total earnings for the year 1964–5 were thirteen per cent lower than 1959–60, despite an increased investment of £700 million and an eleven per cent increase in output.[76] One serious aspect of the situation in the sixties was that, even in periods of record output and capacity utilisation, the profit rate remained low.[77] This was recognised by the Board and taken into account in some of its price determinations.[78] This statement of the general trend for profits made by the steel companies during the years 1953 to 1967 is not to solve a problem but to pose one. What does such a pattern of profit rates tell us about the efficacy of the Iron and Steel Board's supervision?

Before examining this problem it is necessary to consider another matter related to the operation of prices and the level of profit, the question of finance for development in this period of private ownership. In all the determinations of prices by the Board, the need to provide adequate funds for the development programme was one of the most important factors. Whenever it was suggested that the prices were too high, both the Board and the Federation stressed the important part played by the price policy in providing funds for the expansion programme.[79] The amounts of money invested in the steel industry were very large and aggregated more than £1,000 million over the period.[80] Since most expansion occurred in the fifties this was the time when expenditure was at its highest, around £100 million for most years.[81] In the sixties, after a suitable reserve of capacity had been secured, spending on various development schemes dropped dramatically below the levels of the early fifties.[82] Where did all this money come from? Figures produced by the Federation, and supported by other sources, show that about two thirds of this money was provided from the surpluses earned by the steel companies.[83] Though the steel companies occasionally argued that it was a tribute to their financial and sale skills, it is actually a tribute to the price policy. There was nothing exceptional about these figures, as two thirds was the average level of reinvestment for manufacturing industry at this time.

There is considerable evidence to suggest that a substantial part of the additional finance did not come from private investors but from loans arranged by the Government or some government agency, principally the ISHRA.[84] The industry argued that the threat of nationalisation made it difficult to raise money on the open market.[85] Nevertheless some companies did raise money through share issues.[86] It was also argued that the resale of both equity and prior-charge shares restricted the amount of private capital available for steel. The argument does not seem convincing, given the existence of the steel compensation and the low, almost nominal, charges for the steel firms. At no stage did the Board suggest that finance was restricting the development programme. The onset of recession slowed down the rate at which projects were completed.

The decline in investment in the sixties does not appear to be significant since the Board claimed that the focus had changed to projects which would be more technically efficient.[87] But it seems unlikely that wholesale technical modernisation could have been gained without a much larger spending campaign and a determined move to close obsolete plants, neither of which occurred. Thus, it is not likely that the decline in investment in the sixties was the result of a decline in the profit rate. More probably, it showed the industry's habitual response to uncertain market circumstances.

There is one other point to be made about development finance. When the need for a new strip mill was recognised, the Government became involved and gave large loans to make it possible. Consett, the privately owned firm involved in the Scottish development, suffered badly financially.[88] The other firm involved, Richard Thomas and Baldwins, was still publicly owned. At the end of the period comparative figures show that as a result of the investment undertaken by the ISHRA it was the largest steel company.[89]

Another matter which affected the pricing policy and the level of profits was the decision taken by the Restrictive Practices Court against the Heavy Steel Producers, a product conference of the BISF.[90] As indicated earlier in the text, the prices set by the Board were maximum prices. They were intended to be the prices at which steel products would actually sell and they were designed to guarantee a reasonable return on the capital employed by reasonably efficient producers. The various product conferences of the BISF turned them into actual selling prices by a series of restrictive agreements to prevent members from undercutting the price arrangements. These arrangements were referred to the Court as restrictions on free competition and were duly found to breach the Restrictive Practices Act. The Court did not think that the way in which the policy had been designed by the Board infringed the rights of consumers or was of itself against the public interest. But the Court did not want a series of restrictive price agreements between producers. As a consequence, the price agreements were dissolved though the notion of a common selling price remained as 'recommended' by the product conferences. The reality was not much changed by the form of words though it opened up in the industry fears that price competition would be renewed in times of recession.[91] It was accepted by both the Board and the Federation that such a policy would endanger the health of the industry by reducing its ability to accumulate sufficient funds for the continuing investment needed in the steel industry.[92] As a result, the form of the industry's price policy was an issue once again.

Before the Federation, the Board recognised that the conditions in which the price policy was intended to operate had changed.[93] The Board argued that the price policy was designed to protect the consumers in a period when there was a shortage of capacity, a consequent shortage of supply and the possibility that large profits would be gained from excessive price rises. The price policy had been designed to protect steel users in a seller's market. The Board argued that the situation had changed by the early sixties and that the old price policy was inappropriate. On this basis they opened negotiations with the Federation over the terms of a more realistic price policy. The Board suggested a more flexible approach, along the lines of the European Coal and Steel Community (ECSC) arrangements,[94] but this was rejected. During the negotiations over British entry into the Common Market, the Federation and the Board agreed to an experiment, using a modified version of the ECSC scheme. This collapsed when the entry bid failed.[95] After the Labour Government had come to office, the Board and the Federation again agreed to experiment but the Government vetoed the move.[96]

The old scheme of maximum price determination remained. Behind these various initiatives by both parties lay the knowledge of the decline in company profits and the implications of the Restrictive Practices decision. The Federation believed that a more flexible policy would enable company profits to be boosted by higher prices in the period of a boom to compensate for any losses during price competition in the recession. The Board felt that the Restrictive Practices decision undermined its price procedures by making price competition in a recession possible when there was no way in which the Board could allow a price rise to compensate in the period of the boom, even though it may have been both deserved and necessary. It felt that the logic of its price policy had been severely damaged. Though there was an abundance of qualms and fears these did not affect the operation of the price policy and there is no evidence of a dramatic resurgence of price competition.

Before turning to a detailed assessment of the power revealed by the operation of public supervision, it is useful to summarise the situation at the end of fifteen years of private ownership and public supervision. It is clear that the capacity of the industry had been increased substantially through a series of development plans agreed between the industry and the Board. Though these expansion plans included modernisation and technical improvement, the development had not resulted in a thorough transformation. New projects were most often grafted onto pre-existing sites and plant. The question of technical modernisation will be taken up again in the chapter on renationalisation but, at this stage, it can be noted that adequate capacity never implied adequate technical efficiency. The period started with a degree of harmony between the industry and the ISB but this gradually broke down. The financial health of the companies worsened in that period until by 1966 the industry faced a very difficult situation. There was the continued prospect of recession and unused capacity, excess world capacity and the attendant problem of import competition undermining the price stability which the industry believed had been the basis of its success.

What are the implications of these developments for the character of power in the period of public supervision? Did the decline in the health of the steel industry indicate that public supervision had not worked? Did it fail because power had been exercised against the Board or were there other reasons why public supervision had not been able to protect the steel industry and provide the appropriate amounts of steel at reasonable prices to the consumers of steel products?

Power in the period of public supervision

The preceding discussion treated the period as a whole, but the implications for the assessment of power are fundamentally divided by the change from prosperity to potential recession. This contrast between the two periods raises important questions for the evaluation of public supervision and its effectiveness. Most of the important problems arise when trying to discuss the significance of the problems faced by private capital involved in steel production in the sixties. An assessment of public supervision in the fifties would produce one set of conclusions, which are partly challenged, but not refuted, by the relative decline of the steel industry in the sixties. It is necessary to consider the form of power evident in the initial period, before this contrast can be meaningful.

In the fifties there was a profitable, expanding steel industry and its capacity was almost adequate to meet the requirements of the steel-consuming industries. There were often delays and bottlenecks in the delivery of steel, when demand was at its highest. The development plans, prepared by individual companies, processed by the Federation and sanctioned by the Iron and Steel Board, did not radically alter the balance of the industry, though they expanded the quantity and increased the quality of steel production. Furthermore, the price policy operated by the Board secured good profits for the steel companies without exploiting consumers in what was rightly seen as a seller's market. Thus, on the surface at least, there does not seem to have been a contradiction, or any serious tension, in the way in which the prosperity of private capital in steel was assured and the way in which the needs of the consumers were met. If there were tensions, they did not emerge until the sixties, when the effective basis for the harmony between the interests of the steel industry and the rest of private capital was undermined.

The period of prosperity and apparent harmony between the interests of private capital involved in steel production and other sections of the class of capital does raise several problems of interpretation. To what extent was this favourable outcome a product or expression of the power of either that section of private capital involved in steel production, the sections of capital involved in the steel-consuming industries or the class of capital as a whole? In the absence of dramatic and overt conflict, other kinds of arguments need to be considered. One which seems inappropriate at this stage concerns the question of who held the initiative in the relationship between the Board and the Federation. It is a revealing question which cannot be ignored but it can usefully be deferred until the discussion of what happened in the sixties. At this stage, the two bodies broadly agreed on what was wrong and what needed to be done in the steel industry. If the question of who marginally gained by the policies implemented in this period can be used to indicate the distribution of power, an edge must be conceded to capital in the steel industry. For, in this period, the extent and pattern of change broadly accorded with their view of the situation. The industry did not suffer greatly in an effort to meet the high level of demand, and steel imports provided a safety valve.

An assessment of whether the policies of this period actually accorded with the long-term interests of private capital in the industry can only be faced when examining the reasons for the problems which emerged in the sixties. It is possible that the prosperity of the fifties masked the damage being done by the development policies being pursued. Since the steel-consuming industries were only inconvenienced by the delays in the delivery of steel, and did not suffer seriously, it is possible to argue that power was fairly evenly divided between them. The character of power revealed in this 'successful' period of public supervision was of the kind which could adequately meet the different demands of the denationalised industry and the rest of the class of capital. To the extent that power refers to the ability to protect oneself against harmful consequences, the events of the period suggest that the steel industry had not been weakened by the period of public ownership or the form taken by its return to private hands.

There were certain developments in the fifties which emphasised the important part that could be, and was, played by the Conservative Government. The 1953 Act left some residual powers in the hands of the Government, mainly to override decisions in favour of some undefined 'national interest'. This power was used by the Conservative Government in the dispute over the site for the third strip mill.

Despite the technical debate in the industry the Government took the initiative and arranged for the development to be split between Wales and Scotland. It is clear that the decision was made for political and social reasons which identified a need for a major project in Scotland, an area of high unemployment. The action of the Government may well have been influenced by electoral concerns. The consequences of the Government's initiative were significant as it effectively undermined the apparent importance of Federation and Board negotiations over development policy. It also went against the technical judgment of the Board and the Federation, whose doubts were confirmed by the severe financial problems faced by Colvilles as a consequence of their participation in the scheme.

The incident can be used to illustrate an interesting point. As far as the Conservative Government was concerned, and there is no evidence to suggest that a Labour Government would have been less swayed by political and social criteria, there were occasions when the financial health of the steel companies was less significant than the political requirements of the Government. Here the term political is used in its broadest sense, with the emphasis on generating social consensus, or reducing social tension rather than in the derogatory sense of a petty concern with votes and seats. The fact that the Government was able to alter the policy generated by the industry and Board reveals something about its priorities, even in this initial period; there were circumstances when the interests of private capital in steel would be sacrificed to wider social concerns. In this way the Government was using power to advance the wider, social goals of capital at the cost of possible short-term inconveniences for one of the steel firms. The fact that the Government had to intervene to make such a judgment also reveals limitations in the Board/Federation arrangements for public supervision. Their deliberations were almost exclusively focused on economic considerations. Their debates were constricted by the need to organise a balance between competing steel firms, regions and product groupings, and the relations with manufacturing industry. In such a process, the importance of social and political considerations would be either ignored or obscured by reference to various forms of cost-benefit analysis. The residual powers of the Government were an important part of the whole process, and necessary for the protection of the social interests of capital, even if these were achieved by policies initiated for a variety of short-term and opportunist reasons.

Though the prosperous period of the fifties suggests some questions about the efficacy of public supervision and the character of the power involved in the process, it most usefully provides a contrast, against which the developments in the sixties can be assessed. It is the end of prosperity and the succession of boom years and recessions accompanied by the decline in profitability of the major steel companies which raises most questions about supervision and power. For the following discussion, the argument will be divided into two parts: the first will consider the implications of the price policy and the second, the development programmes.

The price dilemma

Before it is possible to argue about the implications of the price policy, it is necessary to decide whether it was a success or a failure. Such a judgment will vary with each section of capital. From the perspective of private capital involved in the production of steel, the policy failed because it did not provide enough profit for the major steel companies. If the price policy failed the steel companies, it is necessary to ask why. Was it the consequence of power or the result of other more technical factors? Some explanations stress the fact that the steel prices set by the Board were too low. In this view, the ISB is blamed for failing to make adequate calculations of costs and margins and generally failing to compensate for the reduced earnings of the industry in the periods of recession when the amount of unused capacity was great. This view was the one most often expressed by individual steel firms and by the Federation. It is consistent with the interpretation of company behaviour identified in the previously cited American studies of public regulation. Such research established that, since the rate of return is directly governed by the prices set by the regulatory commissions, companies saw profit problems in terms of the policies of these regulating bodies. The two large increases given in the sixties suggested that the Board thought their calculations had not been generous enough to compensate for the problems faced by the steel firms. The intervening years of almost completely stable prices suggest that this was not the only relevant consideration.

Though the Federation continually sought greater increases from the Board, and exerted pressure to this end, the Board did not simply acquiesce. It resisted attempts to make the policy work in the interests of the private steel companies. The Board was charged with the duty of ensuring that steel was supplied to home consumers at the lowest reasonable price as this was used to justify the Board's actual policy. There was, however, almost no imperative built into the price policy since what was considered a reasonable level was meant to be one which would give sufficient profits to the steel firms to attract enough private investment and finance to support a large-scale development programme. Other factors or considerations combined to keep steel prices down. An important matter here was the existence of a large volume of surplus steel-making capacity in the world. This meant that there was little scope for the Board to raise steel prices, even if they had wanted to. Such a surplus meant that, precisely in the periods of recession, vast quantities of cheap and very cheap steel would be available for importing. Without a significant degree of tariff protection, which would have 'exploited' the consumers of steel products, such international competition provided a point above which prices could not be raised. Either the price remained low or the demand for domestically produced steel would have dropped. Pressure on the Board to alter the terms of the price policy would have been without effect and pressure for a tariff had to compete with the interests and policy preferences of the rest of manufacturing industry which benefited from the low price of steel and the prospect of cheap imports. The Board, which recognised the implications of the situation, was only willing to press for an end to dumping. It admitted that much of the steel being offered was genuinely 'cheap', and that can only stand as a critique of the technical efficiency of the British steel industry. The recourse to a special duty on imported steel was only a short-term measure.

There was another factor which encouraged the Board's reluctance to increase the price of steel and it had little to do with the market circumstances of the steel firms. The earlier account of how the Board fixed the price levels showed that the increases granted did not always compensate for the full change in costs since the previous review. The difference, which would be needed to maintain the size of the profit margin, had either been provided by an increase in technical efficiency or it was anticipated that such an increase would offset the consequences of the price determination. In this sense, the fixing of steel prices was an integral part of the Board's attempts to improve the industry's efficiency by providing it with an incentive to reduce costs. During the fifties, when the main emphasis of the development policy was on the overall expansion of the industry's capacity, this aspect of the price policy was not very important. When the emphasis of development planning changed to give prominence to projects which would significantly improve technical efficiency, this aspect of the price policy was much more significant. In the Board's *Annual Reports* and *Special Development Reports*, it is

apparent that they were not satisfied with the rate of technical modernisation. This was most clearly shown by their continual references to
the slow rate at which obsolete and outdated plants were being
scrapped and the criticisms of the amount of money being spent on
research and development. The 'failure' of the price policy, from the
perspective of the steel companies, was not the result of the Board's
caprice or the vagaries of the market or Government economic policy,
but an index of the industry's failure to introduce significant and
comprehensive technical modernisation.

In its long-term operations, the price policy neither advanced nor
protected the sectional interests of that part of private capital
involved in the production of steel. That these interests were not
protected can be seen in the decline in the profitability of the major
steel firms. Profitability can only be used as an indication of the
short-term consequences of the price policy for the interests of the
steel industry. It is theoretically possible that the decline in profits
could have been linked with a secure future, an assured market or
substantial technical advantage. But there is no evidence to suggest
that there was such a trade-off between declining profits and some
future benefit. Indeed the decline in earnings may have affected the
rate of technical modernisation, predicated as that was on a radical
change in the structure of the firms. Similarly, the decline in profits
and the apparent inability of the firms to do anything about it, apart
from criticising the Board's policy, exposed the industry to the challenge of nationalisation once again. It also deprived the industry of its
main weapon against the challenge: the sign of its good health, high
profits.

Though the price policy failed to protect the interests of the part of
private capital involved in steel production, that does not stand as
evidence that the price policy was not a success from the perspective
of some other sections of capital or of the class as a whole. Here the
question of the profits earned by the steel companies is almost irrelevant. For the private capital involved in the manufacturing or steel-
consuming industries, the success of the price policy could be measured by its ability to ensure that steel was available in the right
quantities and at the lowest possible prices. Certainly for the period
under consideration, the price policy acted to secure that interest.
Even when the Board granted large percentage increases in the price
of steel, these did not have the effect of raising the cost of steel
proportionally above that of other components of the manufacturing
process, nor of bringing it up to the level of comparable world-market
prices. Given the large surplus capacity available in the world, there

was no possibility that the supply of steel at such low prices would be interrupted. If anything, the changes proposed by the Board for the calculation of costs and prices in the last years of its operation would have made domestically produced steel available at even lower prices. There was only one sense in which the price policy may have had adverse consequences for the interests of the manufacturing industries and this concerned the long-term consequences of low profits for the health of steel industry, measured by its ability to supply steel in the appropriate quantities and at a high level of technical efficiency. The Federation claimed that the very future of the industry was endangered by the price policy. This matter is more appropriately considered along with the rest of the development policy.

What then of the class interests of capital? It is unlikely that the price policy pursued by the Iron and Steel Board would have any impact on the general class interest that capital has in maintaining its social dominance over labour. If the policy had any impact on the interests of the whole class then they must have been of a different kind. For example, though the profits of individual steel companies have almost no relevance to the class as a whole, the source of its finances and the extent to which it represents a drain on the financial resources of the class are important. In one way the decline of the industry's profits could have undermined some of the ideological claims made for the superiority of private capital. The return of the industry to private ownership would have boosted those claims only if the steel industry was efficient, competent and profitable.

An examination of the industry's finances shows that these were not a problem for the class. In the preceding chapter, the financial aspects of the denationalisation scheme and the policies of the Iron and Steel Holding and Realisation Agency were considered. For the whole period of public supervision there was almost no call for finance from the rest of the class of capital, apart from that involved in the reselling of the industry into their hands. The extensive expansion programme was not a financial burden to the banks or other sections of capital. To the extent that the major projects were funded through cheap loans organised by the Government, the costs were spread over the whole of society. To the extent that the expansion programme was funded out of the internal resources of the steel companies, that is, from the earnings guaranteed by the price policy and the Board's cost calculations, there was no drain on the class's capital. Though the costs of the expansion programme were passed on to the consumers as part of the cost calculations of the price policy, the limits within which the prices could be increased meant that the steel consumers were not 'milked' to finance the industry's expansion. On this matter, the price policy implemented by the Board had few, if any, serious consequences for the class interests of capital. For the most part it was irrelevant. For the rest, it prevented the development of potential problems.

It is significant to note the pattern of consequence which the price policy had for various sections of capital and for the class as a whole. For that section involved in the steel industry, the policy had a bad effect; for that section involved in the manufacturing or steel-consuming industry, its consequences were beneficial, at least in the short term. For the class as a whole, the policy was either neutral or positively useful. This differentiated pattern is important for the assessment of the character and operation of power in the period of public supervision. It also reveals that, for one important question, the institutions of public regulation were not adequate to the task of finding policies that could harmonise the interests of the different sections of capital concerned with the operation of the steel industry. In one area at least, the hopes of the Federation had not been fulfilled.

The development policy

As a result of the development policy, sanctioned by the Board during the fifteen years of public supervision, there was a significant expansion of capacity. This was mainly achieved by expanding existing works by the addition of new plant, updated repairs and the introduction of some new technical processes. Though such a pattern of building secured expansion and some modernisation, it did not automatically provide a similar increase in the industry's technical efficiency. The limited improvement in efficiency did not come from a radical, wholesale reconstruction of the industry which scrapped technically outmoded plants, regardless of their formal ability to earn a profit within the price policy and the industry's levy arrangements. It certainly did not come from the building of large-scale works which incorporated the most modern techniques. It is instructive to contrast the modern works of the still publicly owned firm, Richard Thomas and Baldwins, with that of the profitable John Summers. This profit, according to *The Economist* was 'gained by a policy of clever, penny-pinching investment: making do with old plant, wherever possible and keeping in mind that its main function is to make money – to quote Sir Richard Summers, the chairman – and "not to build pretty plant" '.[97]

Though this attitude of Sir Richard's was not entirely representative, it does capture some of the flavour of the development projects suggested and approved in this period. A further indication of the limitations of the development programme can be seen in the length of time it took the industry to approach the targets set in the 1952 productivity report. This is so even if the improvements in steel technology that appeared after 1952 are set aside. Despite the development programme, the industry was as much characterised by small-scale units of production, small financial groups and a corresponding lack of product and regional specialisation as it had been when the productivity report was produced.

At this stage in the argument, it is useful to consider the way in which this expansion without technical improvement affected the interests of the various parties. What were the consequences of the policy for the interests of the section of private capital involved in steel and the class interests of capital?

It is not a simple matter to assess the impact of the development policy on the interests of private capital in the steel industry. In one sense, the policy corresponded with their short-term interests in that it provided for a smooth and orderly expansion of the industry's capacity. The Federation, in generating policies that expressed such a short-term interest, was particularly concerned to avoid any rapid expansion which could have resulted in surplus capacity. Hence the disputes with the Board over the level of projected demands, the missing million tons, and the rate at which new strip-mill capacity should be introduced. The eventual emergence of surplus capacity was as much a product of the problems of the British economy as a consequence of the development programme. The inability of the planning process to force the scrapping of obsolete and backward plants also contributed to this surplus. The continued operation of such outdated plant made sense for each individual company. It was not irrational to keep in production a plant that could return a profit or supply needed raw materials, even if it were technically obsolete. But it did not make sense for the industry as a whole. Though the existence of such plants may have provided reserve capacity to help in periods of high demand, its use at other times was not beneficial. It reduced the overall efficiency of the industry and represented a drain on capital, labour and raw material resources. It is useful to note that, when the recession deepened, there was a move to scrap such plants because they had, in the first instance, become uneconomic with the contraction in demand and they also reduced the working rate of the most modern and efficient plants. On the question of capacity and efficiency, the Board was a much better judge of the interests of the steel industry than either the Federation or the individual steel companies.

Though there was a sense in which the development policy accorded with the short-term interests of the steel industry, this does not imply that the policy was adequate for the long-term situation. It is not surprising that the development programme should have been attuned to short-term interests, given the extent to which it was articulated by a combination of individual companies and the technical committee of the BISF who were more alert to the needs of company and regional balance than they were to the requirements of wholesale technical modernisation. The various programmes, with their emphasis on piecemeal additions, codified the existing structure of the industry and did little to alter the existing relationship between firms, works and districts. Was the pattern of development adequate to the long-term interests of the steel industry? Would the summation of numerous 'patched' projects add up to a radical transformation of the industry's technical structure and dramatically improve the level of efficiency? The assumption here is that it is in the long-term interests of capital involved in the production of steel to operate with the most advanced technology available and with a structure of plants and companies most suited to those techniques. This assumption is not unreasonable, as it is only under such conditions that the industry could supply the appropriate quantities of steel at the lowest cost and with the greatest scope for profit. On the basis of such a view, the industry's development programmes were sorely inadequate. They provided neither that transformation nor the basis for it. Indeed it was the given structure of companies, technology and the institutions of public supervision which stood in the way of such important changes. So long as companies could be profitable without such changes, they would have no incentive to rationalise or improve efficiency. The ability to squeeze a profit out of the existing arrangements was what mattered and the vast expenditure on development had to be measured against the short-term prospects of profit. In this way, the logic of the development process, with its emphasis on the extension of existing plants, placed obstacles in the way of far-reaching changes. Though the Iron and Steel Board worked with slightly broader horizons and a more long-term perspective, evident in their frequent comments on technological innovation, it could not impose such changes on the industry and instead endorsed the *ad hoc* approach.

How did the development programme affect the class interests of capital? As far as can be told, the particular character of development in the steel industry had few if any consequences for capital's class interest in social domination and the recreation of labour as the commodity labour power. The fate of a single industry, even one as significant as steel, is not immediately pertinent to such a class project. In terms of the ability to supply the prerequisites for the other sections of the class involved in manufacturing industry, there are more direct consequences. The process of boom and recession upset the ordered delivery of supplies to these industries, though it is unlikely that an adequate technology and technical efficiency would have reduced these problems. Once again there are relevant long-term interests to be considered. Is it in the long-term interest of capital to have an important industry with a structure and technology that are both wasteful of resources and of capital? On the whole, the answer must be no. There is only a finite amount of resources available to capital to be consumed in the process of production. An industry which consumes more than is appropriate is a drain on the resources of the class and a limit to its successful operations. The steel industry was just such a problem and, though the development projects were in accord with the short-term interests of capital involved in steel production and harmonised briefly with other sections of the class, the programme was not adequate to the long-term interests of either the steel industry or of capital as a class.

Why did the Board not try to do something about the situation? First, it is not clear that the Board recognised the full consequences of the development programmes which it endorsed. In the early stages, at least, the Board accepted the logic already embodied in the Federation's and the companies planning procedures. The Board's *Annual Reports* reveal that they accepted the economic calculations that made patching seem 'logical' and acceptable. Why the Board should have been trapped by the industry's thinking on development is an important matter for the subsequent assessment of power and will be discussed separately. There are some indications that the Board's increasingly frequent comments on technical efficiency were prompted by a recognition of long-term consequences. Regardless of the quality of its vision, and this is the second point, the Board lacked any powers to force the industry to introduce even the limited changes which they thought were necessary. It could not compel, but merely recommend, the closure of outdated plants and it could not enforce the wholesale technological reconstruction of the industry. To a large extent the Board's planning was nothing more than an exercise in the forward calculation of probable demand, with some attempt to fit the industry's intentions into that general framework.

The very nature of Federation/Board relations made it unlikely that the character of the industry could be changed. As such, the general relationship between the Board and the British Iron and Steel Federation needs to be examined more closely.

Board/Federation relations

In examining the relationships between the publicly appointed Iron and Steel Board and the industry's own trade association, the British Iron and Steel Federation, it is necessary to consider both the effectiveness of public supervision and the character of power revealed in the fifteen years of its operation. To discover which of the two bodies had power, it has been traditional to ask which held the initiative and dominated the decision made for the supervised industry. The propaganda put out by the Federation recognised the importance of the question and sought to show that the Board was something more than a cipher merely reflecting the wishes of the industry. They were handicapped in the presentation of this case by the need also to stress the 'responsibility' and adequacy of the Federation's arrangements and the fact that 'real' initiative lay with the individual steel companies. Such a balance was more easily expressed in words than in the relations between the two bodies.

Though the question of who had the initiative is an important one, it starts with the assumption that the two bodies were separate and autonomous, in an analytically meaningful way. With the Federation and the Board this was only true of their institutional forms. There were two distinct sets of institutions and processes for determining the future pattern of the industry's development, one of which was supposed to supervise the other. The meaning of that supervision process was imprecisely defined in the statutes that set up the Iron and Steel Board. If the Board had been intended to be an independent body, it would have been staffed by those with no financial or commercial stake in the industry. Instead, it was manned by 'representatives' of the various relevant 'interests'. The two key terms are in inverted commas to show that they have peculiar meanings. The members of the Board were not representatives in any constitutional or theoretical sense: they were representatives only in that they were drawn from a particular group. Interest is used here in the old-fashioned sense of meaning a group who had direct concern with the way in which the industry was being run. In effect this meant the producers, the consumers, the workers and the government. The only independent on the Board was the Chairman.

The presence of steel producers on the supervisory Board suggests a number of complications for the relations between the two bodies and the reality of public supervision. How can supervision work when those being supervised are represented on the supervising body? The two senior non-independents were people who had either been prominent in the steel companies and the councils of the Federation or in an appropriate steel trade union. Initially, observers felt that the initiative was held by the Federation but this altered when Shone accepted appointment to the Board.[98] Shone had been a very important person in the Federation as he had been involved in working out the techniques for the forward calculation of demand and the monitoring of cost changes for their impact on the price policy. Was his appointment a case of poacher turned gamekeeper or did it mean that the industry's own procedures would be confirmed and further protected by having their designer sitting on the supervisory Board? The answer is not to be found in the movement of personalities from one side to the other; it is the fact of overlapping membership which is important.

The character of the Iron and Steel Board was very much in the tradition of those corporate structures identified by Brady in his important analysis of the postwar Labour Government. Such corporate bodies were distinguished by the attempt to give an institutional expression to the conflicting social 'interests' in a given industry so that comprehensive development programmes could be agreed. In its very construction, the Board was designed so that it could attempt to harmonise the interests of the various sections of capital affected by the operation of the steel industry. The presence of trade unionists on the Board only added an extra factor to complicate the necessary compromises. For such an arrangement to be fully effective, the Board would have needed extensive powers and authority over the whole of the industry. Without these powers, the Board could only react to initiatives made by the Federation or individual steel companies. The basis for conflict and disharmony was built into the membership of the Board, as the supervised industry had an effective power base in the institution itself. With such a structure and supervision procedures, the Board could only work by finding compromise solutions to the problems of the industry.

In terms of the relationship between them, the Federation and the Board operated as two parts of a single mechanism for the supervision of the conduct of the individual steel firms. In such a view, the conflict between them is nothing more significant than the conflict between different parts of the same policy development process.

Thus, the tensions between them represent important indications of the real alternatives faced by the industry in planning its development. To the extent that there was a conflict between them in the sixties, this revealed the tensions between the class interests of capital and the short-term interests of the steel producers. In the period of public supervision, the Board, through its composition and relationship, stood closer to the class interests of capital, and the Federation to the interests of that subsection of capital involved in the production of steel. If the above view is correct, then supervisory is the wrong word to describe the relationship between the Board and the Federation, as it implies both a degree of independence and a sense of being authoritatively in charge of the situation. Another consequence of seeing the Board and the Federation as parts of the same process, is to move the search for the character of power away from the relations between them. Consideration of who held the initiative remains an important part of the description of the way in which the mechanism worked. It does not help in the assessment of the character of power revealed in the period of public supervision.

Before assessing the character of power, it is necessary to examine the implications of the failure of public supervision for the previous argument about the mixed economy. It was argued that the nationalisation of steel was part of an attempt to construct a comprehensive mixed economy in a strategy to solve the problems of the capitalist economy, made evident by the depression of the 1930s. The general strategy required the nationalisation of steel, but in the circumstances of the immediate postwar period no irreparable damage was done to the mixed economy by the omission of steel from the publicly owned base. This was the result of a number of specific factors, including the expansion programme, the profitability of the steel firms and the level of production and demand for steel at the time. Though no immediate problems appeared, because steel was not part of the public base of the mixed economy, it was always possible that there would be serious consequences if those specific circumstances ever changed. The consequences of the denationalisation of steel for the general health of the capitalist economy and the long-term class interests of capital need to be evaluated.

In terms of the argument about the mixed economy, it would be pleasing to argue that the problems increasingly faced by the steel industry and the British economy in the sixties were a result of the rash, politically motivated, denationalisation of steel. The vast array of economic problems could be used to prove the point. Though this reasoning is attractive, it is also wrong. The earlier contention could only be supported at the cost of abandoning a proper perspective on the significance of steel, privately or publicly owned, in a capitalist economy. The two parts of the argument are correct, steel was denationalised and the economy ran increasingly into trouble, but the causal connection is weak. For the argument to be true it would have to show that, under nationalisation, the steel industry would have expanded its production, and rationalised and transformed its technology. Though there is no way in which it is possible to be certain about these things, there does not seem to be any reason to think that this would not have happened. The argument also needs to prove that the contribution of such a changed steel industry would have been such that the problems faced by the rest of the economy would not have been so severe. Though nationalisation could have added stability to the supply and quality of steel products, could probably have reduced the deficit on the balance of payments by reducing the need to import steel and could perhaps have increased its exports at an earlier stage, it is unlikely that these changes would have been sufficient to save the economy from its endemic problems. At best, one problem for the manufacturing sector would have been solved. It would have been possible to concentrate on the other problems of the economy and the social structure, but it would not have stopped the other problems appearing. The obsolete and unrationalised character of so much of the British economy – textiles, ship building, car manufacturing – would still have had to be tackled by both government and private capital. My position on the question is this: the denationalisation of steel had important consequences for the health of the British economy and worked against the long-term class interests of capital but it was not the most significant factor affecting conditions in other sectors of the economy and was itself adversely affected by their problems. As a private industry, steel shared many of the rationalisation and technical problems of the declining British economy: it was part of the problem. If it had been nationalised, in the way suggested above, it may not have been part of the problem, but it would not have been the key element of the solution.

The assessment of power

The preceding examination makes it clear that the policy of public supervision had different consequences for different sections of capital and for the class as a whole. This provides the essential background for the analysis of the power evident in the various phases of the interaction between the Federation, the Board and the government as part of the interaction between different sections of the class of capital. It was only in the short term that the policies produced benefits for both the steel industry and the rest of manufacturing and industrial capital. In the long run, the policies complicated the situation and worked against the interests of the various sections of capital and the class as a whole. The main evidence for the failure of public supervision was the fact that it could not maintain the harmony between the sectional interests of capital in steel and the class interests of capital. The institutional arrangement which was supposed to make nationalisation irrelevant proved to be unable to solve the problems of the steel industry as it could not promote its adequate technical transformation. It is the pattern of this failure, and the complications generated by the process of supervision, which need to be considered in the analysis of power. Problems are raised here about the limits on the effective action of capital and government. Similarly, the period of public supervision reveals a change in the power, signified by the ability to have interests protected or advanced, of a section of capital, a problem rarely identified or analysed.

At the start of the period, that section of capital involved in the production of steel had power, and this was revealed by the following features. First, its solution to the problem of the future development of steel was legislated in the setting up of the Iron and Steel Board to supervise the conduct of the industry. Secondly, the major firms in the industry were initially assured good rates of profit. Thirdly, the expansion projects proposed by the individual companies and processed by their collective organisation, the British Iron and Steel Federation, were endorsed by the Board. Also the price policy and the Government's finance scheme were able to provide the funds needed for those investment programmes. The effective working of public supervision was evident in the harmonious relations that existed between steel and other sections of manufacturing industry.

As the period developed the power of that section of capital waned. This was indicated by the gradual erosion of its secure position. The Iron and Steel Board could no longer harmonise the relations between the steel industry and the rest of the class of capital. After the period of expansion came a succession of boom years and recessions. In these conditions, the emphasis of the development programme had to shift towards the substantial modernisation of the industry's technology. However, supervision could no longer assure an adequate surplus for this purpose nor could it enforce the necessary changes. Furthermore, the profitability of the steel companies was gradually and seriously undermined. In one sense it was the decline in the profitability of the

steel firms that most clearly indicated the waning of that section of
private capital's power. Under a capitalist system, the strength and
viability of each section is revealed by its profitability which is an
indicator of that section's potential for expansion and accumulation.

Though the period of public supervision saw a decline in the power
of that section of capital involved in steel, the power did not 'flow' to
other sections or to the class of capital. The consequences for industrial capital can be discussed along with the class interests of capital.
The problem is: how were the class interests of capital affected by
what happened and what does this reveal about the class power of
capital? In the conclusion to the chapter on the form of denationalisation, I argued that the solution proposed by the steel industry and
legislated by the Conservative Government was a conditional one.
That is, the class interests of capital, relevant to the production of
steel, would only be served to the extent that the public supervision of
steel proved to be effective. Hence in the fifties, the supervision
worked and the interests of capital were secured, but in the sixties the
situation changed. Public supervision, though partly expressing the
collective needs of capital, failed and the steel industry once again
became a problem for the class of capital as a whole. The institutional
arrangements were not adequate to the task of solving this, a new form
of the problem. Indeed, it was the fact and the failure of public
supervision which gave the problem its new and distinctive character. Hence, the power of private capital, as a class, was not such that it
could work through the institutions of public supervision to secure an
outcome that advanced its collective interests. It is not that the class
did not have the power but that the power was not of the kind that
could prove effective, given the existing institutions. For the interests
of the class to be secured, it would be necessary for these institutions
to be changed in such a way that they would enable the wholesale
reconstruction of the steel industry, with rationalisation of both its
technology and its plant structure.

There was a further limit revealed to the class power of capital. One
of the factors which compounded, and provided a safety valve for, the
difficulties of the steel industry was the international context. This
international dimension included both the fact of surplus steel-
making capacity and the comparative efficiency of the British industry. In this period, British capital could not control this international environment. The sectional claim of steel to a tariff had to be
balanced against the possible consequences which this could have on
the exports of the rest of manufacturing industry, and of steel itself.
Here, the international context acted as a constraint on the effective-

ness of the actions of British national capital and that section of it involved in the production of steel. The only way in which the international situation could be controlled was through an improvement of the industry's technical efficiency.

What does the period of public supervision reveal about the power of government? If we return to Rose's arguments about regulation, it is possible to argue that, in the initial period of supervision, the arrangements enabled the industry to prosper – but in a way that revealed little about the respective power of either private capital in the steel industry or the government. The important intervention of the Government over the third strip mill showed that it had the formal power to override and ignore the supervision process. It did not ensure that the strip mill would be a commercial success. Market relations and the demand for steel in Scotland were such that it would have required decisive government action to make the new mill financially viable. This action the Conservatives were not willing to take. Though the choice of Scotland was a political decision, related to the electoral needs of the Conservatives, it was also an attempt to face a real social problem in the level of unemployment in the area. Though the decision made sense in these terms it did not meet the narrowly defined economic needs of the steel industry even though it was ratified without complaint by the Iron and Steel Board.

With the increasing uncertainties of the sixties the Conservative Government made some moves to offset the problems. It negotiated aid deals to absorb some of the surplus capacity of the industry and it sought to control dumping and low-priced imports of steel. When these proved ineffective, it introduced a special duty to reduce steel imports. In these actions the Government was acting to back up the needs of the steel industry as articulated by both the Board and the Federation. However, many of the immediate problems faced by the steel industry were a consequence of the Government's strategy for managing the general problems of the British economy. The stop–go character of economic policy had adverse consequences for the demand for steel and the Government made few exemptions to help the industry. The tax burden was not eased for the industry, though the Federation often urged the Government to make steel a special case. These actions all illustrate the general competence of the Government to regulate the level of economic operation. Though this matter will be treated more fully in the conclusion, a few observations are appropriate here. It would seem that the Government's actions were both an expression of its formal powers and an indication of the balance that had to be constructed between the needs of the steel industry and those of capital as a whole. The economic strategy could not be arranged so that the general interests of capital could be advanced, without creating problems for various subsections of the class, amongst which were the problems it created for steel. Built into the situation was a serious tension between class and sectional interests, and endemic in government policy were the complications that this entailed.

So far in this chapter, there has been no mention of the interests of the working class, as a whole or just that part of it employed in the steel production, though they were obviously affected by the development policies and fluctuating fortunes of the industry. At the level of the class's interest in the abolition of the commodity status of labour, these changes had no impact. For the steel workers' immediate interest in the continuation of employment and the improvement of the conditions of work, the period was one of mixed significance. Safety in steel improved with the modernisation of the steel works. Technological change, to the extent that it was labour-saving, reduced the demand for workers. Fluctuating fortunes in the industry were reflected in the increased insecurity of employment and the increased prospect of redundancy and short-time working. There was, however, nothing distinctive in this pattern. The workers in steel were no better or worse off than those in other sections of British industry, who all faced similar problems in the face of a declining economy and the attempts of government and private capital to improve its viability. There was no general change in the way in which the interests of the work force were taken into account when considering technical modernisation.

In conclusion, it is possible to make several comments which summarise important features of the period of public supervision. First, it marked a significant decline in the ability of the steel industry to secure, or have secured, its interests, either through the actions of the Federation, the Board, or the Government, or as a consequence of its health and place within the processes of capitalist production and accumulation. Secondly, public supervision failed in that it could not harmonise the sectional interests of capital in the steel industry with interests of the class as a whole. This was signified by the failure of the industry to modernise either its structure or its technical processes. As a consequence of that failure, the whole question of how the industry should be organised and its relations with the rest of the class was reopened. Thirdly, the period of public supervision revealed that the power of capital is affected and constrained by the institutions through which it has to work and the actual form of those arrangements is important. The power of the class is not such that it can have its interests advanced regardless of the particular shape of the institutions through which its interests are articulated and in which it has to struggle for their protection and advancement. Furthermore, the international context also limited the potential effectiveness of the class of capital.

8

The renationalisation of steel

The election of 1964 saw the return to office of a Labour Government after thirteen bitter years in opposition. Though it had campaigned with a buoyant determination to 'get the economy moving' through government initiative and the sponsorship of new technology, its small parliamentary majority limited the amount of its programme which it could introduce. Steel nationalisation was delayed, despite the fact that it had been promised at every election since the Party was defeated in 1951. After another election in 1966, the Government was returned with a large majority and was easily able to implement its policies. This provided the secure basis upon which steel could be returned to public ownership and once again form part of the publicly owned base of the mixed economy. Much had changed during the thirteen years in opposition, not just the attitudes of the Labour Party, but also the significance of the move to nationalise steel. What had been seen as a crucial challenge to the power of capital now appeared as a move against a much weakened and less important industry. As well as considering the changed significance of the move, this chapter examines the new struggle over nationalisation, the form of nationalisation proposed the second time, and the implications which these factors had for the assessment of power. The general argument about the successive changes in the ownership of the industry will be taken up in the conclusion.

The Labour Party and nationalisation

Electoral defeat in 1951, and the others which followed, provoked a critical examination of the Party's position on nationalisation and the objectives of its political action. The achievements of the postwar Government had almost completely exhausted the Party's thinking on social and economic policy and it was nationalisation, as both a means and an objective, which was at the centre of the dispute about the future character of the Party. Extensive details of what became known as the revisionist controversy, and the fight over clause 4, are to be found in the various studies of the contemporary Labour Party and the adequacy of its policies.[1] I do not wish to go over these arguments here. Instead, it is important to show how the Party's thinking had changed on nationalisation and the effect that this had on the many calls to nationalise steel.

In the programmes of the thirties, the Labour Party had argued that nationalisation was important because it would bring under public control the major resources of the capitalist economy and enable them to be co-ordinated through a system of democratic planning. The Attlee Government laid the foundations for such planning with its nationalisation programme. Unfortunately, observers suggest, the Party's enthusiasm ebbed with its time in office and this malaise continued in the initial years of opposition. The Party needed a new sense of purpose. This it found in the work of Tony Crosland, and the policies advocated by Hugh Gaitskell in the mid-fifties. Both downgraded the importance of nationalisation for any future Labour Government's programme. Nationalisation was also thought to be an electoral liability. Crosland claimed that the success of the Attlee administration had transformed capitalism and that the Labour Party required new means to reach its unchanged goals.[2] In the changed situation, ownership was increasingly irrelevant. There would be little need for further nationalisation, though competitive public enterprise might be occasionally useful. These views were also stated in works by Gaitskell[3] and in the Labour Party pamphlet, *Industry and Society*.[4] The change in private industry with the separation of control from ownership and the rise of 'autonomous' professional managements, was stressed. This was thought to have significant implications for Labour's social policies. It was agreed that the scope for fiscal management had been increased and that the Government could control the level and pattern of economic activity without needing to expand the nationalised sector. The extension of ownership, without government control, was also canvassed as a way of promoting equality. The dispute over clause 4 reinforced the impression that the Labour Party had moved away from support for an extension of public ownership. Furthermore, the rejection of a 'shopping list' of industries to be nationalised by any future Labour Government reduced the significance of the theoretical arguments that were still being adduced in its favour.

Amidst such trends, the call to renationalise steel at the earliest opportunity must have seemed a little strange. Why did the Labour Party remain committed to the nationalisation of steel, despite both the changing fortunes of the industry and the changed perspective of the Party itself? Part of the answer lay in the Party's need to assert its continuity, legitimacy and authority. Steel was the one measure of the Attlee era which had been solidly fought by vested interests, and denationalisation had rewarded their defiance. Thus it was necessary to renationalise steel to make it clear that the Party could not be thwarted by a Conservative programme to dismantle the changes introduced by Labour. The need to renationalise steel was a symbolic one. So was the need to assert the continuity of the Party, by referring back to its first period of majority rule when it had made its most dramatic impact on society. In a symbolic form, it provided a way to reduce the tensions between the centre and the left wing of the Party who were otherwise dissatisfied with the policies being introduced by the new leadership. All these symbolic purposes held good, regardless of the health of the steel industry, and provide reasons for thinking that steel would have been renationalised even if its performance had been faultless. There were other reasons for the renationalisation of steel which fitted the revisionists' account of the circumstances of future Labour Government action.

Even though the revisionists expressed severe reservations about the expansion of public ownership in the future, they did not seriously denigrate the achievements of the Attlee Government. Indeed, for their position to be tenable, it was important that they preserve both the image and the significance of the changes introduced in that period of Government. This meant seeing the nationalisation of steel and road haulage as important parts of that achievement, though most emphasis was on steel. Furthermore, their argument depended upon a particular view of the public base of the mixed economy, and what this would allow the Government to do without further encroaching on the sphere of private capital. Again this spelt out reasons for the renationalisation of steel. Without steel, the mixed economy was incompletely structured and, without an adequate mixed economy, the rest of the argument would be seriously weakened. So on these grounds alone, the revisionists and the left of the party would be united in pursuing the nationalisation of steel. They might disagree on the priority but not on the need for the action itself. The only thing which could have weakened the revisionist resolve, if only slightly, was the performance of the industry. If public supervision had been an unquestioned success, producing both reasonable profits and adequate modernisation and expansion, then the need to renationalise might have appeared less urgent. As it was, the circumstances of the industry when Labour returned to office left no reason for delay.

The struggle over nationalisation

In giving an account of the second struggle over the nationalisation of steel I do not want to follow Ross's example. He gives a very full account of the conflict between the Labour Government and the British Iron and Steel Federation and the way in which it was resolved. What I want to do here is far less detailed, providing only the information which will be useful to show the contrast with the previous period, and which will help in the assessment of the character of power revealed by renationalisation. The incident is not as significant as that studied by Ross, nor does it reveal the democratic dilemma of a conflict between a reforming Labour Government and a resisting section of private capital. The Labour Government no longer had the same reforming ambitions and the steel industry no longer attempted to act, or speak, on behalf of the class. These changes reduce the important lessons that can be learnt from the struggle over steel nationalisation the second time round. What is provided in this account is a brief outline of the tactical skirmishes between the Federation and the Labour Government, necessary for an evaluation of the meaning and significance of the outcome.

Before going into the details of these manoeuvres, it is useful to make a few comments on the distorting effect which the parliamentary arena had on the expression and appearance of the conflict. In Parliament, the issue was fought out between the Labour and Conservative Parties, along traditional lines. Consequently the debates are full of quibbles and side issues. The question of what was at stake in the nationalisation of steel was not confronted clearly or directly but through the focus of long-standing disagreements. There are numerous and irrelevant references to the theory of mandates, the significance of changes in voting patterns in the steel electorates and the attitude of the Liberal Party.[5] The effect of past disputes was most evident in the prolonged exchanges over the significance of the Restrictive Practices Court decision as a measure of the competition in the industry and the efficacy of the Iron and Steel Board.[6] Such comments moved attention away from the real issues and focused it on the degree of future competition in either the Tory or the Labour solution to the problem posed by the steel industry. The only useful thing about the Parliamentary Debates is that they provide evidence for the way in which the Parties made political sense of the issue, by linking it with their past positions and disagreements. They do not provide a good guide to what the actual significance of steel was for the various sections of capital involved or for the system as a whole.

The Labour Government came to office with a very small majority and this affected the way in which the question of steel nationalisation was approached. In some circumstances, it would have made no difference but steel nationalisation united the opposition of the Conservative and Liberal Parties and this made the Government vulnerable.[7] This was especially so since two Labour backbenchers, Woodrow Wyatt and Desmond Donnelly, were committed opponents of nationalisation.[8] Wyatt, in particular, went out of his way to find compromise proposals that would save the industry from complete take-over. His efforts were, in part, thwarted by the attitude of the Federation and its reluctance to state a negotiating position.[9] The situation was further complicated by the attitude of George Strauss who had been responsible for introducing the original nationalisation proposal and who also sought some compromise proposal.[10] As far as one can tell from Wilson's recollections of this period, the question of numbers and majorities conditioned the whole approach to steel nationalisation.[11] As a consequence, the White Paper on Steel Nationalisation was published in 1965 and this formed the basis of the first debate about the industry.[12]

The Steel White Paper showed that the Labour Government had learnt the tactical lessons of the previous conflict with the industry. Built into the proposals were ways of avoiding many of the earlier criticisms and obstacles. These included the decision not to nationalise the whole industry, as was done before, but just the thirteen largest steel producers.[13] Richard Thomas and Baldwins was to be the fourteenth company to become part of the newly constituted National Steel Corporation (NSC) (at a later date, the name was changed to the British Steel Corporation). No attempt was made to define the precise structure which this National Steel Corporation was to assume after vesting day.[14] Instead an organising committee, under the chairmanship of the designated future chief of the NSC, and staffed by those with an interest in the steel industry, was to decide the most appropriate organisational shape of the nationalised industry. There would be no basis for a charge that nationalisation would impose a rigid and bureaucratic structure on the industry. It did leave them open to the accusation that, without specific proposals, it was impossible to argue about the necessity or consequences of nationalisation. Significantly, the Government confronted the problem of the British Iron and Steel Federation directly. Not wanting to be faced with its organised opposition, the Government chose to weaken its power base as quickly as possible. It intended to do this by simply having the fourteen largest companies, which were being nationalised, withdrawn from the Federation and to make arrangements for the central services to be transferred to the National Steel Corporation.[15] The Government made it clear that if this could not be done amicably, then it would introduce legislation to force the change. The proposed Act would not nationalise the Federation but it would effectively bring it to an end.

The White Paper was the first move but the weakness of the Government's parliamentary situation meant that it was not followed up. There was no reference to steel nationalisation in the next Queen's speech. This was justified solely on the basis of the numbers and the attitude of the Liberals. Naturally, the left wing of the party, whose position at this time was most eloquently expressed by Michael Foot, carped about the delay and the Government's sense of urgency and priority, but they created no trouble.[16] The subsequent election and the increased Labour majority removed the tactical obstacles, and the measure to nationalise steel proceeded. It was only delayed by the longest committee hearings on any nationalisation proposal. Without any serious difficulties and without raising any serious constitutional questions, the industry was nationalised in 1967.

The Labour Government's case against the steel industry, and in favour of nationalisation, had several different strands and harked back to the work done by several pamphleteers in the period of opposition.[17] Though some leading Labour speakers in the Debates did not attack the industry's record (the most prominent person to praise the industry was George Strauss who had been impressed by the changes since he had confronted the industry) most were concerned to show that the industry had failed to make the significant progress which was to have been expected in the years of public supervision.[18] In this way the critique had two edges, one directed against private ownership in the industry and the other against the efficacy of public supervision and its potential variants. The industry was criticised for its failure to modernise its technology or to rationalise its structure.[19] Its comparatively poor performance, if compared with the industry in Japan, America and Europe, was continually highlighted. The point of these criticisms was not just to suggest that the industry had failed the nation and to refute the Federation's claim that they should 'Leave Well Enough Alone',[20] but to show that private ownership was a barrier which stood in the way of a progressive steel industry. Here the case was simple: if private ownership had been unable to produce the needed changes since the industry was returned to their hands, and despite the amount of public money invested in the industry, then there was no way in which private ownership could be capable of implementing such drastic changes.[21] This argument was needed to counter the steady flow of claims made by the Federation to suggest that things would be better in the future.

Both the White Paper and the Debates included arguments to explain why the Iron and Steel Board had failed and why alternative forms of public supervision were unlikely to work. In their comments on the efficacy of public supervision, the Labour Party was helped by the last few years of the Board's own *Annual Reports*. These showed that the Board's powers were insufficient for the task and that they could not compel the industry to change the pattern of its investments to accord with the Board's projections.[22] This point was picked up and reiterated in the account of public supervision. Government spokesmen also argued that there was no alternative scheme which could effectively produce the required changes while still retaining private ownership. As the position was expressed in the White Paper, 'The Government do not believe that the system of private ownership, in the main part of the steel industry, combined with the present form of public supervision, or indeed any workable variation of such supervision, can be reconciled with the national interest and with the proper functioning of the private enterprise itself.'[23] The problem was that any more powerful form of public supervision would have meant the Board overriding the commercial judgments of the separate companies, to the possible detriment of the shareholders.[24] Similarly, schemes in which the Government owned a majority or substantial number of shares would have involved contradictory pressures on the managing boards of the companies who would be torn between their duty to the private or public shareholders, in circumstances where this could not be mutually satisfactory.[25] That is why the Government was not enthusiastic about Wyatt's attempts to revive a hybrid proposal. The case for a reformed Board, or one with stronger powers, was also weakened by the belief that the privately owned steel companies would be no more serious about change than they had been under the old arrangements.

There was one further point raised in the Labour Government's critique of the steel industry and this centred on the Restrictive Practices Court decision and the degree of competition in the industry as indicated by the price policy. The Court's decision was used to show that there existed a significant degree of monopoly in the steel industry.[26] This made mockery of the 1953 Iron and Steel Act's claim that the return of the industry to private ownership under the supervision of the Iron and Steel Board would promote competition.[27] Unfortunately, the Party's position was complicated as they were not trying to extol the virtues of price competition as such. What they wanted to show was that competition was impossible in the steel industry and that it could not provide a solution to the problem of steel. Hence, nationalisation was the only way in which the anti-social consequences of that monopoly could be avoided.[28] Such a line of reasoning went back to the theme of democratic control of irresponsible private power which had been a prominent part of the first nationalisation dispute.

Though the price policy and the Court's decision gave the Labour Party a useful weapon to use against the steel industry, it was actually a false perspective. Not only did it give a wrong emphasis to the significance of competition, one that was consistent with the views of the revisionists,[29] but it also distorted the real problems faced by the steel industry and the solution posed by nationalisation. There was no prospect of a return to anything like a free-price system under any form of ownership or organisation of the industry. Nor would nationalisation lead, in the short run, to lower prices, though this is what the argument on prices implied. If the industry was to produce steel and to modernise its technology, prices would have to be controlled. The only question was who was to fix the level of prices and who was to get the reward, in the form of profits, as a consequence of that controlled price policy. Far too often in the Party's arguments, the discussion of prices lost sight of this important focus and concentrated instead on the general bad consequences of monopoly. This, of course, left them open to the attack that nationalisation would not solve the problem, since it would necessarily create an even larger and more effective monopoly.

There were other, subsidiary strands in the argument over nationalisation. Concern was expressed about the ability of a privately owned industry to raise the large sums of money needed to finance the substantial investment programme associated with large-scale rationalisation.[30] The industry's record on imports, exports and the balance of payments was also assessed. Mention was made of the social consequences of rationalisation which, it was thought, private ownership would not be able to handle in a humane manner.[31] The main feature of the Government's argument remained the industry's poor performance, the failure of supervision and the impossibility of a return to competitive conditions. These three points owe their strength, not to the actual implications of the nationalisation proposals, which will be considered below, but to the traditions of parliamentary procedure and the issues raised in previous arguments over nationalisation. They do not provide a clear guide to the significance of the move to renationalise the steel industry.

The Conservative Party's opposition to the proposed nationalisation of steel shows similar marks of the parliamentary arena and the past exchanges with the Labour Party. Thus it was that the Conservatives immediately pledged themselves to the denationalisation of steel when they returned to office.[32] When the nationalisation of steel had been previously debated, their case had been closely co-ordinated with the position of the Federation. It had also revitalised the spirits of the party. This time there was no such revival and little sign of effective co-operation with the steel producers. The Conservatives were uncertain about the position that they should take on the present health of the industry and the efficacy of public supervision. Some complained about the state of the industry, emphasised its shortcomings and argued that under a Conservative Government some new arrangements would have to be made.[33] Some expressed themselves quite pleased with the existing situation and saw little need to change the present form of supervision as they believed it worked quite well.[34] Despite this division, the main position taken by the Conservative Party stressed the need to work out new ways of stimulating the industry and increasing the effectiveness of public supervision. There was some confusion over the part that competition was to play in the new arrangements. They were willing to recognise the absence of competition as one of the weaknesses of the existing arrangements, but it was very difficult for them to find an adequate way to describe a new form of supervision which could combine private ownership, rationalisation, competition, and a secure future for the industry.[35] On such a basis, it was quite easy to criticise the Labour Government's proposals for failing to provide adequately for competition and for destroying the limited amount of competition that did exist by introducing a comprehensive state monopoly that would discriminate against the small, residual private sector. Their efforts throughout the long committee stage to promote competition within the nationalised industry and protect the remaining steel makers, whilst confining the National Steel Corporation as much as possible, failed to win the admiration of either the Federation or a commentator in *The Economist*.[36] Certainly, the Conservative opposition was nowhere as effective as it had been in the first dispute and it did not significantly delay the introduction of the measure.

The Federation's position was as fraught with difficulty as that of the Conservative Party, which had spoken on its behalf in Parliament.

During the long period of the Labour Party's electoral failure, the Federation had sponsored campaigns against the renationalisation of steel and published pamphlets and speeches to support its position.[37] Whether as a result of complacency or as a question of tactics,[38] the Federation based its case on the bombastic assertion that everything was well with the steel industry and that the Iron and Steel Board was a perfect safeguard of the public and the steel consumer's interests.[39] The propaganda issued at the time of the 1964 election suggested that they felt certain the Labour Party would lose again, and their efforts were largely a formal exercise.[40] They did make some attempt to answer the points made by critics of the industry but they were more concerned to complain that the Labour Party would not clearly state the case against the steel industry.[41] When the Labour Party won the election, the Federation seemed convinced that the Government would not last and that private ownership of steel would be saved by another election. In a sense their judgment was sound: the Government did not attempt a full term in office and they did not force through the Nationalisation Act. But the steel industry was not saved by the electorate in 1966.

The Federation did not use the period between the two elections wisely, though they sought to refute the main parts of the Government's case against the industry. They stressed both the industry's technical improvements, particularly the use of oxygen in steel production, and its ability to finance future expansion.[42] Their main initiative at this time was to endorse the statement issued by the Chairman of the Steel Companies which were destined to be taken over under Labour's nationalisation scheme.[43] This statement was issued at the time of the debate on the Steel Nationalisation White Paper. Its main purpose was to devise a formula which would not only protect private ownership of steel but would concede enough to 'take steel out of politics'. In this document it was stated:

We do not stand on the *status quo*, but accept that to take steel out of politics, revision of the legislation currently governing the industry's affairs is necessary . . . We suggest that the new legislation should establish a new Authority, charged with the supervisory control of the Industry and having powers to this end.

We believe that fully adequate control is obtainable without the need for State shareholdings in the individual companies. We envisage the need for close links between the Authority and the companies to ensure that their policies in regard to industry development conform to the general lines laid down by the Authority.

We accept that further rationalisation may well be necessary over the coming years.[44]

It looked like the old 'stronger Board' ploy all over again and was certainly not part of a strategy to avoid nationalisation by a determined Labour Government.

From this time on, the Federation was involved in a succession of attempts to devise formulas which would satisfy the Government and preserve an ever-decreasing share of private ownership in the major steel firms. In patching together these proposals they were faced with a serious dilemma. Each new concession had to be based on the recognition that something was wrong, either in the supervision arrangements or in the policies of the companies. So each concession further undermined their general case against nationalisation and made their overall strategy untenable. This can be seen in their changed attitude to both the price policy and the necessary powers of the supervisory authority.[45] It was even more evident in the last desperate attempt to stave off nationalisation, represented by the Benson Committee, which was set up ostensibly to consider the future structure of the industry.[46] The Stage One Report of this Committee appeared on the weekend before the Second Reading Debate on the Nationalisation Act.[47] Its recommendations about the size of plant and the weaknesses of the company structure, far from indicating an industry which wanted change, confirmed the general criticisms made by their opponents. In the closing stages, before the passing of the Bill into law, the Federation issued a pathetic plea against nationalisation. 1967 was another of the industry's bad years and so they claimed, 'The hard fact remains that these entirely unnecessary disruptions ought not to have been conjured up at a time of such considerable difficulty for the Steel Industry, especially since the problem of Industry rationalisation, which is put forward as the main reason for the Government's present step, is being effectively tackled by private initiative.'[48] The irony of this remark can not go unnoted. It was rationalisation that had been the key issue in the debate on the granting of the tariff, thirty-five years before! As Richard Marsh observed, there had been more rationalisation of the industry during the six months that the Nationalisation Act was being discussed, than in the previous fifteen years.[49]

All this manoeuvring by the Federation provides a pitiful contrast with their vigorous counter-attack in 1949. What had gone wrong in the councils of the steel industry? Whereas in the first dispute about nationalisation the industry had been able to speak with a progressive voice, defending itself while advocating advanced structures for reconciling the operations of private capital with the long-term planning perspectives of government, that was no longer possible. The problems in the steel industry and the failure of public supervision would have made such claims sound false. This time, the industry did not even attempt to act on behalf of the class but was concerned with a shrill defence of its own position. In contrast with the previous positions, leading figures in the industry and the Federation spoke of steel nationalisation as a threat to freedom and to the very existence of capital; a last-gasp, rhetorical claim for support from the rest of the class.[50] Here was the second problem they faced in defending their position. Previously they had been supported by vocal opinion from other sectors of the class and the press.

Though the Confederation of British Industry came out with an expected, but belated, condemnation of the proposed nationalisation,[51] the old supporters of the industry were now deserting. It was not that these old friends supported the nationalisation of steel in a strong or positive sense but that they joined their voices with the critics of the industry. Duncan Burn, the steel historian frequently referred to here, was still opposed to nationalisation but criticised the industry for its lack of rationalisation and technical innovation.[52] Various comments in the press undermined the Federation's case and were used by the Labour Government to support their policy.[53] But the most surprising indication of the decline of the industry's position and influence was provided by that 'radical' journal of capital, *The Economist*. This magazine had never supported the conservative and restrictive actions of the steel masters, but its comments in the period surrounding the debate on steel nationalisation made the Federation's position even worse. In an article published before the 1964 election they calmly faced the prospect of nationalisation and outlined five different variants, some of which were used by the Federation in their later attempts to escape nationalisation.[54] The journal also criticised the industry and stated that there were important problems which needed attention and that: 'Not only are these problems unchanged by the structure of the industry, many of them could only be approached from some quasi-nationalised central planning point.'[55] It also argued that nationalisation would make it easier to solve the problem of obsolete capacity. Though it still opposed and ridiculed nationalisation as tending towards over-centralisation and bureaucracy,[56] it also criticised the Federation for the way in which it went about its opposition to the Government's proposals.[57]

The weakness in the Federation and the industry's opposition to nationalisation can be traced back to the significant decline in the fortunes and circumstances of the steel companies. The self-confidence and the assurance of the industry's spokesmen was directly related to the health and profitability of the industry. Even though the leaders of the Federation in the sixties lacked the stature of Sir Andrew Duncan and Sir Ellis Hunter, it was the change in the circumstances rather than personalities which had the most telling effect. Not even a master tactician like Sir Andrew could have found a way to press the claim of private capital in the steel industry effectively. A policy of minimum co-operation and obstruction might have worked when the Government's will was apparently declining and the industry's position was secure but it could not even be suggested when the positions were reversed. Thus it was that leading figures in the industry, even those vehemently opposed to nationalisation like MacDairmid, were willing to sit on the organising committee designing the future shape of the nationalised industry.[58] Such a sharp contrast between the form and success of the industry's opposition to its nationalisation can be used to reveal a lot about the character of power in the interaction between government and private capital.

What was at stake

The 1967 Nationalisation Act was not just the reintroduction of the previous measure, though it contained many of the same provisions.[59] The terms for compensation were far more generous than had been suggested at the time the industry was denationalised.[60] Compensation was to be based on the stock exchange quotation for the companies and there was the routine dispute about whether or not the shareholders were being cheated. There were two ways in which the 1967 Act differed markedly from its postwar predecessor. When steel was first nationalised, the measure had applied to all firms involved in the production of steel and had included almost three hundred firms. This time the measure was far more selective and only applied to the major steel producers, those whose works produced more than a stipulated tonnage of ingot steel (475,000) in a fixed twelve-month period.[61] Hence only thirteen companies were to be taken into public ownership. The fourteenth was Richard Thomas and Baldwins which was still owned by the ISHRA.[62] As a result, there would still be a significant private sector, made up of many small firms, some of which were involved in the highly profitable business of special finishing processes.[63] Though the British Iron and Steel Federation dissolved itself as a consequence of the nationalisation measure, a new body, the British Independent Steel Producers Association, was set up to cover the private sector.[64]

The second major difference between the two forms of nationalisa-

tion lay in the character of the legislation and the proposed organisational shape of the National Steel Corporation. As Richard Marsh
commented, the legislation was in some senses enabling legislation,
as the precise details of the nationalised structure were not stipulated.
Instead, an organising committee under Lord Melchett, a Conservative merchant banker, was set up to consider the most appropriate
arrangements.[65] As Vaizey noted, they initially came up with a
scheme that was very similar in its suggestions to the Brassert report
to Sir Montagu Norman and the industry's own Benson Report.[66] It
was intended to work on the basis of regional groupings, while still
preserving the existing company units.[67] Subsequently, the whole
basis of the Corporation's organisation and finance was changed so
that it would resemble more the financial shape of its competitors.[68] I
do not want to consider here the actual working of the nationalised
steel industry, as that would raise a completely different set of problems. It is not that these problems are unrelated to issues already raised
in the discussion of power but that they would divert attention away
from the central questions so far considered in the succession of
the nationalisation, denationalisation and renationalisation of the
industry.

As with the first nationalisation of steel, the interests of the various
parties to the dispute were affected in different ways by this piece of
government action. Some of the issues previously considered are
once again relevant. In the earlier discussion it was necessary to
recognise that it was unlikely that the industry would remain
nationalised. This influenced the assessment of how nationalisation
affected interests and also the implications for the character of power.
This time there is no need for the discussion to be qualified by the
imminent prospect of denationalisation.[69]

The nationalisation of steel in 1967 meant that private capital
would no longer be directly involved in the major part of the industry.
To that extent its interests were overridden. Despite the industry's
attempt to protect itself, and to preserve some scope for private
ownership in this part of the industry, it was unsuccessful. The
compensation policy had the same consequences as before and meant
that, though private capital was not involved in steel production,
those who had held shares in the industry were either guaranteed a
stable return or were able to sell their stock and invest in some other
section of industry. The managing directors did not have to leave
their places in the steel companies in the initial period and they were
well represented on the first board of the British Steel Corporation.[70]
Undoubtedly some managing directors had their freedom of action

reduced and others would not be as significant in the nationalised industry as they had been before.[71] Any extensive rationalisation of the Corporation's structure or the elimination of the old company identities would further erode their positions. If nationalisation was a struggle between the Labour Government and that section of private capital directly involved in steel production, then that section of private capital had lost. The significance of the part of the industry left to private capital should not be underestimated.

To say that nationalisation eliminated the direct involvement of private capital in the production of steel is not to suggest that the industry escaped from the hegemony of capital: it did not. But the form of capital's domination and control of the industry changed. In Poulantzas's words about nationalisation, it was now owned and operated by the state in the collective interests of capital.[72] This way of stating the consequences of piecemeal nationalisation that does not break, or contribute to the breaking of, the hegemony of capital, is particularly apt. It highlights precisely the significance of the change in ownership. The collective interests of capital were advanced to the extent that nationalisation provided a basis for the effective solution to the problem which the industry represented for other sections of capital and the class as a whole. There seems to be no reason to doubt that nationalisation finally broke the constricting pattern that private ownership, tariff protection and public supervision had formed round the steel industry. The fact of nationalisation did not guarantee substantial progress, just that the starting point for such progress had been made.

Even in the kind of political struggle that ushered in the nationalisation legislation there were hints that the implications of the move for manufacturing industry and the rest of capital were recognised. Thus it was that Francis Lee, in the first debate over the proposal, stated:

On any reckoning the iron and steel industry plays a most formidable role in the economy. Its efficiency is vital to the efficiency of those other major industries which use the products – motor manufacture, shipbuilding, engineering to quote but a few. In the Government's view this industry is one of the 'commanding heights' of the economy which must be brought into public ownership.[73]

Though the rhetoric of the 'commanding heights' remains, the meaning has changed. Previously it had shown the need for democratic control of the economy, now it referred to an industry which had to be publicly owned so that it could make a greater contribution to the efficiency and health of other sectors of the economy. Though there

were references to the anti-democratic implications of private mono-
polies such as the steel industry, more reference was given to the
implications this had for rationalisation, output and efficiency. In
another way, the connection between the nationalisation of steel and
the needs of other sectors of capital was recognised in the general
statement of the National Steel Corporation's duties. The main task of
the Corporation was:

to promote the efficient and economical supply by the Corporation and the
publicly owned companies of iron and steel products, and to secure that such
products produced by the Corporation and the publicly owned companies are
available in such quantities, and are of such types, qualities and sizes, and are
available at such prices, as may seem to the Corporation best calculated to
supply the reasonable demands of persons (including those in Northern
Ireland) who use such products for manufacturing purposes and to further the
public interest in all respects.[74]

Hence it can be seen that, although the move to nationalise was
prompted by a variety of political motives related to the internal
character of the Labour Party and its past experience, the legislation
introduced for steel facilitated the advance of the interests of capital,
even though it required the sacrifice of the sectional interests of one
part of the class.

Securing the class interests of capital through the final nationalisation of steel was not without its disadvantages and difficult side
effects. Partly, it undermined the image of private enterprise as vigorous and effective, and weakened its claim to be the most appropriate
way of organising economic life. Not only did it reveal that a very
substantial industry was unable to rationalise its structure under
private ownership but it also implied that a nationalised enterprise
could be effective. Of course, such implications were not clearly and
dramatically evident, and if they emerged at all it was in the midst of
the continuing assault on the wasteful bureaucratic character of
nationalised industries. But it was an implication that the ideologues
of capital had to work to conceal. Regardless of the timid and unsub-
stantial character of nationalisation, it does raise questions about the
efficacy of private enterprise. Furthermore, the nationalisation of
another area of production further reduced the area in which capital
was free to operate. It also changed the very shape of the arena in
which economics and politics were to operate, giving the state, itself,
an enhanced role. The nationalisation of steel did not make any
dramatic change in the situation. It completed and made more comprehensive the publicly owned base which had been constructed in
the years 1945–51.

When considering the first nationalisation and its effects upon the interests of the working class, the argument suggested that these had not been changed in any significant way. The class's interest in breaking the social domination of capital and the process by which labour was re-created as the commodity labour power, was not helped by the nationalisation then, and it was not helped this time. It was possible to argue that the circumstances of the struggle over steel in the postwar period helped those who were making an attempt to break that social domination. There was little in the rhetoric of the 1964–70 Labour Government to assist those who wanted to encourage the Party to take the path of socialism. The first nationalisation had few implications for the sectional interests of the working class employed in the steel industry, since the actions of the Steel Corporation were contained by the desire not to upset the old management and later, by the 'standstill' memorandum and the prospect of denationalisation. This time there was no such restraint. It was argued that one of the reasons for the good labour relations evident in the industry was the fact that the steel companies did not rationalise and thus increase the displacement of labour. In other words, it was suggested that the immediate interests of the steel workers were protected by the poor development programmes introduced in the industry. Given that one of the main reasons for nationalisation was to change that situation, it meant that, to the extent that the policy was a success, the steel workers would be faced with the prospect of unemployment and redundancy. That there would be such consequences for the steel workers was recognised both in the debates and in the provisions of the Act. Though the Government may have intended to deal with the problems in a 'humane' manner, the fact that there would be a problem was an inescapable consequence of the nationalisation project. Thus, paradoxically, though it was the workers in the steel industry and the Labour M.P.s returned from steel constituencies who pressed most strongly for nationalisation, it was the steel workers who stood to lose by the policies implemented. Those who remained employed would have gained the advantage of working with more modern and technically efficient equipment but the overall level of employment would have to fall. Nationalisation, instead of securing an advantage for the steel workers, left them more exposed.

Government action and the assessment of power

It is significant that the renationalisation of steel should have been initiated by a social democratic government. Though the Conservative Opposition was forced, partly as a result of the logic of parliamentary opposition, to state that they would have changed the arrangements for public supervision, it is extremely unlikely that they would have had the necessary vision or resolve either to nationalise the industry or to force it to make the necessary and substantial changes which could have endangered the profitability of some of the individual steel firms. So once again, it was the change of government which provided the conditions for significant changes in the institutions that affected the interests of capital and the fate of one of its subunits. This will be considered more fully in the conclusion which focuses on the succession of governments and the changes in policy and strategy for capital development.

Certainly, the renationalisation involved a large amount of conflict between the Labour Government and the Federation as the representative voice of private capital in the steel industry. This time there was little doubt that the government would win the conflict, impose its rather open-ended wishes on the steel industry, and gain certain limited goals. Some of these have been discussed earlier in the chapter, specifically those relating to legitimacy and the assertion of continuity with the heritage of the Attlee Government. Gaining these goals was not without its problems. For instance, it would seem, on the basis of opinion poll evidence cited by both the Federation and Conservative spokesmen, that the nationalisation of steel, as a separate issue, was not popular. The 1966 result showed that the issue was not one that would lose the Labour Party an election. The most important political gain which the Labour Party had from the nationalisation of steel was the fact that it asserted the Party's ability to implement policies against the resistance of significant sections of capital. This enhanced its position against those who sought to criticise the Party as an inadequate vehicle for social transformation. It also enhanced its standing in the eyes of capital, by giving evidence of a firm resolve to act and to win, despite long delays and periods out of office.

This raises the question of the significance and meaning of the Labour Government's action. Though the initiative or motives for the action can be found in the logic of the political process and the ongoing conflict with the Conservative Party, the significance of the action derived from the impact which it had on the relationship between capital as a whole and that section of the class which was involved in the production of steel. The actions of the Labour Government were crucial for altering the balance between the steel industry, other sections of manufacturing industry and the class as a whole.

It was through the action of the government that the short-term and long-term interests of the steel industry were sacrificed for the long-term benefits of the class of capital, even though the nationalisation of steel was not introduced with that end in mind. Once again, it is most appropriate to see the government as a mediating institution, uniquely placed to effect changes in the relations between the various sections of capital when the class lacks internal arrangements capable of doing so in an organised and deliberate manner. But the government is not a passive instrument of mediation, somehow receiving messages or hints that there is a problem and then by means of its internal structures or procedures managing to translate these requirements into policies that are roughly attuned to the needs of the class. The institutions and procedures of government, and significantly party government, play a decisive role in both the recognition of problems and the formulation of programmes which are implemented to solve them. The important thing to note about these processes is that they are not automatically, necessarily or frequently based on a direct recognition of the way in which the planned actions will affect the interests of the various classes or the fractions of classes. Though the initiative and internal reasoning may be concerned with other issues, the actions are nonetheless significant for these class consequences.

The above discussion of the varied way in which steel nationalisation affected the interests of the class of capital and its component subgroups and the interests of labour, and also the part played by governmental action in the process, provides important information and problems for the assessment of power. The full implications cannot be considered here as many of them relate to the period as a whole and will be taken up in the general conclusion. There are some points which relate solely to the process of renationalisation. For instance, this end to the changes between private ownership and public ownership, and the significance attached to these changes indicates that power finally resided with the class of capital as a whole. The power of that section of capital in steel was not such that it could secure its own future or serve the needs of other sections of the class, mainly the part of capital involved in the industrial and manufacturing process. The class power of capital was, however, manifest in the ways by which its collective interests were secured against the steel industry. It is important to note that this power was not directly exercised by the class, which lacked institutions and processes of its own to do so. Instead, the interests of the class were protected and advanced by the actions of a government ostensibly acting against one of its subunits in the steel industry. The power exercised by the government was the class power of capital as it secured and advanced capital's collective interests. This is true regardless of the grounds upon which the government conceived its actions or the goals it sought to achieve. These factors remain important, though, for the way in which they shaped the policies through which the interests were, in practice, secured.

Though the part played by the working class and the political organisations of the working class, the trade unions and the Labour Party, has not been treated directly, some things are revealed by the eventual renationalisation of steel. The form of its power, and the institutions through which its interests were expressed, was not such that its general or sectional interests could be protected and secured, even when the party in office claimed to be the party of the workers. It was the efforts of the class and its political organisations which kept steel nationalisation alive as a political issue. It was this part of the struggle of labour with capital which left nationalisation on the political agenda. However, it could ensure that the form of nationalisation would protect its interests. As such, this meant that the sectional interests and claims of the steel workers would have to be pursued against the management of the National Steel Corporation in the same way as they were against the management of private capital in the steel industry. Nationalisation had the effect of changing the way in which the problems would appear, and the arena in which their sectional battles would have to be fought.

The eventual nationalisation of steel by the 1964–70 Labour Government brought the succession of changes in ownership to an end. It concluded both the attempt of one section of private capital to maintain its right to operate in a particular industry and the attempt by the Labour Governments to construct a comprehensive mixed economy based on an integrated publicly owned base. Throughout the period there was a continual interplay between the government, labour and capital, and within the class of capital between the various subsections of the class. The combination of successful and unsuccessful struggles with periods of co-operation which failed to produce desired and agreed ends, provides a fruitful basis for a detailed consideration of the character, form and purpose of power in a major interaction between government and private capital. It is this matter which will be taken up in the concluding discussion.

Conclusion

Government action and the power of private capital

The account provided of the conflict over the status of ownership of the steel industry, and the way in which the different arrangements introduced by a succession of governments affected the interests of the relevant parties, provides an effective background for a detailed discussion of the character of power evident in the relations between government and private capital. Aspects of the incident chosen for analysis limit the scope of the general conclusions that can be established about power. Nationalisation of steel was examined because it would focus attention precisely on the relations between a succession of governments and a section of private capital. Though the conflict over nationalisation was closely related to the actions and institutions thrown up by working-class experience, it does not follow that the example can be as useful for revealing the character of power in either the relations between labour and capital or in the interactions between government and labour. Without an extensive argument, it would be wrong to assume that power is the same in all social interactions under capitalism. Indeed, I think it very unlikely that power in the relationship between labour and capital would be the same as that present within the class of capital or in its interactions with government. Taking this into account, the arguments in this conclusion concentrate on the power involved in the conflict and co-operation between private capital and governments. The assessment of the character of that power depends on the identification of the significance of government action and its consequences for the fortunes of one section of capital and for the class as a whole.

Before considering these matters it is useful to summarise what was involved in the various conflicts over the status of the steel industry. It is unnecessary to restate all the arguments given in the preceding chapters. Rather I want to identify what actually changed in the various moves from private to public ownership. The term 'public ownership' is ideological as it implies that the community as a whole owns the steel industry. This is not correct. The community only owns the industry to the extent that it controls the government. At

176

best that control is formal and so is the ownership. The community's other stake in the industry is through taxation and the national debt, which are used to buy the industry and to provide it with needed additional funds. More accurately, nationalisation makes an industry state-owned. With the recognition that nationalisation leads to state, rather than public ownership, it is possible to see that what is mixed in the mixed economy is not capitalism and socialism. If the mixed economy stands as a transitional stage between any two forms of social organisation, it is between private and state capitalism. Within the mixed economy are combined two different forms of capitalist domination of the process of production. This can be illustrated by reference to the different arrangements found in the steel industry during the period considered here. At the outset, capital dominated the process of steel production through a system of private ownership and private management. This was replaced, under the quasi-nationalisation of 1951 and before the resale of the companies to private owners, by a form of state ownership and private management. As the firms were resold, capital again dominated through private ownership and management, subject to the supervision by the Iron and Steel Board. After the final nationalisation in 1967, capitalist domination was provided through state ownership and with the industry organised as a public corporation such that its actions accorded with the needs of other, privately owned and managed, units of capital. The emphasis given to the struggles over the forms of ownership may have concealed the extent to which these were actually disputes about the forms of domination of the process of steel production.

The succession of governments

In considering the period as a whole, it is impossible to ignore the close correlation between the changes in the legal status of the industry and changes in the party-political character of the government. Though none of the changes occurred immediately after a new government came to office, it was the change in government which formed the necessary basis for the major changes in the ownership of the industry: nationalised under Labour, twice, and denationalised by the Conservatives. This point cannot be over-generalised to suggest that all major changes in the government's strategy towards private capital depend on changes in the Party in office. This is clearly not the case. It ignores the significant changes which can occur in the course of a Party's period in office, such as the Conservatives' setting up of the National Economic and Development Office, and the important degree of continuity which exists between governments. For example, the consolidation of the mixed economy owed as much to the Conservatives' period in office as it did to the initial action by the Labour Party or its struggle to include steel in the state sector. If the error of exaggeration is avoided, then it can be seen that the nationalisation of steel, and the conflict over the size and character of the state-owned base of the mixed economy, were incidents in the conflict between the two major British political parties over forms of capitalist organisation and the strategies for social development.

There are a large number of studies of the particular character of the Labour and Conservative Parties. There are also books and articles on the complications that follow from party government. There is almost nothing written about the importance of the struggles and conflicts between these Parties for the continuity of the strategy to be pursued by governments towards the development of capitalism as both an economic and a social system. Though there is other evidence, the dispute over the nationalisation of steel can be used to show that the two major political parties complement each other. The actions of the Labour Party are consistent with it being the progressive voice of capitalist development. This can be seen in its early recognition that government should play a greater part in ensuring the stability and expansion of the system and that the success of such a policy would depend on the construction of a comprehensive, state-owned sector. Even though it pursued these policies for other reasons, and they were conceived with other purposes in mind, its actions had the effect of creating the base of a mixed economy which could provide for the profitable expansion of private capital. If the Labour Party's programmes are judged by the pattern of capitalist development encouraged, it would have to be concluded that the party was seeking a progressive solution to the problems faced by capital. It was progressive in that it was undogmatic about private ownership and it was willing to alter the existing character of the class of capital and the areas of its action. The Conservative Party, on the other hand, spoke with the voice of caution tinged with reaction. It was, so to speak, the conservative voice of the class, standing on the abstract rights of private ownership, as responsive to the needs of small capital as to those of large capital, and to those in old areas of production as opposed to encouraging the expansion of new areas. It was unwilling to tamper with the existing character of the class or its internal relations, beyond minor and piecemeal changes. This portrait of the differences between the two major political parties is not new. It is a modified form of the old view of Labour Parties as the parties of initiative and Conservative Parties as the parties of resistance. What is different is the link with a conception of alternative strategies of capitalist development. I do not want to suggest that only the Labour Party introduces progressive policies for the class of capital, but that this pattern makes sense of the differences between the two parties on the question of steel and can be roughly applied to other policy questions as well.

It was the interaction between these two Parties, expressing different strategies for the development of the system, which gave the dispute over steel its decisive characteristics. The conflict between them conditioned the ways in which the ownership of the industry changed and the times of those changes. Only such an interaction could determine the general pattern of the government's initiative towards private capital. Given the unorganised state of the class of capital, the most appropriate government strategy can only be established by trial and error. Neither capital as a class, nor government as an institution, possesses the kind of consciousness that can overcome this problem. Within the class there are no procedures which can guarantee that implemented policies will be transformed to serve the collective needs of the class. In such circumstances, where the consequences of policy cannot be assured, certain and deliberate conflict between political parties and conflict between sections of capital and governments are the only ways in which general policies can be adjusted to serve, more effectively, the needs of capital. Once again, it should be stressed to prevent misunderstanding, this does not mean that government policies are conceived clearly with such intentions but that they necessarily have implications for the class relations both within capital and between labour and capital.

Though the above comments have focused on the interaction between political parties and the consequences which this has for the class of capital, the important implications for the class of labour cannot be ignored. One of the Parties has a distinctive relationship with the working class through the trade unions, other institutions of the labour movement, and its electoral appeals. This relationship certainly affects the way in which the Labour Party formulates its policies and the way in which it comes to recognise the problems which need to be tackled by government action. In the dispute over steel, it was the Labour Party's connections with the trade unions, as much as anything else, which kept nationalisation on the political agenda. The consequences of the social democratic form in which the class interests of labour are represented in the political sphere have been considered at a later stage in the conclusion.

The status of government action

As indicated in the chapter on power, the pluralist model used for the assessment of government action has normally made two assumptions about the character of governments. First, pluralists assumed that governments have interests to defend and advance, and that these are derived from the political processes of parliamentary and electoral democracy. Secondly, they assumed that governments were pressure-influenced bodies, essentially without interests, whose actions could be used to measure the strengths of contending classes and social groups. These assumptions have rarely been examined for the implications they have for the analysis of power as a social process within a class-structured society. The analysis of the role of government action in the conflict over steel nationalisation provides a basis for judging these and other assumptions about the character of government action.

The examination of the status of government action in the conflicts over the nationalisation of steel suggests that there is only a small portion of truth in the assumptions summarised above. Essentially, the pluralists were correct to assume that governments derive their programmes and policies from the arena of political struggle and that the political process had its own logic which it stamped on the policies of successive governments. They were wrong, however, in not considering the consequences that this had for the study of power. Pluralists have no difficulty in showing that governments formally control the process of economic and social development, but they lack any criteria to assess the significance of the actual policies implemented. They are unable to consider, in an adequate manner, the consequences of government action. Though it is true that the goals and policies pursued by political parties are a product of political contests, struggles and arguments, it is also true that government actions have consequences for other areas of society and that these consequences can be of a kind unrecognised in the initial conception of the policy. No matter how goals are conceptualised, or represented in the thoughts of political actors, they have consequences for the fortunes of the two major classes and their constituent subgroupings. For example, the initial move to nationalise steel, and to create a comprehensive state-owned base for the mixed economy, was conceived in terms of the prerequisites for the democratic control of the economy, seen through the lens of socialist rhetoric about the 'commanding heights' of the economy. Nevertheless, what was construed was a mixed economy that faced the long-term and system interests of the class of capital. In other words, it was through the particular conceptions of the political actors that formed the Government that the policy was introduced and the long-term interests of capital as a class were advanced.

The argument here is not that governments conceive of their political tasks directly or clearly in terms of the consequences that their actions will have for the basic classes or subclass groupings. Indeed, given the earlier argument about the character of interests and the structure of the two classes, it is highly unlikely that a government could ever exist which had such perception that it could recognise these in a direct form. Instead, it is being argued that governments represent the task of advancing or affecting the interests of classes and class fractions in terms of the political programmes they introduce. Sometimes this representation is of an indirect kind, as in the Attlee Government's pursuit of democratic control of the economy, or more directly, as in the previously cited duties of the nationalised Steel Corporation. The particular terms in which policies are conceived have important consequences for the way in which the interests of the various classes and fractions will be influenced. For example, the terms in which the 1953 legislation on public supervision and the powers of the Iron and Steel Board were conceived, had very serious effects upon not only the health of the steel industry and its relations with other sections of manufacturing industry, but also its long-term prospects for remaining privately owned.

It is not that the policies which become government action contain indirect representations of their consequences for the classes in society but that the situation in which they are introduced is such that government action must necessarily have direct and immediate implications for the classes and their various constituent fractions and sections. Thus, despite intention and often beyond conception, government action has a reference point external to that of the political process in which it was developed. This external point of reference has an important part to play in assessing the meaning and significance of government action as expressed by the pattern of consequence which it has for the various classes. As such it is relevant both to the consideration of the status of government action and the assessment of the power revealed in the struggle over the nationalisation of steel.

In the course of presenting the discussion on the struggle over the nationalisation of steel, there were many indirect attempts to answer the question of the status, as opposed to the significance, of government action. It was in those terms that the argument over the initial nationalisation of steel included the suggestion that the government was best treated as a mediating institution. In terms of the specific example, government action appeared as a form of mediation between the class of capital as a whole and that section of the class which was involved in the production of steel, and as a mediation between industrial capital and the steel industry. In the relationships between these parts of the class of capital, the government existed as an institution whose actions facilitated the solution to problems which existed in these relations. Government action was part of the process by which the collective and sectional interests were harmonised. For this to be the case it was not necessary for the government to be aware of this role; it could happen both unconsciously and against the will or intentions of the government. Government action also existed as a point of mediation in the relations between labour and capital, by securing situations in which social harmony could be preserved. Here the important thing to note is the complex transformation which occurred to turn the interests of the working class into policies which would formally encapsulate their demands but would have the effect of securing their continued social subordination. In the case of the second nationalisation of steel, it did not even secure the employment future of those who worked in the industry.

The view of the government as a mediating institution in the relations both within capital and between capital and labour, has the benefit of focusing the discussion, not just on the ability of the government to have its will implemented in the passing of laws, but also on the content of those laws and their consequences, intended or otherwise, for the interests of the various classes. Changing the emphasis from the formal fact to the consequences of government action has important consequences for analysis based on the pluralist model. It reduces the possibility that government action can be used to assess the relative power of contending parties, especially if it were intended to show that capitalist societies were democratic because the government dominated economic developments. The success of the government in introducing legislation against the resistance of a section of capital (or the class as a whole) cannot be used to prove that government actually dominates the economic process, that politics is in command, or that the democratic procedures of capitalist society are significantly effective in ensuring that the benefits of government action will go to the majority of the people. Though governments have formal powers, it is the content of their actions which is important for the assessment of the power revealed in the interaction between government and private capital. It is quite possible that the government may act against a particular section of capital, and be opposed by it, but its actions may be fully or largely consistent with the long-term interests of capital as a whole, or the interests of some other section of capital. In such a case, the government may have exercised power against one section of capital, but it may also have exercised power on behalf, or to the advantage, of the other sections of capital or the class as a whole.

In specific terms, the nationalisation of steel was achieved against the opposition of that section of capital, a combination of owners and managers, directly involved in the production of steel. Though the Labour Government was not overtly or enthusiastically supported by other sections of the class, or manufacturing industry, the form of nationalisation was such that their interests were advanced by it. Thus the nationalisation of steel, against the opposition of a section of capital, cannot be used to show the general power of the state over the class as a whole, or, in the terms of the pluralist analysis, of government power over business. Nor can it be used to show that the political order is more significant than that of the economy.

Rose, in *The Power Structure*, is suspicious of such arguments. He notes both business opposition to government action and the fact that business has benefited from it. He then observes (p. 486, n.2):

It has been argued that this businessman's ideology represents a 'false consciousness' – that is, it claims to represent an economic interest, but is in fact, contrary to the economic interests of businessmen. The factual argument is that businessmen gain most economic benefits when the government actively promotes the welfare and education of even its poorest citizens, when it maintains a regularly unbalanced budget, and when it reduces tariffs – all policies most businessmen oppose.

It is possible to ignore both the misrepresentations of his opponents' case, signified by limiting the benefits that could accrue to capital to 'economic' ones, and the specific programmes he mentions. What he is disputing is the possibility that the long-term class interests of capital could be advanced by policies which 'most businessmen oppose'. In fact, it is not true that business groups are unaware of the benefits of such progressive policies. There are sufficient studies of the American situation which show that there were businessmen and sections of business who were not merely aware of the benefits of these policies, but organised themselves to campaign for their introduction by postwar governments. Similarly in Britain there were business people who recognised the advantages which would follow from both the construction of the mixed economy, the use of Keynesian fiscal policy and even the nationalisation of steel. However, Rose's case rests on an unacceptable assumption about the consciousness of business groups. Why is it that their views should coincide with what is in the long-term interests of the class as a whole? Rose relies on an appeal to common sense, which in this case obscures the necessary consideration of how government policy actually affects not only class but also sectional interests.

It is both comfortable and reassuring to assume that people or businessmen know their own interests; it also has the effect of simplifying the analysis of power and the interaction between classes and with the government. The need to argue about the consequences of action is removed. It is enough to be able to show that it was supported or opposed by the groups arguing about a policy. Apart from the fact that there is no logical reason why a class or a fraction of the class of capital should be fully conscious of their immediate and long-term interests, and the full implications of any policy which may affect these, there is the matter of the context in which these complicated assessments are being made. There is not, as I have argued earlier, any simple correlation between an interest and the policy which most adequately expresses it, or which will secure or advance it in the best manner. These are all questions of judgment, in complicated situations, which require contradictory and complex matters to be balanced. It is the very structure of classes and the complications of interests which makes it unlikely that most or all businessmen will be competent to establish what is, or is not, the most appropriate course to advance or protect their position, as individual concerns or as part of the collective interests of the class as a whole. The whole matter is one of conflict, struggle, organisation and dispute. These circumstances make it possible for a fraction of capital to try to speak on behalf of the whole class and to reorganise its areas of operation. It also allows governments to act as institutions of mediation to produce strategies with far-reaching consequences for the internal structure of the class.

The government is not a simple mediating institution in the sense that its actions merely reflect the intentions, demands and compromises worked out within the class of capital. If it were a simple reflecting mediation, the view of government as a pressure-influenced body would have been reinstated, dressed in conceptually different clothes. As I have argued before, the class lacks the internal arrangements to make decisions or organise solutions to these kinds of problems. In this sense, any solution must be developed and implemented by an external mediating institution, and one which plays an active part in working out what needs to be done. It is not necessary that governments should be aware that their policies have such a dimension: the character of the difficulties as they appear in the political sphere, and the context in which governments act, will have the effect of making their actions relevant, if not adequate, to these tasks.

In these terms, the particular character of the government and the kinds of programmes which it tries to introduce are crucial parts of the process by which the internal relations within the class of capital are regulated, maintained or changed. It is in these terms that government action in the dispute over the form of ownership of the steel industry is best considered. The succession of governments, by their actions to alter the forms of ownership in the steel industry, for whatever reason, altered the internal balance of fractions and sub-units within the class of capital. The final nationalisation confirmed a complete change in the internal structure of the class by removing steel from the domination of one set of private owners and managers. Government action mediated the relations within the class and constructed a new balance between the various parts of capital and their areas of action. It would be wrong to see this process in too abstract a manner. Government action was needed as a response to particular problems evident in the health of the industry, its relations with other sections of manufacturing industry and the demands of the steel unions for action on the question of steel. Furthermore, the move to nationalise steel prompted vigorous opposition from the industry and so the whole process of government action was conditioned by the need to solve the problem of relations with that particular section of capital. On the basis then of the consideration of the various aspects of the dispute over the steel industry, it is possible to undermine the dominant pluralist assumptions about the character of government upon which is predicated their analysis and assessment of power. It is also possible to suggest a conception of government as an agency of active mediation, with its reference point in the consequences of government action for the relations within the class of capital and between capital and labour. Again this conception of government is relevant to the analysis of the social process of power in advanced capitalist countries.

The consequences of government action: the mixed economy

The central point in the argument about the status of government action and its consequence for the balance within the class of capital depends upon an argument about the significance and character of what was achieved, the mixed economy. Given Rose's scepticism, it is more necessary to spell out these implications since they do relate directly to the question of whether the collective interests of capital can be advanced despite significant opposition from particular industries and sections of capital. Though part of the argument depends on establishing the long-term contribution of the mixed economy to the viability of capitalist society, I do not want to tackle that question directly. Instead I want to comment on the implications of the mixed economy for the assessment of the character of government action and the problems for which the mixed economy provided some solutions.

Though the mixed economy was created in Britain by the actions of a social democratic government seeking to gain democratic control of the economy, it was directed to solving the problem of unemployment. This desire to remove unemployment and operate a full-employment policy was shared by all political parties and was one of the main forms in which the problem of the depression was represented in the field of political struggle. In its essence, the mixed economy provided the basis for the revival and continued successful operation of private capital. It did this in a number of ways, by removing areas of unprofitable action from the hands of private capital and by rationalising the infra-structural base of capitalist production. This was not done directly by private capital but indirectly through the actions of the government and state institutions. In that the mixed economy could not be constructed by private capital directly, its implications for the significance of government action need to be considered further.

A mixed economy, that is, one which combined two forms of capitalist domination of the production process, through private ownership and management and through state ownership and control, could not be constructed by private capital. On a matter like this, private capital could not act as a class and in a co-ordinated manner, no matter how important the mixed economy may have been for its survival. The mixed economy could only be built under the direction of a government, acting in a manner similar to that of the Bank of England during the depression. A mixed economy cannot be built without the subordination of some sections of private capital. It is necessary for their short-term interests, in particular areas of production, to be sacrificed to secure the long-term interests of private capital as a class. As such, it involved the restructuring of the class of capital. Some sections would gain in importance, others would decline and some would disappear completely. As argued above, nationalisation would not free the state-owned sector from the domination of capital but it would change the form of that domination. Such a change had important consequences. For one thing, the apparent significance of private capital would be diminished, as the rise of a state-owned sector implied both a rivalry and tension between the two parts of the capitalist economy. For nationalisation to achieve its social objective, and to give the appearance of politics dominating economics, the actual continuity of capitalist domination had to be concealed in the change of ownership. This had its ideological costs, not only in the appearance of an alternative to private ownership but also in the fact that sections of private capital were hostile to any increase in the area of government action, regardless of how useful it might be for the class as a whole.

The advantage of the mixed economy for restoring and maintaining the health of the capitalist economy lay in the fact that the necessary base for profitable expansion could be constructed by government action. To the extent that those industries were either not profitable or required massive programmes of reconstruction, modernisation and rationalisation, the costs could be socialised. That meant that they would be borne by government finances in the form of taxes and additional claims on the national debt. Unlike the relations between other areas of capitalist production, unless organised by a comprehensive monopoly, the base of the mixed economy could be planned and co-ordinated. The relations between the two sectors could be regulated by government policy on prices, supply and finance. Naturally, one consequence of the creation of a mixed economy was that it increased both the sphere of government action and its significance. As such, it altered the arena of political conflict and it changed the character of the issues that were raised within it. This was as true of capital's relationship with government as it was for the working class. As an important consequence, it meant that the conduct of the economy, and the strategies for its development, would be political issues. Though governments in Britain had always been concerned with the conduct of the economy, their positive role had been limited. Successive governments had accepted that their actions ought to be minimal. After the construction of the mixed economy, through the Labour Party's nationalisation programme and its consolidation through thirteen years of Conservative Government, the conduct of the economy was irreversibly a political issue. Whatever the symbolic value of the 1953 denationalisation of steel, it could not alter the new status of government action.

The appearance of the economy as a political issue in the wake of the postwar Labour Government, and the implied alternative to private ownership, had consequences for the politics of the working class. When the Labour Party wished, it could argue that the mixed economy stood as a transitional stage between capitalism and a more planned and brighter future. Some of the more short-sighted may have thought it was part of the transition to socialism. But this whole position was an illusion, based as it was on a belief that the opposition between state ownership and private ownership implied an opposition to the domination of capital. As argued above, if the rise of a state-owned sector makes the mixed economy into a transitional form, then it lies somewhere between private and state capitalism. Nationalisation, implemented in a piecemeal manner by a social democratic government, does nothing to alter the commodity status of labour. It does, however, alter the context within which the struggle for its abolition has to be fought.

Though the nationalisation of steel was not the most important part of the policy to construct the mixed economy, the struggle and delay that surrounded the move was significant. As argued in the text, the steel industry lay at the boundary between an infra-structural process and manufacturing industry. It occupied a position on the logical point of separation between the state-owned sector and the area for private capital. The initial resistance to nationalisation focused attention on both the specific character of the steel industry and the appropriate limit to the size of the state sector. In the course of the initial conflict, the Labour Government was forced to clarify what it understood to be the ground rules for the conduct of the state-owned sector in its relations with the privately owned industries. These ground rules were further elaborated during the period of Conservative Government. When Labour renationalised the industry, it sought to solve the problem of the dual character of the steel industry by only nationalising firms on the basis of the quantity of basic steel produced. This excluded from the state sector those parts of the industry which made special steels or which were involved in the finishing processes similar to parts of manufacturing industry.

The dispute over steel, and its denationalisation by the Conservatives, conferred legitimacy on the remaining part of the state-owned base of the mixed economy. It also set the limits of legitimate state action for almost fifteen years and confirmed that the renationalisation of steel would be the end point in the construction of the mixed economy. Such a claim might seem a little strange after a decade during which the range of government action has been increased and in which there have been a number of industries nationalised and calls for further nationalisation. Though the 1973 Labour Party manifesto spoke the language of democratic control which had heralded the initial construction of the mixed economy, the meaning of that call had changed. The nationalisation of Rolls Royce by the Conservative Government and British Leyland by the Labour Government had nothing to do with the construction or extension of the mixed economy. They were moves as a response to new problems faced by private capital, some of which were related to the operation of the mixed economy. Though they too increased the importance of state action, these nationalisations were unrelated to the task of creating a comprehensive state-owned base for the mixed economy. The renationalisation of steel in 1967 was not the start of this new period: it was an end to the process started in 1945. It set the limit to the base of the mixed economy and confirmed, both in the terms in which it was introduced by the Labour Government and in the definition of the National Steel Corporation's tasks, the rules that governed the relationship between the state-owned and private sectors. In this, the state-owned base of the mixed economy was subordinate to the needs of the private sector and would be operated to enhance that sector's smooth operation and profitability.

The argument about the mixed economy, and the points made in the course of the analysis of steel nationalisation, have consequences for the analysis of the process of power. It also affects the terms in which government action has been treated in the works of various pluralists. It counters Rose's suggestion that actions against the wishes of business but which bring them benefits, are not relevant to the assessment of the character of power. Though the construction of the mixed economy was opposed by capital, and opposed for good reasons because it eliminated private ownership from some sections of the economy and also restricted the range of free action for private capital, it was, nonetheless, in the long-term interests of capital. By providing the basis for a new period of profitability for the privately owned sector of the economy, it gave a material benefit to the class as a whole. By attempting to remove unemployment as a serious social problem, it helped the class maintain its social domination. Furthermore, the ideological form of the mixed economy, with a publicly owned sector, weakened the struggle against the commodity status of labour. The new situation was more complex and the work experience of those in nationalised industries increased disillusionment. For a time, the basis for a new socialist challenge was unclear. None of these matters were pertinent to the opposition of specific industries in defending themselves against nationalisation, though the leaders of the Federation in 1949 realised that they had to come up with a solution that could give similar benefits to nationalisation while retaining private ownership. These alternative arrangements failed and the construction of the mixed economy was completed, against their will, in 1967.

The character of power

The discussion of the significance of government action has refocused the account of the character of power in the general interaction between government and capital. The argument that governments act as a mediation between the various parts of the class of capital, or as a mediation between capital and labour, removed the significance from an isolated consideration of power in the relations of capital and government. Instead, the analysis must concentrate on the character of power revealed by government action in its impact on the relations between the constituent parts of the class of capital and the relations between labour and capital. Power is involved in the relationship between government and private capital, but its character can only be seen in the consequences that government action has for the various fractions of capital and subunits of the class.

The analysis is now concerned with the character of power in the relations between capital as a class and one of its subunits, the steel industry, and in the relations between the steel industry and other sections and fractions of capital, principally industrial or manufacturing capital. In examining these relations, the analysis is confronted with a paradoxical situation that concerns action and the exercise of power. It is the government which acts, exercises power, and secures outcomes. In the process examined, this varied from the nationalisation of steel to the setting up of forms of public supervision. Though these actions had a significance in terms of the political and social goals of the particular governments, they were also significant for the internal relations between the different constituent parts of the class of capital. That is, the changes in the ownership of the steel industry had a set of different consequences for the industry, other fractions and sections of capital, and the class as a whole, which are relevant to the analysis of power. It was the section of capital directly involved in the production of steel which was most crucially affected by government action. That section of capital, organised and represented by the Federation, struggled to secure its interests and in the short term, its continued existence. In the first phase it was successful, though the continuation of private ownership in steel depended upon the action of a government. There was no other way in which it could be secured. Though there followed a period in which it was not seriously challenged by the Iron and Steel Board, the government or the workers in the industry, that section of capital was not able to create the conditions to make it immune from the threat of renationalisation. It could not harmonise its interests with the requirements of the rest of industrial capital and its viability declined. Despite its opposition, the second move to nationalise the industry was successful and private capital ceased to have a direct stake in the production of steel. That part of private capital ceased to exist as part of the class of capital.

So far there is no paradox. It is a simple matter of conflict between a section of private capital and various governments and a series of changes which affected the status and significance of the industry. The paradox is evident when the consequences of government action for industrial capital and the class as a whole are considered. Throughout the various struggles over the nationalisation of steel, industrial capital played a minimal role. Though it lacked any form of organisation equivalent to that of the British Iron and Steel Federation, its approximate voice in the Federation of British Industries and the Confederation of British Industries supported the industry in its struggle against nationalisation. The strength of their opposition may have changed between 1949 and 1967 but they never issued a call for the nationalisation of steel. Individual users of steel may have complained about the delivery and quality of steel available from the British industry but they did not mount a campaign in favour of nationalisation. And yet, it has been argued here, industrial capital's interests were secured by a policy of which it did not approve, and for which it certainly did not fight. Though it might be possible to argue that nationalisation did not have material benefits for the rest of industrial capital, what cannot be disputed, for the period under consideration, is that the form of nationalisation was such that advantages would flow to those industries that used steel as a raw material.

If the position of the class of capital is considered, many of the comments made about industrial capital can be repeated. The class lacked a representative organisation like the Federation. It had no institutional forms to articulate its interests or to formulate them into coherent, class-relevant policies. Nevertheless, those who spoke on behalf of the class were not in favour of nationalisation. In 1949 they had been quite resolute in their opposition, though by 1967 the sturdiness of their support for the industry had gone. As The Times and *The Economist* show, they did not approve of the move to nationalise steel in 1967 but they minimised the seriousness of its consequences and recommended trying to work with the nationalised steel industry. In general, their comments undermined the Federation's case by pointing out the shortcomings of the industry. Though sections of the class were willing to co-operate with the Labour Government in the nationalisation of the industry, this did not amount to a campaign of support. Once again, I have argued that the nationalisation of steel, in completing the state-owned base of the mixed economy, secured the long-term interests of the class.

Here then is the paradox: that section of capital which struggled most, and had an institution to co-ordinate its actions, was not in the long run able to protect its interests though it was well aware of what they were. Those sections of the class, and the class as a whole, which lacked any effective form of organisation, did not act but still they had their interests secured by the actions of the governments. This raises the question of not just the character of power, but what part, if any, did power play in the process by which the interests of one section of capital were subordinated to those of others and the class as a whole. The need to confront that question is reinforced by the need to consider and explain the gradual decline in the industry's ability to secure its interests. What part did power play in undermining the industry's competence for successful action?

The problem partly arises from the 'language of power', some of the implications of which were considered in the opening chapter. As Lukes correctly points out, the common use of the term power implies both responsibility, in the sense of being able to do something else, and agency, in that it is something that is actively done. In such usage there is an almost unbreachable gap between the notions of power and structure. But it is precisely the interconnection between these two that needs to be considered if the problem is to be solved. In the first chapter I argued that the common language of power was of limited use since it construed power relations as those between autonomous and individual subjects, whether people, groups or social institutions. It is in the consideration of the paradox, such as the one outlined above, that the limitations of common usage are most clear. The language of power has the dual effect of destructuring the context in which power interactions occur and of attributing the outcome, almost exclusively, to either the imbalance in the distribution, or the skill in the use of, power or power resources. In focusing attention on who acts, even if this is conceived in the broadest possible sense to include inaction or passivity, it is impossible to understand or analyse actions that advance the interests of others if they take no part in the interaction or if they overtly oppose the actions being taken. The significance of government action as a form of mediation in the relationships between the constituent parts of capital, must remain invisible to such an approach.

The outcome and the character of power evident in the process of conflict over the nationalisation of steel can only be understood on the basis of close attention to the effects of the context in which the interaction occurs, and the part played by the structure in conditioning the outcome. In looking at this matter it is necessary to refer back to the statement about the character of power, where I argued that power was revealed by the ways in which the interests of class and subclass groups were affected by action. There, I also set up a distinction between the exercise of power, the ability to act and to secure outcomes, and the fact of having power, which was revealed when interests were secured by the normal operations of the system. In considering the change in the significance of the steel industry and the way in which the interests of industrial capital and the class of capital were advanced, it is possible to elaborate the following view. Power is a property of the structured relations between classes, and the constituent groups within classes, that enable them to secure their various sectional and class interests. With this perspective, it can be seen that the role of government action in mediating between the constituent parts of capital confirmed the power of the class of capital, and in this instance, the power of industrial capital over the power of that section of capital involved in the production of steel. In this process it was not necessary for industrial capital or the class as a whole to act to secure these interests. They were secured for them by the action of the mediating institution of the government. Power then, in the relations within the class of capital, is a structural property that can be expressed in the actions of various sections of capital, or other intermediary institutions, but its presence and potency are revealed as the capacity to secure interests.

The point of this argument is to locate the source, character and significance of power for relations within the class of capital. It is not to undervalue the importance of the struggles and conflicts that actually occur. The pattern of who acts and who exercises power and for what reason is central to the understanding of what happened. But it is necessary to refer these actions to the structured context in which they occur. Throughout the consideration of the series of disputes about the ownership of the steel industry, I have stressed the important part played by the actual ways in which actions have been conceived by the political actors and the importance of the logic of the political process. Struggle between governments and fractions of capital or industries is important, given the lack of an effective form of internal class organisation. It is the structured context within which these conflicts occur which ensures that they have significance for the internal relations within the class of capital. The social process of power, and the role of government as a mediating institution, are important for the consequences they have for the interests of the various parts of the class of capital. It is in the pattern of the consequences of government action that the form, distribution and significance of that power is revealed.

In the analysis of this particular interaction between the steel industry, industrial capital and the class as a whole, several things stand out as being important. The first of these is the role of organisation and power in the articulation of interests into more or less coherent policies. This was most obviously significant in the case of the steel industry, with the British Iron and Steel Federation. Though its efforts to protect private ownership were unsuccessful in the end, it had devised and operated a comprehensive form of organisation which was able to secure some sort of balance between the diverse concerns of its disparate elements. With steel, it was the presence of organisation that was important; with industrial capital and the class as a whole, it was the lack of organisation. Capital lacked any comprehensive and conscious form of organised unity, internal to the class. As has been argued earlier, this provided not only the scope but also the importance of the actions of external institutions, such as political parties and governments, to organise the unity of the class and to seek strategies for development which would harmonise the interests of the constituent parts of the class. It should be noted that the absence of such internal arrangements increased the difficulties of creating policies that could adequately express the diverse interests that had to be harmonised in collective, class-relevant policies. It is this absence which gives the political process, the struggle between different parties and the conflicts between government and capital, its distinctive importance. Given that the actions of government define the general pattern of capitalist development, alter the internal balance of the class, and enable it to secure its long-term interests, it could be argued that the government is not exercising an independent power but the power of the class as a whole. Clearly, the long-term consequence of government action was to secure the class interests of capital against the sectional interests of the steel industry. In that sense power, in its exercise, is a facilitating medium for achieving, securing and reconciling the interests of various sections of capital and the class as a whole. However, and this is the point, the fact that some interests are secured and others subjugated is not just a product of will and struggle but is related to the structured context in which the conflicts occur. Considering the period as a whole, it would be wrong to see that structuring as static or unchanging, prefiguring consequences consistently in the favour of one section of the class. The balance of the structured relations is changed, as was shown in this study, by the effects of government action and the strength and viability of various parts of the process of capitalist production.

It is also important to note that an analysis of steel nationalisation indicates some of the limits which exist for the effective action of private capital. Capital, and its fractions, are not omnipotent: there are certain things, in certain circumstances, which they cannot do. Apart from what can be deduced from the steel industry's eventual nationalisation, the period of public regulation can be used to show some of those limits. International circumstances, in this instance the state of the world steel market, limit what can be done by declining industries or those facing economic problems. In the case of steel, the international context provided a cushion during the period of high domestic demand, but reduced the industry's manoeuvrability in the period of recessions and undermined the industry's ability to both modernise and earn a profit while selling at a competitive price. The whole period also indicates that the pattern of property relations within a particular sector may place obstacles in the way of needed changes. This is particularly true if the problems of the development programmes are considered. The failure of the process of public supervision also shows that the institutional forms through which capital has to operate may work against its success, and that these arrangements may need to be changed before the continued health of the class can be assured. When considering this set of limits and constraints on the power of capital, it should be noted that they are not the product of the wills or struggles of others, or the result of an overt exercise of power, but that they are the consequence of certain features of the structured context within which capital has to act. It is not that all the limits on capital are of this kind but that there are limits set by circumstance and not the exercise of power, which should be recognised.

The example of the struggle over the nationalisation of steel is not very appropriate for considering the character of power in the relationship between labour and capital or between labour and government action. Intentionally, the example was selected to form the basis of arguments on the interactions between government and private capital. Nevertheless, the interaction with labour was an important part of the process. Though the arguments advanced here are limited by the kind of example being considered, a few tentative observations on the character of power in the relationship with labour can be made. As suggested earlier, the significance of power in the interactions between labour and capital is quite likely to be of a different kind from that evident in the relations between the constituent parts of the class of capital. For one thing, the structure, rather than providing a context which prefigures the outcomes of power interactions, stands as an obstacle to the class gaining one of its key interests, the abolition of the commodity status of labour. Even if the reforming or ameliorative interest is considered, it is much more a struggle of will and agency than the interactions within the class of capital. Once again, however, an important part of the process is the way in which the interests of the class are organised, articulated as collective policies and fought for in the political context. The impact which labour has both on capital as a class and on the process of capitalist development is strongly conditioned by the particular way in which this is done. Some aspects of this process, and of the power of labour, can be seen in the paradoxical conclusion to the struggle for the nationalisation of steel as viewed from the perspective of the working class.

As indicated in the text, the move to nationalise steel came from the steel unions, was endorsed by the TUC and became Labour Party policy. Its relevance as an issue after steel was denationalised was as much a product of these labour institutions as of anything else. The move to nationalise steel was carried through by a Labour Government which was supposedly in tune with the interests and needs of the working class. Despite all these factors, the eventual form of nationalisation was such that it advanced certain of the class interests of capital but it failed to secure even the limited, short-term interests of the steel workers. Indeed, in this particular instance, it was the action of labour, via the distorting processes of the trade union movement and a social democratic political party, which provided capital with both the solution for one of its problems and the impetus for the introduction of that solution. This certainly reveals something about the power of labour and the crucial consequences of the institutions and processes by which its interests are organised and articulated into policies. Despite its exertions and its formal successes, the power of labour, organised through social democratic institutions, was unable to secure either its sectional or class interests.

Though the main emphasis in this argument has been on the

character of power evident in relations between governments and a section of the class of capital, there have also been references to different ways of approaching the analysis of power. The traditional approach to power, which encompasses much of the arguments of people as diverse as Dahl and Lukes, conceives the conditions in which power can be studied in fairly definite terms. The procedures rely on the use of the formula, 'A has power over B to the extent that A can get B to do something which he would not otherwise do'. On the basis of Lukes's arguments about the connection between power and interest, and after a more extensive consideration of a framework within which interests can be treated, I sought to establish a different way of treating the analysis of power. One of the side considerations in the arguments was to show that the approach was more revealing than that using the 'A has power over B' formula. Traditional analysis has used the category of power to account for the gaining of outcomes. What I have done is to show that power is the term to describe the process by which interests are secured, protected and advanced within a given social setting. The existence and character of power has been discerned by considering the different consequences which a particular government action has for the interests of various classes and subclass groupings. The consequences of the approach used can be briefly summarised. Rather than developing an abstract argument about the general character of power, the analysis is focused on a detailed examination of a specific social process. As a result, the actual incident is treated as being worth considering in its own right. Furthermore, theorising about the character of power is closely rooted to a social context and useful issues. By examining a specific process, the nationalisation of steel and its relationship to the mixed economy, it was possible to consider power in the relations within the class of capital, something which had not been studied before in anything other than an abstract manner.

The study of the various conflicts over steel, and the periods of co-operation between the industry and the government, reinforced the earlier arguments about the limited efficacy of the traditional approach and the 'A has power over B' formula. The consequences of the prevailing pluralists' assumptions about the character of government action have been mentioned. Methodological approaches which relied on the existence of clear and overt conflict for their assessment of the character of power would not have been relevant to the analysis of a large number of incidents considered in the central arguments. Over and above those considerations, the approach taken has shown the importance of considering the significance and meaning of outcomes, beyond using them to discover who prevailed in any conflict. In the preceding discussion of the nationalisation of steel, the key points often rested on what could be shown about the consequences of the outcome for the various parties involved in or relevant to the issue. As a result, the approach taken in emphasising the importance of the effects of actions on the interests of various parties opened up more for investigation than was treated by Dahl and his associates. The arguments developed here all show the importance of considering power in the context of a social process that is to be approached through an examination of the consequences of action, rather than as part of a limited exercise to identify the distribution of power, or who triumphed in a particular dispute.

Notes

Introduction

1. R. A. Dahl, 'The Concept of Power', *Behavioural Science*, 2 (1957), pp. 459–77; 'Power' in D. L. Shils (ed.), *International Encyclopedia of the Social Sciences* (New York, 1968), vol. 12; *Modern Political Analysis* (Princeton, 1970), ch. 3; *Who Governs? Democracy and Power in an American City* (New Haven and London, 1961).
2. P. Bachrach and M. S. Baratz, 'The Two Faces of Power', *American Political Science Review*, 56 (1962), pp. 947–52; 'Decisions and Non-decisions: An Analytical Framework', *American Political Science Review*, 57 (1963), pp. 641–51; *Power and Poverty: Theory and Practice* (New York, 1970).
3. N. W. Polsby, *Community Power and Political Theory* (New Haven and London, 1963).
4. A. M. Rose, *The Power Structure: Political Process in American Society* (New York, 1967).
5. C. Hewitt, 'Policy Making in Postwar Britain: a Nation-level Test of Elitist and Pluralist Hypotheses', *British Journal of Political Science*, 4:2 (1974); 'Elites and the Distribution of Power in British Society' in P. Stanworth and A. Giddens (eds), *Elites and Power in British Society* (Cambridge, 1974).
6. R. Miliband, *The State in Capitalist Society* (London, 1973; originally published 1969); G. W. Domhoff, *Who Rules America?* (New Jersey, 1971).
7. See the previously cited works of Dahl, Polsby and Rose and also R. A. Dahl, 'A Critique of the Ruling Elite Model', *American Political Science Review*, 52 (1958), pp. 463–9.
8. See the previously cited works of Miliband and Domhoff, also G. W. Domhoff, *The Higher Circles: The Governing Class in America* (New York, 1971), ch. 9, and J. Playford, 'The Myth of Pluralism', *Arena* (Melbourne), 15 (1968), pp. 34–47, reprinted in F. G. Castles, D. J. Murray and D. C. Potter (eds), *Decisions, Organizations and Society: Selected Readings* (Harmondsworth, 1971).
9. A. Glyn and B. Sutcliffe, *British Capitalism, Workers and the Profit Squeeze* (Harmondsworth, 1972), ch. 1.
10. G. Kolko, *The Politics of War: The World and the United States Foreign Policy, 1943–1945* (New York, 1970), pp. 224–63; G. D. H. Cole, *Great Britain in the Post-War World* (London, 1942), pp. 33ff.

11. For a brief account of what that Government did, see D. Coates, *The Labour Party and the Struggle for Socialism* (Cambridge, 1975), ch. 3.
12. For a brief discussion of the changes in the industry see G. Turner, *Business in Britain* (London, 1969), ch. 6.
13. G. W. Ross, *The Nationalisation of Steel: One Step Forward, Two Steps Back?* (London, 1965).
14. D. L. Burn, *The Steel Industry 1939–1959: A Study in Competition and Planning* (Cambridge, 1961).
15. B. S. Keeling and A. E. G. Wright, *The Development of the Modern British Steel Industry* (London, 1964).
16. J. Vaizey, *The History of British Steel* (London, 1974).

1 Problems in the analysis of power

1. From *Max Weber: Essays in Sociology*, translated, edited and with an introduction by H. H. Gerth and C. Wright Mills (London, 1948; seventh impression, 1970), p. 180.
2. M. Weber, *Economy and Society: An Outline of Interpretive Sociology*, edited by G. Roth and C. Wittich (New York, 1968) vol. 1, p. 52.
3. N. Poulantzas, *Political Power and Social Classes* (London, 1973; originally *Pouvoir politique et classes sociales*, Paris, 1968), p. 104.
4. S. Clegg, *Power, Rule, Domination: a critical and empirical understanding of power in sociological theory and organisational life* (London, 1975).
5. S. Lukes, *Power: A Radical View* (London and Basingstoke, 1974).
6. Poulantzas, *Political Power*, p. 104.
7. Lukes, *Power*, pp. 52ff.
8. N. W. Polsby, *Community Power and Political Theory* (New Haven, 1968); 'How to Study Community Power; The Pluralist Alternative', *Journal of Politics*, 22 (1960).
9. Dahl, 'The Concept of Power', p. 203. For variations see *Modern Political Analysis*, p. 17, and 'Power', p. 407.
10. Dahl, 'Power', p. 410.
11. Dahl, *Modern Political Analysis*, pp. 18–25; 'The Concept of Power', pp. 205ff; 'Power', p. 410.
12. Dahl, *Modern Political Analysis*, p. 17.
13. Dahl, 'A Critique of the Ruling Elite Model'; *Modern Political Analysis*, p. 27.
14. Dahl, *Modern Political Analysis*, pp. 28ff; 'Power', p. 409.
15. Bachrach and Baratz, 'The Two Faces of Power'.
16. ibid. pp. 947–9.
17. 'power is also exercised when A devotes his energies to creating or reinforcing social and political values and institutional practices that limit the scope of the political process to public consideration of only those issues which are comparatively innocuous to A', ibid. p. 948.
18. Bachrach and Baratz, 'Decisions and Non-decisions'.
19. The main focus of these criticisms was not Dahl but an older order of

theorising associated with H. D. Laswell and A. Kaplan's *Power and Society: A Framework for Political Inquiry* (London, 1952).

20. Bachrach and Baratz, 'Decisions and Non-decisions', p. 635.
23. ibid. p. 641.
22. ibid. p. 952.
23. Bachrach and Baratz, *Power and Poverty*.
24. M. A. Crenson, *The Un-Politics of Air Pollution: A Study of Non-Decision Making in the Cities* (Baltimore, 1971).
25. Lukes, *Power*, p. 34.
26. ibid. pp. 14, 20, 25, 34–5, 45.
27. W. E. Connolly, 'On "Interests" in Politics', *Politics and Society*, 2:4 (1972). I. D. Balbus, 'The Concept of Interest in Pluralist and Marxian Analysis', *Politics and Society*, 1 (1971).
28. Lukes, *Power*, p. 14.
29. ibid. p. 25, n.
30. ibid. p. 24.
31. ibid. p. 41.
32. T. Parsons, 'The Distribution of Power in American Society', in M. E. Olsen (ed.), *Power in Societies* (New York, 1967), p. 273; Rose, *The Power Structure*.
33. Rose, *The Power Structure*, p. 31.
34. Parsons, 'American Society', p. 274.
35. S. E. Finer, 'The Political Power of Private Capital', pts I and II, *Sociological Review*, 3:2 (1955) and 4:1 (1956).
36. Domhoff, *Who Rules America?*
37. Miliband, *The State in Capitalist Society*.

2 State theory and the question of class interests

1. Miliband, *The State in Capitalist Society*, pp. 46–7.
2. L. Althusser, 'Ideology and the State' in *Lenin and Philosophy and Other Essays* (London, 1971); N. Poulantzas, 'The Problem of the Capitalist State', *New Left Review*, 58 (1969), reprinted in R. Blackburn (ed.), *Ideology in Social Science: Readings in Critical Social Theory* (London, 1972), pp. 250–3 (all references to this article will be to this reprint); N. Poulantzas, *Fascism and Dictatorship: The Third International and the Problem of Fascism* (London, 1974), pt VII (1).
3. R. Miliband, 'Reply to Nicos Poulantzas', *New Left Review*, 59 (1970), reprinted in Blackburn, *Ideology in Social Science*, pp. 261–2. All references to the article will be to this reprint.
4. Miliband, *The State in Capitalist Society*, p. 47.
5. P. Mattick, *Marx and Keynes: The Limits of the Mixed Economy* (London, 1971); *Critique of Marcuse: One Dimensional Man in Class Society*
   See the account given of the implementation of the nationalisation
6. J. O'Connor, *The Fiscal Crisis of the State* (New York, 1973).
7. H. J. Laski, *The State in Theory and Practice* (London, 1935).
8. S. Aaronovitch, *Monopoly: A Study of British Monopoly Capitalism* (London, 1955); *The Ruling Class: A Study of British Finance Capital*

(London, 1961); J. Harvey and K. Hood, *The British State* (London, 1958).

9. J. Westergaard and H. Resler, *Class in a Capitalist Society: A Study of Contemporary Britain* (Harmondsworth, 1976).

10. Miliband, *The State in Capitalist Society*, pp. 132, 139, 145, 150. Normally when using the term in this sense, Miliband places it in quotation marks.

11. ibid. ch. 6.

12. ibid. pp. 139ff.

13. ibid. pp. 15ff.

14. It is published as a debate both in the previously cited collection edited by R. Blackburn, and in J. Urry and J. Wakeford (eds), *Power in Britain: Sociological Readings* (London, 1973). There were two other exchanges, R. Miliband, 'Poulantzas and the Capitalist State', *New Left Review*, 82 (1973) and N. Poulantzas, 'The Capitalist State: a Reply to Miliband and Laclau', *New Left Review*, 95 (1976). See also E. Laclau, 'The Specificity of the Political: The Poulantzas–Miliband Debate', *Economy and Society*, 4:1 (1975).

15. C. Offe, 'Structural Problems of the Capitalist State: Class Rule and the Political System. On the Selectiveness of Political Institutions', *German Political Studies*, 1 (1974).

16. Miliband, *The State in Capitalist Society*, p. 63.

17. Westergaard and Resler, *Class in a Capitalist Society*, p. 249.

18. Miliband, *The State in Capitalist Society*, p. 73; 'Reply', p. 258.

19. Miliband, *The State in Capitalist Society*, ch. 4.

20. Westergaard and Resler, *Class in a Capitalist Society*, pt III.

21. C. Offe and V. Ronge, 'Theses on the Theory of the State', *New German Critique*, 6 (1975), p. 140.

22. Westergaard and Resler, *Class in a Capitalist Society*, p. 248.

23. Poulantzas, *Political Power*.

24. ibid., compare the discussion in pt I with that in pt IV.

25. ibid. pt I.

26. ibid. p. 104.

27. ibid. pp. 105, 109ff.

28. ibid. p. 111.

29. ibid. p. 112.

30. ibid. pp. 109ff.

31. ibid. pts III and IV.

32. ibid. pp. 284ff, and pt IV, ch. 4.

33. ibid. p. 247.

34. Poulantzas, 'The Capitalist State'.

35. Poulantzas, 'The Problem of the Capitalist State', pp. 242, 245, 246.

36. N. Poulantzas, *Classes in Contemporary Capitalism* (London, 1976), pp. 97–8.

37. J. Holloway and S. Picciotto (eds), *State and Capital: A Marxist Debate* (London, 1978).

38. J. Holloway and S. Picciotto, 'Capital, Crisis and the State', *Capital and Class*, 2 (1977).

39. P. Connerton (ed.), *Critical Sociology* (Harmondsworth, 1976).
40. E. Altvater, 'Notes on Some Problems of State Interventionism', *Kapitalstate*, 1 (1973), 2 (1973); 'Some Problems of State Interventionism', in Holloway and Picciotto, *State and Capital*.
41. This may be because the translations in *Kapitalstate* and *State and Capital* omit some sections of the original article.
42. J. Holloway and S. Picciotto, 'Capital, the State and European Integration' (unpublished paper, circulated March 1976), pp. 7–9.
43. J. Hirsch, 'The State Apparatus and Social Reproduction: Elements of a Theory of the Bourgeois State', in Holloway and Picciotto, *State and Capital*.
44. ibid. pp. 57, 61.
45. ibid. pp. 61–2.
46. ibid. p. 63.
47. ibid. p. 66.
48. J. Holloway and S. Picciotto, 'Introduction: Towards a Materialist Theory of the State', *State and Capital*; 'Capital, Crisis and the State'; 'Capital, the State and European Integration'; 'A Note on the Theory of the State', *Bulletin of the Conference of Socialist Economists*, V:2 (1976).
49. Holloway and Picciotto, 'Capital, the State and European Integration', pp. 7–9; 'Capital, Crisis and the State', Section 1.
50. Holloway and Picciotto, 'Capital, the State and European Integration', pp. 9ff; 'Capital, Crisis and the State', pp. 79ff.
51. Holloway and Picciotto, 'Capital, the State and European Integration', p. 17.
52. ibid. p. 8; Holloway and Picciotto, 'Capital, Crisis and the State', pp. 79–85.
53. W. Muller and C. Neususs, 'The Illusion of State Socialism and the Contradiction between Wage Labour and Capital', *Telos*, 25 (1975), p. 9.
54. Hirsch, 'The State Apparatus', p. 65.
55. Holloway and Picciotto, 'A Note on the Theory of the State', p. 5.
56. Offe, 'Structural Problems of the Capitalist State'; Offe and Ronge, 'Theses on the Theory of the State'; C. Offe, 'The Theory of the Capitalist State and the Problem of Policy Formation', ch. 5 in L. N. Linberg, R. Alford, C. Crouch and C. Offe (eds), *Stress and Contradiction in Modern Capitalism: Public Policy and the Theory of the State* (Cambridge, Mass., 1975); 'Further Comments on Muller and Neususs', *Telos*, 25 (1975).
57. Offe, 'Structural Problems', p. 33.
58. Offe and Ronge, 'Theses on the Theory of the State'.
59. Offe, 'Structural Problems', pp. 36ff.
60. Offe, 'State and Policy Formation', p. 144.
61. Poulantzas, *Classes in Contemporary Capitalism*.
62. Connolly, 'On "Interests" in Politics'.
63. Balbus, 'The Concept of Interests in Pluralist and Marxian Analysis'.

3 The steel industry 1919–1945

1. D. L. Burn, *The Economic History of Steel Making, 1867–1939: A Study in Competition* (Cambridge, 1940), chs XIV–XVI; J. C. Carr and W. Taplin

(with the assistance of A. E. G. Wright), *History of the British Steel Industry* (Oxford, 1962), chs XXXI–XLVIII; Keeling and Wright, *The Development of the Modern British Steel Industry*. This study was commissioned by the British Iron and Steel Federation and gives an approximate view of developments as seen by them.

2. Vaizey, *History of British Steel*, ch. 1.
3. Burn, *Steel Making*, chs IV, V, X, XI, XIII. Carr and Taplin, *British Steel Industry*, pt III.
4. Committee on Commercial and Industrial Policy, *Final Report* (London, 1918), Cd. 9035 (1918), XIII, 239. In the text the committee is referred to as the Balfour Committee and the report as the Balfour Report.
5. *Report of the Departmental Committee Appointed by the Board of Trade to consider the Position of the Iron and Steel Trades After the War* (London, 1918), Cd. 9071 (1918), XVIII, 433. In the text the committee is referred to as the Scoby-Smith Committee and the report as the Scoby-Smith Report.
6. Burn, *Steel Making*, p. 370.
7. Scoby-Smith Report, p. 3.
8. ibid. pp. 14–15.
9. ibid. pp. 4–5, 19.
10. ibid. pp. 14–17.
11. ibid. p. 17.
12. ibid. p. 21.
13. ibid. p. 21.
14. Carr and Taplin, *British Steel Industry*, p. 344.
15. ibid. pp. 344–5.
16. Burn, *Steel Making*, ch. XIV.
17. Keeling and Wright, *Development*, p. 3.
18. Balfour Report, p. 26.
19. Carr and Taplin, *British Steel Industry*, p. 345.
20. Burn, *Steel Making*, p. 375–6.
21. Keeling and Wright, *Development*, p. 2.
22. R. Skidelsky, *Politicians and the Slump: The Labour Government of 1929–1931* (London, 1967), p. 151.
23. Sir Henry Clay, *Lord Norman* (London, 1957), ch. VIII; A. Boyle, *Montagu Norman: A Biography* (London, 1967).
24. Clay, *Lord Norman*, p. 323.
25. Carr and Taplin, *British Steel Industry*, pp. 440–5.
26. Clay, *Lord Norman*, pp. 345–6.
27. ibid. pp. 328–9.
28. Burn, *Steel Making*, pp. 437–8.
29. Keeling and Wright, *Development*, p. 4.
30. Clay, *Lord Norman*, pp. 323, 348, 354–5.
31. Skidelsky, *Politicians and the Slump*, p. 153; Boyle, *Montagu Norman*, pp. 207–9.
32. Burn, *Steel Making*, pp. 441–2.
33. ibid.
34. Clay, *Lord Norman*, p. 358.

35. Burn, *Steel Making*, ch. XVI; Carr and Taplin, *British Steel Industry*, ch. XLIII.
36. Keeling and Wright, *Development*, p. 5.
37. Burn, *Steel Making*, pp. 426ff.
38. ibid. pp. 436–8.
39. ibid. p. 448.
40. ibid. pp. 449–50.
41. Carr and Taplin, *British Steel Industry*, p. 484.
42. Burn, *Steel Making*, p. 451; Keeling and Wright, *Development*, p. 9.
43. Clay, *Lord Norman*, pp. 325, 355.
44. Carr and Taplin, *British Steel Industry*, p. 484.
45. ibid. p. 560; Burn, *Steel Making*, pp. 470ff.
46. Keeling and Wright, *Development*, p. 2; Carr and Taplin, *British Steel Industry*, pp. 387–8.
47. Burn, *Steel Making*, p. 499.
48. ibid. pp. 488ff and 496–7.
49. Keeling and Wright, *Development*, p. 17.
50. Burn, *Steel Making*, p. 475.
51. Keeling and Wright, *Development*, p. 20.
52. Burn, *Steel Making*, pp. 511ff.
53. E. Wilkinson, *The Town That Was Murdered: The Life-Story of Jarrow* (London, 1939).
54. Burn, *Steel Making*, pp. 460–3.
55. Clay, *Lord Norman*, pp. 347–9.
56. IDAC, *Report on the Present Position and Future Development of the Iron and Steel Industry* (London, 1937), Cmd. 5507.
57. ibid. p. 12.
58. Burn, *Steel Making*, pp. 470–1.
59. ibid. p. 458.
60. ibid. pp. 511–12.
61. Iron and Steel Trades Confederation, *What is Wrong with the British Steel Industry?* (London, 1931).
62. Burn, *Steel Industry*, pp. 114–15.
63. ibid.
64. Trades Union Congress, *Annual Report* (1934), pp. 189–205.
65. Labour Party, *For Socialism and Peace* (London, 1934), p. 17.
66. 'Ingot', *The Socialisation of Iron and Steel* (London, 1936).
67. H. Dalton, *Practical Socialism for Britain* (London, 1935); D. Jay, *The Socialist Case* (London, 1938); *The Nation's Wealth at the Nation's Service* (London, no date given, but circa 1938).
68. G. D. H. Cole, *Plan for Democratic Britain* (London, 1939), pp. 163ff.
69. J. Hurstfield, *The Control of Raw Materials* (London, 1953), ch. 4. His discussion is also useful in that it uses the iron and steel industry as an example of the way in which the structure of wartime administration grew out of government/industry relations in the 1930s.
70. ibid. p. 68.
71. Vaizey, *History of British Steel*, p. 93.
72. Hurstfield, *Control of Raw Materials*, p. 69.

73. ibid. Duncan Burn argues that the Control was not simply the Federation drafted for government service. Though the point is accurate it should not detract from the fact of the close relationship between the industry and the Control. Burn, *Steel Industry*, p. 5, n.4. It should be noted that Burn served as a member of the Control.
74. Vaizey, *History of British Steel*, p. 96.
75. Keeling and Wright, *Development*, pp. 32–7.
76. *Report from the Committee of Public Accounts, 1940–1941* (105) ii.I (London, 1941), p. 4.
77. Hurstfield, *Control of Raw Materials*, pp. 394–6.
78. ibid. p. 261.
79. ibid. pp. 312–13.
80. ibid. p. 335.
81. ibid. pp. 335, 342.
82. ibid. p. 345; W. Ashworth, *Contracts and Finance* (London, 1953), p. 176.
83. For details of the wartime arrangements see Ashworth, *Contracts and Finance*, pp. 164–76; *Vote of Credit Appropriation Account, 1941, Report of the Comptroller and Auditor General* (London, 1943), paras 49, 50; *Fourteenth Report from the Select Committee on National Expenditure*, Session 1942–3, 'War Production: Methods of Settling Prices for War Stores' (London, 1943), paras 183–5.
84. Hurstfield, *Control of Raw Materials*, pp. 366ff.
85. ibid. p. 377.
86. For the clearest account of how the profit fixing mechanism worked see Ashworth, *Contracts and Finance*, pp. 164–5.
87. *Fourteenth Report of the Select Committee on National Expenditure*, para. 194; *Report from the Committee of Public Accounts* (London, 1941), p. xxv; *Report from the Committee of Public Accounts* (London, 1943), para. 55.
88. Keeling and Wright, *Development*, p. 11.
89. *Fourteenth Report of the Select Committee on National Expenditure*, pp. 68, 75.
90. Ashworth, *Contracts and Finance*, p. 166.
91. Hurstfield, *Control of Raw Materials*, p. 372.
92. Ashworth, *Contracts and Finance*, p. 167.
93. *Report from the Committee of Public Accounts, 1943*, paras 55–6; *Vote of Credit Appropriation Account, 1941*, para. 47 and *Vote of Credit Appropriation Account, 1942*, para. 52, *Reports of the Comptroller and Auditor General* (London, 1941 and 1942).
94. Ashworth, *Contracts and Finance*, pp. 175–6.
95. For a discussion of the role of banks see P. M. Sweezy, *The Theory of Capitalist Development: Principles of Marxian Political Economy* (New York and London, 1968), pp. 262–9.

4 The first nationalisation of steel: conflicting proposals

1. R. Miliband, *Parliamentary Socialism* (second edition, London, 1973),

ch. IX; D. Coates, *The Labour Party and the Struggle for Socialism* (Cambridge, 1975), ch. 3.

2. R. A. Brady, *Crisis in Britain: Plans and Achievements of the Labour Government* (Berkeley, 1950).
3. A. A. Rogow (with the assistance of P. Shore), *The Labour Government and British Industry, 1945–1951* (Oxford, 1955).
4. G. D. H. Cole, *Principles of Economic Planning* (London, 1935) and the previously cited works of Dalton and Jay.
5. E. Eldon Barry, *Nationalisation in British Politics: The Historical Background* (London, 1965).
6. W. A. Robson, *Nationalised Industry and Public Ownership* (London, 1960), ch. 11.
7. See the account given of the implementation of the nationalisation programme in Brady, *Crisis in Britain*.
8. Labour Party, *Let Us Face the Future* (London, 1945), p. 5.
9. ibid. pp. 5–7.
10. Cole, *Plan for Democratic Britain*, ch. XX.
11. J. Hughes, 'Nationalisation and the Private Sector', in Urry and Wakeford (eds), *Power in Britain*.
12. H. Morrison, *Socialisation and Transport: The Organisation of Socialised Industries with particular reference to the London Passenger Transport Bill* (London, 1933); L. Tivey, *Nationalisation in British Industry* (revised edition, London, 1973), pp. 35ff.
13. D. N. Chester, 'Organisation of the Nationalized Industries', *The Political Quarterly*, XXI:2 (1950).
14. Ross, *Nationalisation of Steel*, p. 30.
15. Burn, *Steel Industry*, p. 111. See also Ross, *Nationalisation of Steel*, p. 30.
16. *Report by the British Iron and Steel Federation and the Joint Iron Council to the Minister of Supply* (London, 1946), Cmd. 6811.
17. Ross, *Nationalisation of Steel*, pp. 36–40.
18. ibid. p. 42.
19. Keeling and Wright, *Development*, pp. 160–1.
20. Cited in Ross, *Nationalisation of Steel*, p. 48.
21. Keeling and Wright, *Development*, p. 161.
22. Ross, *Nationalisation of Steel*, pp. 55–8.
23. Burn, *Steel Industry*, ch. V.
24. Keeling and Wright, *Development*, pp. 168–71; Ross, *Nationalisation of Steel*, pp. 66–8.
25. Ross, *Nationalisation of Steel*, p. 66.
26. Keeling and Wright, *Development*, p. 164.
27. For both a summary of the Act and a description of its passage through Parliament see W. Gumbel and K. Potter, *The Iron and Steel Act, 1949* (London, 1951).
28. Ross, *Nationalisation of Steel*, pp. 79–83; Keeling and Wright, *Development*, p. 172.
29. C. Wilson, *A Man and his Times: A Memoir of Sir Ellis Hunter* (Middlesborough, 1962), ch. 2.

30. H. H. Wilson, 'Techniques of Pressure – Anti-nationalization Propaganda in Britain', *Public Opinion Quarterly*, 15 (Summer, 1951).
31. Ross, *Nationalisation of Steel*, pp. 79–83.
32. ibid. pp. 110–16.
33. ibid. pp. 127–8.
34. ibid. pp. 126–32, 136–44; Burn, *Steel Industry*, p. 317.
35. Burn, *Steel Industry*, p. 313.
36. Ross, *Nationalisation of Steel*, p. 138.
37. Burn, *Steel Industry*, p. 317; Keeling and Wright, *Development*, p. 176.
38. E. Bond, *The Facts About Steel* (London, no date but circa 1949), p. 12.
39. Sir Ellis Hunter, *A Stronger Board* (London, 1949); Wilson, *A Man and his Times*, pp. 27–35.
40. BISF, *Planning and Competition in the Industry* (London, 1949); *Progress of the Steel Development Plan* (London, 1949).
41. BISF, *Iron and Steel Bill: Arguments For and Against* (London, circa 1949), pp. 1–8.
42. Bond, *Facts About Steel*, p. 13.
43. BISF, *Iron and Steel Bill*, p. 8.
44. BISF, *Iron and Steel Bill*, pp. 9–10.
45. Bond, *Facts About Steel*, pp. 12–13; BISF, *Iron and Steel Bill: Discussion in Committee* (London, circa 1949), p. 3.
46. BISF, *The Policy for Steel* (London, 1953), p. 32; Bond, *Facts About Steel*, pp. 10–11.
47. BISF, 'Organisation in the Steel Industry', *Monthly Statistical Bulletin*, 23:10 (1948), p. 5; Bond, *Facts About Steel*, p. 11.
48. The critics of the industry were not, on the whole, as crude as the Federation described them. They did believe that the organisation of the steel industry was monopolistic and that the form of centralisation proved this. For their criticisms see G. D. H. Cole, *Why Nationalise Steel?* (New Statesman and Nation, revised edition, 1948), p. 29; H. Owen, *Steel: The Facts about Monopoly and Nationalisation* (London, 1946), chs 4 and 5, and W. Fienberg and R. Evely, *Steel is Power: The Case for Nationalisation* (London, 1948) ch. V and VI, p. 114.
49. BISF, *Policy for Steel*, p. 6.
50. G. D. H. Cole, cited by Bond, *Facts About Steel*, p. 29.
51. BISF, 'Organisation in the Steel Industry', p. 2.
52. ibid. p. 6.
53. BISF, 'Iron and Steel Prices', *MSB* 23:6 (1948).
54. BISF, 'Organisation in the Steel Industry', p. 2.
55. Burn, *Steel Industry*, p. 201.
56. BISF, 'Organisation in the Steel Industry', p. 2.
57. Bond, *Facts About Steel*, ch. 10.
58. Burn, *Steel Industry*, p. 546.
59. BISF, 'Organisation in the Steel Industry', pp. 4–7; *Planning and Competition in the Industry*.
60. BISF, 'Organisation in the Steel Industry', pp. 2–3.
61. ibid. pp. 4–7.
62. ibid. p. 5.

63. BISF, 'Iron and Steel Prices', p. 3.
64. Burn, *Steel Industry*, p. 176.
65. BISF, *Planning and Competition in the Industry*, p. 4.
66. G. D. H. Cole, cited in Bond, *Facts About Steel*, pp. 26–7.
67. *Reports by the British Iron and Steel Federation and the Joint Iron Council to the Ministry of Supply*, Cmd. 6811.
68. Burn, *Steel Industry*, p. 173.
69. BISF, *Planning and Competition in the Industry*, p. 5.
70. BISF, 'Organisation in the Steel Industry', p. 7.
71. BISF, *Progress of the Steel Development Plan* (London, 1949). R. M. Shone, 'The Iron and Steel Development Plan: Some Statistical Considerations', *Journal of the Royal Statistical Society*, pt IV (1947).
72. BISF, 'Steel's Record Performance', *MSB*, 23:4 (1948).
73. BISF, 'Capital Expenditure and the Steel Industry', *MSB*, 22:12 (1947); 'Steel Making Capacity', *MSB*, 23:9 (1948).
74. BISF, 'General Summary', *MSB*, 21:5 (1946).
75. BISF, *Annual Report*, 1951.
76. BISF, 'Steel's Record Performance', p. 2.
77. BISF, 'Progress of the Development Plan', *MSB*, 22:5 (1947), p. 3.
78. ibid. p. 2; BISF, 'Steel Making Capacity', p. 6.
79. ibid. p. 6.
80. ibid. pp. 5–6.
81. BISF, 'Organisation in the Steel Industry', p. 8.
82. BISF, *Planning and Competition in the Industry*, p. 7.
83. BISF, 'Organisation in the Steel Industry', p. 7.
84. ibid. p. 8.
85. See the discussion in Brady, *Crisis in Britain* and Rogow, *The Labour Government and British Industry, 1945–1951*.
86. Bond, *Facts About Steel*, pp. 13, 18, 37; BISF, *Planning and Competition in the Industry*, p. 12.
87. Cited in many places, see BISF, 'Organisation in the Steel Industry', p. 7.
88. Burn, *Steel Industry*, pp. 191–2.
89. ibid. ch. V.
90. Hunter, *A Stronger Board*.
91. BISF, *The Iron and Steel Bill*.
92. 'After all, the major part of British industry will remain under private enterprise for many years to come and the socialists' main problem must, therefore, be how to secure the most effective combination of public control with private enterprise.' Bond, *Facts About Steel*, p. 12.
93. The terminology here comes from J. Weinstein, *The Corporate Ideal in the Liberal State: 1900–1918* (Boston, 1968).
94. BISF, 'The Iron and Steel Bill: Likely Effects on Organisation', *MSB*, 23:11 (1948), p. 7.
95. G. Hodgson, 'The Steel Debates' in M. Sissons and P. French (ed.), *Age of Austerity* (London, 1963).
96. See Fienberg and Evely, *Steel is Power*, Owen, *Steel*, and Cole, *Why Nationalise Steel?*.
97. Owen, *Steel*, pp. 57–79.

98. Fienberg and Evely, Steel is Power, p. 107.
99. Owen, Steel, pp. 108–13.
100. ibid. ch. 4; Fienberg and Evely, Steel is Power, chs 5, 6, 11; Cole, Why Nationalise Steel?, p. 29.
101. Owen, Steel, p. 113.
102. Cole, Why Nationalise Steel?, p. 22.
103. Owen, Steel, p. 83.
104. Fienberg and Evely, Steel is Power, pp. 9–16.
105. ibid. p. 114.
106. Cole, Why Nationalise Steel?, pp. 4–5.
107. ibid. p. 39.
108. Gumbel and Potter, Iron and Steel Act, p. 9.
109. ibid. pp. 16, 17.
110. Cole, Why Nationalise Steel?, pp. 37–9.
111. Gumbel and Potter, Iron and Steel Act, p. 9.
112. D. N. Chester, 'Organisation of the Nationalised Industries'.
113. Ross, Nationalisation of Steel, pp. 90–2.
114. Keeling and Wright, Development, p. 176.
115. ibid. pp. 175–6.

5　Steel nationalised and the role of power

1. Brady, Crisis in Britain.
2. Miliband, Parliamentary Socialism, pp. 301, 311.
3. Coates, The Labour Party and the Struggle for Socialism, pp. 69–71.
4. Finer, 'The Political Power of Private Capital', pts I and II.
5. F. Castles 'Business and Government: A Typology of Pressure Group Activity', Political Studies, XVII:2 (1969), pp. 160–76.
6. Finer, 'Political Power of Private Capital', pt I, p. 291.
7. ibid. pt II, p. 15.
8. ibid. p. 17.
9. Castles, 'Business and Government', p. 175.
10. Hewitt, 'Policy Making in Postwar Britain'; 'Elites and the Distribution of Power'.
11. Hewitt, 'Policy Making in Postwar Britain', p. 213; 'Elites and the Distribution of Power', p. 60.
12. Rogow (with Shore), Labour Government and British Industry.
13. Ross, Nationalisation of Steel, p. 88.
14. Keeling and Wright, Development, p. 164.
15. ibid. pp. 161, 164.
16. ibid. pp. 169–71.
17. Wilson, A Man and his Times, p. 24.
18. See the accounts of the incident in H. Morrison, An Autobiography (London, 1960) and H. Dalton, High Tide and After: Memoirs 1945–1960 (London, 1962).
19. Wilson, A Man and his Times, pp. 24ff.
20. See Finer's discussion of the Federation's position in 'Political Power of Private Capital', pp. 17–18.

21. BISF, *Iron and Steel Bill: Discussion in Committee*, p. 3.
22. Keeling and Wright, *Development*, p. 160.
23. ibid. pp. 174ff.
24. Hodgson, 'The Steel Debates'.
25. BISF, 'Steel's Record Performance', *MSB*, 23:4 (1948); 'That "Ten Percent More"', *MSB*, 23:2 (1948).

6 The denationalisation of steel

1. 'Steel Workers Opposed to Government Plan; Grave Concern over Denationalisation', *The Times*, 21 November 1951, p. 6; 'Private Ownership of Steel; TUC. Views on Letter from Ministry', *The Times*, 13 December 1951, p. 6; 'Iron and Steel', *The Times*, 20 December 1951, p. 4; 'Unions Concern at Steel Confusion', *The Times*, 27 December 1951, p. 4.
2. D. Burn, *Steel Industry*, p. 537 n.1.
3. Iron and Steel Corporation of Great Britain, *Report and Statement of Accounts for period ended 30 September 1951*, H.C. 294 (London, 1952), p. 3, para. 13; 'Challenge on Steel Plans', *The Times*, 13 November 1951, p. 4.
4. Wilson, *A Man and his Times*, p. 33.
5. Enoch Powell argues that the action of backbench Conservatives was the main factor that forced a reluctant Cabinet to denationalise, see his article in *The Spectator*, March 1959.
6. 'Who Buys Steel Shares', *Economist*, 9 February 1952, pp. 353–4.
7. 'Can Steel be Supervised', *Economist*, 23 February 1952, pp. 478–80.
8. 'Challenge on Steel Plans', *The Times*.
9. Cmd. 8619; 'The Iron and Steel White Paper', *The Times*, 29 July 1952, p. 9.
10. 'Denationalisation; The Problem and the Pitfalls of Transfer', *The Times*, 28 January 1952, p. 5.
11. 'Steel in Suspense', *The Times*, 13 November 1951, p. 5.
12. 'Iron and Steel White Paper', *The Times*.
13. *Iron and Steel Act, 1953*, clause 19.
14. 'Government Policy for Steel', *The Times*, 24 October 1952, p. 3.
15. *Iron and Steel Act, 1953*, pt III.
16. ibid. clause 18.
17. ibid. clause 20.
18. ibid. clause 19 especially subsection (2).
19. ibid. clause 19(7).
20. ibid. clause 20.
21. Burn, *Steel Industry*, pp. 539–47. My account is based on Burn's work but also draws on the information provided by Keeling and Wright, *Development*, pp. 178–80 and Vaizey, *History of British Steel*, pp. 153–6. I found such arguments invaluable in unravelling the details provided in the *Annual Statement of Accounts* of the Iron and Steel Holding and Realisation Agency, 1953–67.
22. Burn, *Steel Industry*, p. 539.
23. Vaizey, *History of British Steel*, pp. 153, 156.

24. ibid. p. 156.
25. Keeling and Wright, *Development*, pp. 179–80.
26. ibid. p. 179.
27. Burn, *Steel Industry*, p. 451.
28. ibid.
29. Vaizey, *History of British Steel*, p. 156.
30. Burn, *Steel Industry*, p. 542, particularly table 71 and the argument around it.
31. ibid. p. 541.
32. ISHRA, *Report and Statement of Accounts – 1959–64*.
33. ISHRA, *Report and Statement of Accounts for the period 1st October, 1962 to 30th September, 1963*, H.C. 108 (London, 1964).
34. Burn, *Steel Industry*, pp. 544–5.
35. Vaizey, *History of British Steel*, p. 156.
36. Burn, *Steel Industry*, p. 544.
37. *Iron and Steel Act, 1953*, pt II.
38. Wilson, *A Man and his Times*, p. 33.
39. *Iron and Steel Act, 1953*, clause 29.
40. ibid. appendix three.
41. ibid. clause 2.
42. ibid. clause 3.
43. 'The Steel Transfer', *The Times*, 29 July 1952, p. 7.
44. *Iron and Steel Act, 1953*, clause 6(3) and (4).
45. ibid. clause 5(4).
46. ibid. clauses 8, 9 and 10.
47. 'The Steel Transfer', *The Times*.
48. Hunter, *A Stronger Board*.
49. Burn, *Steel Industry*, p. 539.
50. An adequate refutation of these arguments is to be found in Miliband, *The State in Capitalist Society*, ch. 2, and Westergaard and Resler, *Class in a Capitalist Society*, pt III, ch. 2.
51. Burn, *Steel Industry*, pp. 319–20.
52. For an interesting discussion of the Conservatives' attitude to nationalisation and denationalisation, see N. Harris, *Competition and the Corporate Society: British Conservatives, the State and Industry, 1945–1964* (London, 1973), chs 6, 12.
53. E. Schneker, 'Nationalisation and Denationalisation of Motor Carriers in Great Britain', *Land Economics*, 39:3 (August 1963), pp. 219–30; J. J. Richardson, 'The Administration of Denationalisation: The Case of Road Haulage', *Public Administration*, 49:4 (1971), pp. 385–402.
54. For a more extensive account of the Conservative Party's accommodation of its defence of private ownership and the increased necessity for state action, see Harris, *Competition and the Corporate Society*.

7 Power in the period of public supervision

1. Rose, *The Power Structure*, pp. 98ff.
2. ibid. p. 125.

3. C. Wilcox and W. G. Shepherd, *Public Policies Toward Business*, fifth edition (Chicago, 1975) pt IV.
4. G. Kolko, *Railroads and Regulation 1877–1916* (Princeton, 1965); Weinstein, *The Corporate Ideal in the Liberal State*.
5. Iron and Steel Board, *Annual Report, 13 July 1953 to 31 December 1954*, H.C.138 (London, 1955), ch. 3.
6. ISB, *Development in the Iron and Steel Industry, Special Report, 1957*, H.C.214 (London, 1957). Others were issued in 1961 and 1964.
7. ibid. p. 3.
8. ibid. ch. 11.
9. ISB, *Annual Report*, 1954, p. 12.
10. ibid. ch. 3.
11. ISB, *Annual Report*, 1957, H.C.246 (London, 1958), p. 22.
12. ibid.
13. ISB, *Development of the Iron and Steel Industry, 1953–1958*, H.C.49 (London, 1955).
14. ISB, *Annual Report*, 1953–54, p. 11.
15. ibid.
16. BISF, *Annual Report, 1960* (London, 1961), p. 5.
17. BISF, *The British Iron and Steel Federation: An Account of the Central Organisation in the Steel Industry* (London, 1958), p. 11.
18. ibid. p. 18.
19. BISF, *Annual Report, 1952* (London, 1953), p. 34. BISF, *Annual Report, 1960* (London, 1961), p. 4.
20. BISF, *Annual Report, 1958* (London, 1959), President's address.
21. Burn, *Steel Industry*, pp. 657ff.
22. ibid. pp. 658–9.
23. Keeling and Wright, *Development*, chs IV and V.
24. ibid. pp. 188–9.
25. 'Steel: Whose Responsibility?', *Economist*, 25 July 1959, p. 236.
26. 'Rise in Output of Steel – Productivity Teams' Recommendations', *The Times*, 30 June 1952, p. 4.
27. Burn, *Steel Industry*, pp. 661ff.
28. 'Steel: Whose Responsibility?', *Economist*.
29. *Development in the Iron and Steel Industry, Special Report, 1961*, H.C.164 (London, 1961), p. 4.
30. R. Pryke, *Why Steel?*, Fabian Research Series, No. 248 (1965), pp. 15ff.
31. See ISB, *Annual Reports*, 1962–6.
32. ISB, *Annual Report*, 1961, p. 28.
33. ISB, *Annual Report*, 1961, p. 2.
34. J. Hughes, *Plan for Steel Re-Nationalisation*, Fabian Research Series, No. 198 (1958), pp. 5–6.
35. 'Technical Advance: A Check List', *Steel Review*, 39 (1965), pp. 6–8.
36. See tables 30–34 in ISB, *Special Development Report, 1957*, pp. 68–70.
37. ISB, *Special Development Report, 1964*, p. 62.
38. 'Big Enough?', *Steel Review*, 44 (1966), pp. 4–7.
39. 'Automation in the U.K. Steel Industry', *Steel Review*, 32 (1963), pp. 34–40. 'At the Technological Frontiers', *Steel Review*, 35 (1964), pp. 24–9.

40. ibid. Notice how often Richard Thomas and Baldwins is cited as evidence of technological development in steel.
41. ISB, *Annual Report, 1962*, pp. 2, 4.
42. 'Rough Seas Ahead', *Steel Review*, 41 (1966), pp. 2–5.
43. ibid. p. 3.
44. ISB, *Annual Report, 1963*, pp. 3ff.
45. ISB, *Annual Report, 1965*, p. 2.
46. Burn, *Steel Industry*, pp. 639ff.
47. ibid. pp. 645–6.
48. 'Flaws in the Pattern', *Economist*, 14 February 1959, pp. 620–2.
49. 'Steel Companies: Development Finance', *Economist*, 13 February 1960, p. 648.
50. Vaizey, *History of British Steel*, p. 175.
51. 'Flaws in the Pattern', *Economist*.
52. Keeling and Wright, *Development*, pp. 192–3.
53. ISB, *Annual Report, 1966*.
54. The adequacy of this capacity is disputed by both Pryke and Hughes.
55. ISB, *Annual Report, 1953–4*, ch. 4.
56. ibid. pp. 18–19.
57. ibid. p. 15.
58. ibid. p. 20.
59. ISB, *Annual Report, 1955*, p. 26.
60. For an example of a standard price determination, see ISB, *Annual Report, 1956*, ch. 4.
61. ISB, *Annual Report, 1958*, ch. 4.
62. ISB, *Annual Report, 1960*, p. 2, ch. 4.
63. ISB, *Annual Report, 1961*, p. 22.
64. ISB, *Annual Report, 1956*, ch. 4.
65. ISB, *Annual Report, 1957*, p. 24.
66. ibid. p. 25.
67. 'Steel Board Below Capacity', *Economist*, 4 January 1958, pp. 51–2.
68. BISF, *Annual Report, 1962*, p. 30.
69. ISB, *Annual Report, 1961*, ch. 4.
70. ISB, *Annual Report, 1961*, p. 22 (3.5% rise in 1961); ISB, *Annual Report, 1965*, p. 3. (4% rise on top of interim rise of 1% early in 1965).
71. 'Financing Further Expansion', *Steel Review*, 19 (1960), pp. 2–3; 'In Tune With the Times: Steel Development Today', *Steel Review*, 39 (1964), pp. 9–15.
72. ISB, *Annual Report, 1956*, p. 26.
73. Burn, *Steel Industry*, pp. 232ff. Table 22 argues that profit as a percentage of turnover after tax was, for the years from 1948 to 1954, 6.7%, 7.2%, 8%, 5.8%, 4.9%, 5.6%, 6.0%. Using table 23 for the period 1951–56, we get 5.5%, 6.6%, 4.9%, 4.9%, 6.4%, 6.4%. Using table 39 for the earnings of ten largest steel firms we get, for the period 1953–58, 6.6%, 7.0%, 7.9%, 6.4%, 6.0%, 5.1%.
74. British Steel Corporation, *Report on Organisation, 1967*, Cmnd. 3362 (London, 1967), p. 18, gives the figure for 1958 as 13.5%; Vaizey, *History*

of British Steel, p. 178, gives the figure for 1958 as 17.3% and for 1960 as 18.8%; D. Bailey cites the *Benson Report* as giving a figure of 15–20%; 'Forward Projections', *Economist*, 3 December 1960, p. 1058, cites a set of figures which indicate that steel company profits averaged between 8.3% and 25.9% for the years 1954–9.

75. BSC, 3.7% for 1966; Bailey, 4.3% for 1963 and 2.0% for 1967; Vaizey, 4.8% for 1963 and 1.9% for 1967.
76. 'Rough Seas Ahead', *Steel Review*, p. 5.
77. 'Steel Trade at Mid-Year', *Steel Review*, 39 (1965), p. 6.
78. ISB, *Annual Report, 1965*.
79. ISB, *Annual Report, 1956*, p. 26; ISB, *Special Report, 1957*, p. 73; 'Steel Pricing: A Lesson Retaught', *Steel Review*, 34 (1964), pp. 6–9.
80. Vaizey, *History of British Steel*, p. 178.
81. Keeling and Wright, *Development*, p. 129, table 26.
82. Vaizey, *History of British Steel*, p. 159.
83. 'British Steel in 1960', *Steel Review*, 17 (1960), p. 4; Vaizey, *History of British Steel*, p. 178.
84. D. L. Burn, 'Steel', ch. 7 of D. L. Burn (ed.), *The Structure of British Industry: A Symposium* (Cambridge, 1958), p. 291; 'Funding Steel', *Economist*, 17 December 1960, pp. 1251–2.
85. See BISF, *Annual Reports*, 1955, 1959 and 1964.
86. 'Funding Steel', *Economist*.
87. ISB, *Annual Report, 1966*.
88. Vaizey, *History of British Steel*, pp. 173–5.
89. BSC, *Report on Organisation*, p. 19.
90. Keeling and Wright, *Development*, pp. 187–8.
91. 'Stirring Times', *Steel Review* 37 (1965), pp. 2–4.
92. ISB, *Annual Report, 1964*, p. 27.
93. ibid. pp. 25ff.
94. ISB, *Annual Report, 1961*, p. 22.
95. ISB, *Annual Report, 1962*, pp. 22–3.
96. ISB, *Annual Report, 1965*, p. 3.
97. 'Steel's Maverick', *Economist*, 9 April 1966, pp. 163–4.
98. Shone subsequently became the first head of the National Economic Development Council. It is interesting to note that the steel industry was one of the first to co-operate with NEDC and the drawing up of the ill-fated National Plan.

8 The renationalisation of steel

1. Miliband, *Parliamentary Socialism*, ch. X; Coates, *The Labour Party*, ch. 4; S. Haseler, *The Gaitskellites* (London, 1969).
2. C. A. R. Crosland, *The Future of Socialism* (London, 1956).
3. H. Gaitskell, *Socialism and Nationalisation*, Fabian Tract, No. 300 (London, 1956); H. Gaitskell, 'The Economic Aims of the Labour Party', *Political Quarterly*, XXIV:1–4 (1953).
4. Labour Party, *Industry and Society: Labour's Policy on Future Public Ownership* (London, 1957).

5. For instance there was a running dispute about the meaning of the electoral results for various districts and members from the Sheffield area.
6. See both the Steel Nationalisation Debate, *Hansard*, vol. 711, cols. 1571–1700 (6 May 1965) and the Second Reading Debate, *Hansard*, vol. 732, cols. 1215–1364 (25 July 1965).
7. Mr Grimmond, *Hansard*, vol. 701, col. 253 (9 November 1964).
8. See their speeches in the Debate on the Iron and Steel Industry, *Hansard*, vol. 701, cols. 663–793 and the Steel Nationalisation Debate, *Hansard*, vol. 711, cols. 1571–1700.
9. As he stated in the Second Reading Debate on the Iron and Steel Bill, *Hansard*, vol. 732, col. 1246. 'I begged and implored the steel industry to come forward with proposals for something less than 100% ownership on which the Government could compromise. It offered to make concessions on almost every point but it would not give way as to one single share. . . . It was not until after the General Election that the steel industry was willing to consider the Government having a half share in the industry.'
10. Mr G. Strauss, *Hansard*, vol. 711, cols. 1603ff. and vol. 732, cols. 1257ff.
11. H. Wilson, *The Labour Government, 1964–70: A Personal Record* (Harmondsworth, 1974), pp. 56, 142–5, 185, 231–2, 289.
12. *Steel Nationalisation*, Cmnd. 2651 (London, 1965).
13. ibid. pp. 36–7.
14. ibid. clauses 25 and 26.
15. ibid. clauses 41ff.
16. M. Foot's speech, *Hansard*, vol. 720, cols. 202ff (10 November 1965).
17. Hughes, *Plan for Steel Re-Nationalisation* and Pryke, *Why Steel?*
18. See the speech by Francis Lee, Minister for Power, *Hansard*, vol. 701, cols. 1336ff.
19. R. Marsh, Minister for Power, *Hansard*, vol. 732, cols. 1223ff.
20. The title of one of the Federation's anti-nationalisation tracts.
21. Marsh, col. 1226.
22. ISB, *Annual Report*, 1960–6.
23. Cmnd. 2651, clause 10.
24. Lee, col. 686; R. Marsh, *Hansard*, vol. 732, col. 1227.
25. F. Lee, *Hansard*, vol. 732, cols. 1575–1577.
26. Cmnd. 2651, para 12.
27. F. Lee, *Hansard*, vol. 701, col. 677.
28. ibid. col. 679.
29. Labour Party, *Industry and Society*.
30. Cmnd. 2651, para. 11.
31. Cmnd. 2651, para. 15.
32. Mr McLeod, *Hansard*, vol. 701, cols. 633ff, and Mr Barber, *Hansard*, vol. 732, cols. 1255–1256.
33. Barber, cols. 1253–54.
34. Mr Sandys, *Hansard*, vol. 732, cols. 1265ff.
35. Sir W. Robson Brown, *Hansard*, vol. 732, col. 1285 and Sir Keith Joseph, cols. 1336ff.

36. 'Steel Nationalisation: The Importance of Being Controlled', *Economist*, 10 December 1966, pp. 1164–65.
37. BISF, *Annual Report, 1958* (1959).
38. E. Senior's comments in D. L. Burn, *The Future of Steel*, Institute of Economic Affairs, Occasional Paper, No. 6 (London, 1965).
39. 'Steel and the Nation', *Steel Review*, 33 (1964), pp. 2–3.
40. 'Leave Well Enough Alone', *Steel Review*, 34 (1964), pp. 2–3.
41. 'Why and How', *Steel Review*, 35 (1964), pp. 2–3.
42. 'At the Technological Frontiers', *Steel Review*, 38 (1964), pp. 24–9, and 'Technical Advance', *Steel Review*, 39 (1965), pp. 6–8.
43. 'Too Much Politics', *Steel Review*, 39 (1965), pp. 2–4.
44. 'Statement to Company Chairmen of the 12 Companies recommended for Nationalisation in the Steel White Paper', *Steel Review*, 39 (1965), p. 4.
45. 'Piling it on', *Steel Review*, 44 (1966), pp. 2–3.
46. 'Organisation, Rationalisation, Pricing', *Steel Review*, 42 (1966), pp. 2–5; 'Benson 1 . . . and after', *Steel Review*, 44 (1966), p. 8.
47. *Hansard*, vol. 732, cols. 1215–1364.
48. 'Heading Down', *Steel Review*, 45 (1967), pp. 2–3.
49. R. Marsh, *Hansard*, vol. 739, col. 1798.
50. BISF, *Annual Report, 1963*, President's speech by Sir Julian Pode; 'The Moral of the Steel Bill', *Steel Review*, 43 (1966), pp. 2–3.
51. For an account of the CBI's actions over steel renationalisation see W. P. Grant and D. March, *The Confederation of British Industry* (London, 1977), pp. 168–73.
52. D. L. Burn, *The Future of Steel*, esp. pp. 18–21.
53. R. Marsh, *Hansard*, vol. 732, col. 1223 where he cites *The Guardian* and *The Times* for 2 July 1966.
54. 'Steel: If Nationalisation Comes', *Economist*, 9 May 1964, pp. 567–9.
55. 'Steel: The Shadow of Nationalisation', *Economist*, 24 October 1964, pp. 418–21.
56. 'The Domestic Choice', *Economist*, 3 October 1964, pp. 15–17.
57. 'Now Who Gets the Chop?', *Economist*, 15 May 1965, pp. 735–6.
58. 'Steel Nationalisation: In Embryo', *Economist*, 8 October 1966, pp. 180–1; 'Steel Nationalisation: Meaningless Gesture', *Economist*, 18 February 1967, p. 646; British Steel Corporation, *Report on Organisation, 1967*.
59. R. Marsh, *Hansard*, vol. 732, cols. 1224ff.
60. 'Steel in Suspense', *The Times*, 13 November 1951, p. 5.
61. Iron and Steel Act, 1967, ch. 17, in *The Public and General Acts and Church Assembly Measures, 1967*, pt I (London, 1967), clause 4, para. 3a.
62. Schedule One to the Act listed the companies.
63. 'Public and Private Sectors – The Pattern of Production', *Steel Review*, 47 (1967), pp. 3–5.
64. 'Leading Article', *Steel Review*, 47 (1967), p. 2.
65. 'Steel Nationalisation: In Embryo', *Economist*.
66. Vaizey, *History of British Steel*, pp. 181–2.
67. British Steel Corporation, *Report on Organisation*, pp. 22ff.
68. Vaizey, *History of British Steel*, pp. 182–3.

69. Nothing was done to denationalise steel when the Conservative Party came back to office in 1970. In 1977, however, Margaret Thatcher, Sir Keith Joseph and William Whitelaw backed a move to have the industry denationalised. This opens interesting prospects in view of the Conservatives' success in the general election of 1979. In this particular instance it was almost certainly a symbolic gesture. 'Tories back bid to denationalise Steel', *Financial Times*, 20 January 1977, p. 13.

70. British Steel Corporation, *Report on Organisation*, p. 34 Appendix B.

71. 'Steel Nationalisation: Meaningless Gesture', *Economist*.

72. This description of nationalisation was used by Poulantzas in reply to a question at the C.P. Sociology Group's conference on Class, 1976. It seems much too useful to be lost, just because it was not written down.

73. F. Lee, *Hansard*, vol. 701, col. 685.

74. *Iron and Steel Act*, 1967, clause 3. This is the same phrasing as was used in 1947.